THE
NEW PROFESSOR'S
HANDBOOK

THE
NEW PROFESSOR'S
HANDBOOK

A Guide to Teaching and Research in Engineering and Science

Cliff I. Davidson
Susan A. Ambrose
Carnegie Mellon University

Foreword by Herbert A. Simon

Anker Publishing Company, Inc.
Bolton, MA

THE NEW PROFESSOR'S HANDBOOK
A Guide to Teaching and Research in Engineering and Science

ISBN 1–882982–01–0

Composition by Deerfoot Studios.
Cover design by Deerfoot Studios.
Cover art by Douglas Cooper.

Anker Publishing Company, Inc.
176 Ballville Road
P.O. Box 249
Bolton, MA 01740–0249

To
Professor Ted Fenton,
devoted teacher and friend

ABOUT THE AUTHORS

Susan A. Ambrose is Director of the University Teaching Center and a Lecturer in the Department of History at Carnegie Mellon University. She grew up in Belle Vernon, Pennsylvania, just south of Pittsburgh. Ambrose received her B.A. degree (1979) in political science and her M.A. (1981) in history from Indiana University of Pennsylvania, and her doctoral degree (1986) in American history from Carnegie Mellon University. At Carnegie Mellon, she has created faculty and graduate student development programs at the departmental, college and university level. She has also designed and conducted seminars for faculty in colleges and universities throughout the United States and Canada. Ambrose has made presentations at regional, national, and international conferences on issues around faculty and graduate student development, and has publications in those areas. She also teaches courses on immigration and ethnicity.

Cliff I. Davidson is Professor of Civil Engineering and Engineering and Public Policy, and is Director of the Environmental Institute, at Carnegie Mellon University. He grew up in Des Moines, Iowa. Davidson received his B.S. (1972) in electrical engineering from Carnegie Mellon, and his M.S. (1973) and Ph.D. (1977) in environmental engineering science from California Institute of Technology. In addition to publishing and lecturing widely on environmental topics, he is on the editorial boards of three journals and has been a member of more than a dozen government committees. He currently serves on the Board of Directors of the American Association for Aerosol Research. He has taught both undergraduate and graduate courses since 1977.

CONTENTS

About the Authors   *vi*

Foreword   *x*

Acknowledgements   *xiii*

Preface   *xv*

PART I – TEACHING

1. CHARACTERISTICS OF STUDENT LEARNING   1
   Introduction
   Understanding Expertise
   Knowing Your Students
   Understanding the Learning Process
   Considering Educational Goals
   Summary

2. PLANNING A COURSE   19
   Introduction
   Helping Students Learn: Eight Principles of
       Undergraduate Education
   Analogy Between Planning a Research Project and
       Planning a Course
   Steps in Planning a Course
   Summary

3. CONDUCTING DISCUSSIONS   35
   Introduction
   Preparing for the Discussion
   Providing Effective Leadership During the Discussion
   Evaluating the Success of the Discussion
   Summary

4. LECTURING   53
   Introduction
   Preparing the Lecture
   Making an Effective Delivery
   Evaluating the Lecture
   Summary

5. PREPARING ACTIVITIES FOR STUDENTS: EXAMS AND ASSIGNMENTS   65
    Introduction
    Objectives of Exams and Assignments
    Designing Appropriate Problems
    Administering Exams and Assignments
    Interpreting the Results of Exams and Assignments
    Summary

6. WORKING WITH TEACHING ASSISTANTS   81
    Introduction
    Attitudes: The Professor-Teaching Assistant Relationship
    Responsibilities of Teaching Assistants
    Ways of Helping Your Teaching Assistants to
        Meet Their Responsibilities
    Special Considerations for International Teaching Assistants
    Summary

PART II – RESEARCH

7. SUPERVISING GRADUATE RESEARCH   95
    Introduction
    The Graduate School Environment
    Conducting Graduate Research and Completing the Thesis
    Graduate Student Dropouts: The
        "All But Dissertation" Phenomenon
    Summary

8. GETTING FUNDING FOR RESEARCH PROJECTS   113
    Introduction
    Types of Research Funding
    Groundwork: Choosing a Research Topic
        and Identifying Potential Funding Sources
    Preparing to Write the Proposal
    Writing the Proposal
    After the Proposal is Funded
    Summary

9. WRITING RESEARCH PAPERS   127
    Introduction
    Types of Research Papers
    Collecting Background Material and Organizing the Paper
    Writing the Paper
    After the Paper is Submitted: Dealing with
        Rejection or with Acceptance
    Summary

10. REVIEWING RESEARCH PROPOSALS AND PAPERS   145
    Introduction
    Reviewing Research Proposals for Funding Agencies
    Reviewing Research Papers
    Summary

11. PRESENTING TALKS ON RESEARCH RESULTS   159
    Introduction
    The Research Conference Environment
    Preparing for the Presentation
    Delivering the Talk
    Evaluating Your Presentation
    Summary

12. CONDUCTING GRADUATE SEMINAR PROGRAMS   171
    Introduction
    Objective of Graduate Seminars
    Organizing and Conducting Seminars
    Summary

    BIBLIOGRAPHY   183

    INDEX   193

FOREWORD

University faculty members have important responsibilities both for transmitting existing knowledge and for creating new knowledge: for teaching and research. Professors Davidson and Ambrose have written this book to communicate things known about the skills of teaching and research that will help persons beginning academic careers to improve their skills. A couple of central and very important themes run through their discussion of these two components of university life.

TEACHING

Universities have sometimes been described as institutions where amateurs educate students to become professionals. Professors are not, of course, amateurs in their disciplines; they have passed through an arduous education and apprenticeship acquiring knowledge and research skills in their areas of special competence. But most of them have had little or no formal training in the art and skills of assisting others to learn.

Sometimes it is claimed that you are either a born teacher or you aren't. Or it is claimed that the skills of teaching are acquired only through long practice of teaching. Both claims are simply false. There is today a large body of scientific knowledge about how people learn and about how their knowledge must be organized in memory if it is to be usable for professional and personal purposes. These topics have been the object of extensive and successful research, particularly in the discipline now known as cognitive science. Careful experimentation and sometimes computer simulation of human thought processes have provided testable and tested theories of how people solve problems, use language, and learn. Much of this new knowledge has been tested in the classroom and in computer tutoring systems, in domains as varied as mathematics and physics, on the one side, and expository writing, on the other.

This body of knowledge about human thinking and learning can be used even more widely to improve our instructional methods substantially and systematically. Some of it is knowledge that experience can also teach, but usually only slowly and sometimes painfully. Much of it is knowledge that would be very hard for a teacher ever to discover solely through observation of his or her own classroom successes and failures.

In the first half of this book, Professors Davidson and Ambrose use the collective experience of our profession and the new developments in cognitive science to draw lessons that promote effective instruction. They have organized their discussion around the fundamental principle of instruction (so obvious and so often disregarded) that what is important is what students do; what professors do only matters to the extent that they influence students' behaviors and learning practices. So this is a book on learning, and how teaching can contribute to learning. It deals not just with the classroom (important, but only one part of the process) but also with all of the other student and teacher activities that surround it. And it cuts through the voluminous literature on teaching to make the process of learning how to teach more efficient.

RESEARCH

The opportunity to search for new knowledge is one of the strong attractions for most of us to an academic career. An academic appointment is a first step toward that opportunity, but of course only a first step. In the second part of this book, Professors Davidson and Ambrose introduce the world of research and the considerations that determine productivity and success in it. Again they provide practical advice on the everyday activities that go into research.

No one, I think, does successful research of any significance unless there is fun in doing it, and unless he or she believes in the significance, personal and social, of what is being done. Selecting research problems that can produce valuable outcomes is an essential skill. It calls for a blending of what one knows and can do and wants to do, with what is scientifically feasible in the light of existing knowledge and tools of research, and with what the world (one's discipline, society) is interested in and needs to know.

Research generally also calls for resources: for a laboratory, for equipment, for assistants and graduate students, for time released from teaching and other activities. The researcher must believe deeply enough in what he or she is doing to persuade others to provide these resources. Belief must be combined with skills of communicating the promise of research problems and the meanings of research results to others. It calls for great skill and insight to bring together in a project proposal one's sense of what is important and fundamental and doable together with a reasonable idea of what funding sources are willing to support.

Professors Davidson and Ambrose review what is known about these matters and provide practical advice and suggestions on how to advance one's research. These topics are perhaps less informed by theory than is our knowledge of learning and teaching, but there is a large body of solid and non-obvious know-how, available in the environment of every research university, upon which they draw. Much of this information has been gleaned from many years of seminars at Carnegie Mellon on how to conduct research.

So this is a book about the skills that a new professor needs and can acquire. Both authors have impressive records of teaching and research. Susan Ambrose has been engaged for some years as a member of the University Teaching Center at Carnegie Mellon (and is now its Director), where she has worked with a great many faculty members on our campus to improve their teaching effectiveness. Cliff Davidson has organized seminar programs for graduate students in Civil Engineering on teaching and conducting research that have attracted faculty and graduate students from other departments and colleges.

The authors' enthusiasm about their own academic careers shows clearly through the book's pages. I join them in hoping that new faculty members will find it informative and useful to them in launching their careers. And I cannot wish readers any happier outcome of those careers than the deep pleasure and satisfaction I have had in my own teaching and research over the past half century.

Herbert A. Simon
Richard King Mellon University Professor
Departments of Computer Science and Psychology
Carnegie Mellon University
Pittsburgh, November, 1993

ACKNOWLEDGMENTS

We are indebted to many individuals who contributed to this book. The seminar program that led to the final manuscript was organized during the 1986–1987 academic year by a committee of graduate students in Civil Engineering at Carnegie Mellon University: Teresa Adams, Nelson Baker, John Borrazzo, and Ari Trochanis, assisted by Professor Mary Lou Maher and the authors of this book. Throughout the eight years over which these seminars evolved, graduate students too numerous to acknowledge have participated in the program. Many of these have offered valuable feedback on the seminar handouts that eventually became chapters; especially noteworthy were suggestions of Mike Bergin, Darcy Bullock, Jade Goldstein, Tim Gould, Carl Haas, Mark Kantrowitz, Mark Milke, George Turkiyyah, Yee-Lin Wu, and Fang Zhao.

Assistance with preparation of tables in the manuscript and with administrative matters involved in running the seminar program was provided by the secretarial and administrative staff in the Civil Engineering Department: Jenny Cochran, Donna Fillo, Stacy Kabay, Shirley Knapp, Maxine Leffard, Karen Peretin, and Curt Yeske. Additional assistance with manuscript preparation was provided by Michelle Gregg of the University Teaching Center.

All faculty members in the Civil Engineering Department generously gave of their time by participating in panel discussions at the seminars, providing comments on the chapters, and/or contributing ideas to the program: Tung Au, Jacobo Bielak, Larry Cartright, K. Chelvakumar, Paul Christiano, David Dzombak, Steve Fenves, Susan Finger, Jim Garrett, Omar Ghattas, Chris Hendrickson, Jean-Luc Jaffrezo, Haris Koutsopolous, Dick Luthy, Mary Lou Maher, Fran McMichael, Sue McNeil, Irving Oppenheim, Marina Pantazidou, Dan Rehak, Jim Romualdi, Sunil Saigal, Mitchell Small and Chris Thewalt. Professors Maher and McNeil kindly helped run the seminar program for a couple of semesters. Professor Fenves contributed the table on supervising graduate students (Chapter 7) and the anecdote on a Pittsburgh bridge (Chapter 12).

Individuals outside the Civil Engineering Department also provided assistance of various types. Professor Ted Fenton, the first Director of the University Teaching Center and currently Director of the Center for University Outreach, provided valuable assistance throughout the process of planning the seminars and writing the manuscript. His guidance has greatly contributed to our understanding of teaching. Comments on the full manuscript were also provided by Professor Joel Tarr of the Departments of History, Social & Decision Science, and Engineering & Public Policy; Professor William Brown of the Department of Biology; Dr. Benno Bernt, Director of Technology Transfer; Dr. Barbara Gross Davis, Assistant Vice-Chancellor for Educational Development at the University of California at Berkeley; and Dr. Mary Deane Sorcinelli, Director of the Center for Teaching Excellence at the University of Massachusetts at Amherst. Dr. Rea Freeland of the University Teaching Center provided valuable comments on the first six chapters. Professor Fusun Gonul of the Graduate School of Industrial Administration provided suggestions in several of the seminars which led to changes in the manuscript. Professors Granger Morgan and Indira Nair of the Engineering & Public Policy Department gave helpful suggestions during early phases of the program. Dr. Marcia Wratcher helped run the first seminar of the series for a number of years. Other information incorporated in the chapters was provided through informal discussions with Dr. Barbara Lazarus, Associate Provost for Academic Projects, Professor Erwin Steinberg, Vice Provost for Education, and Professor Maurine Greenwald of the University of Pittsburgh. Professor Rudolf Husar of Washington University in St. Louis provided information on the homework assignment concerning statistical treatment of air pollution data (Chapter 5).

We would like to thank Janice McClure of the Design Department, Irving Oppenheim of the Civil Engineering and Architecture Departments, and Douglas Cooper of the Architecture Department for assistance with the cover.

We wish to extend a special thanks to Professor Herbert A. Simon of the Psychology Department at Carnegie Mellon for especially detailed comments on the full manuscript and for writing the Foreword to this book.

Finally, we would like to thank Megan Davidson and Ed Hostetter for being understanding spouses and for contributing in a substantial way by providing suggestions on early drafts of the manuscript.

Although many people have contributed ideas and information to the book, we accept full responsibility for the accuracy of its contents, and for any errors or omissions.

PREFACE

Up to 50% of the engineering and science faculty at our nation's colleges and universities will be retiring over the coming decade. They will be replaced mainly by young men and women just out of graduate school, hardworking and dedicated but inexperienced. How are these individuals going to get the information they need to survive—and flourish—at their new positions?

Much of this information is simply passed along by word of mouth. Young faculty are expected to pick up what they can from senior colleagues, or perhaps from other new faculty with whom they can compare notes. Some new faculty have discussed the ups-and-downs of a professorship with their thesis advisor. Others have discussed the topic with friends or relatives who may be in academia. But whatever the method of getting the information, one thing is certain: learning about the varied tasks of a professor is not likely to be easy.

A review of the literature reveals a curious state of affairs. On one hand, there are copious volumes written on teaching at the college level—which should interest a young professor who is about to teach for the first time and who may never have had guidance in teaching. Unfortunately, extracting practical information from these volumes takes time, which young faculty simply don't have. On the other hand, there is a notable absence of information about how young faculty members in engineering and science should proceed to set up a research program. What research topics should they pursue? Where can they obtain funding? What are the most effective ways of supervising graduate students? Although recent Ph.D. graduates may have some strong opinions on the last of these topics, much of the contact with funding agencies and administration of research projects was probably handled by their thesis advisors. And much of this vital information on supervising research, so important for a new professor to learn, has remained unwritten.

This dual problem of too much literature on teaching and too little on research came to our attention several years ago. After interviewing a number of Carnegie Mellon faculty, new and old, The University Teaching Center set up several unique programs to ease the pain of transition from graduate student to professor. The Center established a series of informal discussions and seminars for new faculty just before the start of the fall semester each year. Individual departments around the University worked with The Center to set up regular seminars for our academia-bound graduate students. Lunch and dinner programs were arranged to complement these activities, bringing together new faculty, senior faculty, and graduate students. The response of participants to all of these programs was overwhelmingly positive.

This book is an outgrowth of The University Teaching Center programs, particularly those developed in cooperation with the engineering and science departments. In the first six chapters, we have distilled the literature and combined it with our own teaching experiences to provide the essence of how to teach courses at the college level. In the second six chapters, we have taken information from numerous seminars, discussions, and interviews, as well as limited published material, to summarize the most important aspects of developing a college-level research program.

The information presented here is vitally important for faculty members at many types of educational institutions. Major universities that have traditionally emphasized research are now reassessing the importance of teaching, especially at the undergraduate level. Colleges and universities where teaching has been the primary emphasis are also reassessing their goals in favor of more research. It is clear that faculty members at almost any college or university must therefore come to terms with these changing priorities, in many cases becoming adept at both teaching and research.

This book covers a wide range of topics, not all of which are relevant in every situation. Early drafts of the chapters were based on engineering, especially civil engineering; these were later broadened to include sciences to some extent. Interactions with colleagues across the university have shown that remarkable similarities exist in the ways professors across disciplines, including those outside of engineering and science, carry out their day-to-day activities. Furthermore, these similarities were not fully recognized by our colleagues—or by us—until the Teaching Center programs brought together groups of faculty from different departments. In some sense, this book opens up the professorship, demonstrating that many idiosyncrasies of our individual academic disciplines are not unique.

We have omitted many topics that are also important for young faculty to consider. Examples include university politics, personal relations with students, staff, and other faculty, service on university committees, and balancing time between career and family. We do not discuss in detail the use of advanced educational technology in courses, since we believe that new faculty must first understand the basic components of effective teaching. We do not discuss issues outside the university such as consulting or professional activities. We also do not deal with the specific question of assembling promotion documents, although the guidelines for teaching and research provided here will, we hope, help the young professor to achieve promotion and tenure.

In essence, this book is about making the jump from graduate student to professor. It is a jump well worth making.

Cliff I. Davidson
Susan A. Ambrose

1

CHARACTERISTICS OF STUDENT LEARNING

INTRODUCTION

Each of us learns differently. Some of us can grasp new information more easily if it is presented visually, while others prefer auditory presentations. Some of us learn in a reflective way, which takes time, while others learn more quickly. Some can learn a subject in great depth, while others must invest an extraordinary effort to understand a concept even superficially. Some students enter our courses with strong prerequisite knowledge and skills, while others are less prepared. And some students are driven by intense interest in our subject, while others need more external motivation. This diversity makes teaching challenging—and fascinating.

The goal of teaching is student learning: we hope that eventually students will use the knowledge and skills gained from our courses in their professional lives as scientists and engineers. To do so, students must be able to transfer the knowledge and skills from the classroom to new situations. How do we help students to accomplish that type of meaningful learning? We can begin by studying *how* students learn, and then use this information as we plan our courses.

The paradox of teaching is that "the teacher must learn from the students…to be more effective in helping students learn from the teacher" (McKeachie, 1980). Teaching is much more than a one-way communication from the blackboard to the class. Rather, it is a complex partnership in which pairs of

1

individuals—the teacher and each student in the class—work together to make permanent changes in their understanding.

The first six chapters of this book are about such a partnership. While all six deal with both learning and teaching, the emphasis of this chapter is on student learning; the other five focus on teaching. As a beginning professor, you have just finished roughly twenty years of learning in a somewhat structured setting: you have had a great deal of personal experience in acquiring knowledge and skills. Nevertheless, a brief summary of the learning process and the factors which influence it can provide insights into the variety of learners you are likely to encounter. Furthermore, it is likely that you were a successful student without explicitly thinking about *how* this learning occurred. You probably mastered good learning habits early, and you now apply them instinctively.

Many of your students will not be so lucky. They may not understand how to channel their energies to be efficient learners, and they may have poor skills in reading, listening, note-taking, and problem solving. They are likely to come from a variety of backgrounds, including those where effective role models were not present. They have a variety of reasons for being in your class: some may want to learn as much as they can, while others may want to put out the least possible effort to get a passing grade. Your job as a teacher is to motivate, challenge, and help students so that as many of them as possible acquire the knowledge and skills they need to successfully perform intellectual tasks.

In this chapter, we first summarize information on characteristics of experts, and suggest ways of using this information to help students learn. Then we discuss the importance of knowing your students, considering their backgrounds, motivation levels, and different ways in which they learn. Third, we discuss current models of the learning process. Finally, we present a classic work on educational goals that helped guide learning strategies for many decades. We use material presented in this chapter as a foundation for discussion presented throughout the rest of the book, but especially in the next five chapters on teaching.

UNDERSTANDING EXPERTISE

For many years, people equated expertise in a subject—demonstrated by earning a PhD—with the ability to teach that subject. This is no longer an acceptable paradigm. All of us have sat through courses taught by people who knew a subject well. In some instances, we completed the course knowing that the teacher was indeed an expert—but without gaining much understanding of the subject matter. What went wrong? In this section, we build on the premise that having expertise is a necessary but not sufficient condition for teaching, and that studying *how* people make the transition from novice to expert can help us to become better teachers. Essentially, we want to use this information to help our students move along a path that enables them to become competent, proficient, and eventually experts. Let us consider what we know about experts, that is, those who have been successful learners.

First, we know that developing expertise is an intensive and time-consuming effort. No one, no matter how bright, can become an expert without long periods of hard work. Simon (1981) suggests that becoming a world-class expert requires at least ten years. Bobby Fisher played chess intensively for a decade before achieving "grand master" status. Mozart began composing at age 4, but he did not begin producing his acclaimed masterpieces until he was a teenager. Richard Feynman built electronic devices as a child, indicating that he learned and practiced the laws of physics at an early age, but he did not develop his Nobel prize-winning theories until the middle of his career.

Second, studies have indicated that world class experts have usually learned—and can use—about 50,000 "chunks" or familiar patterns, such as a pattern of chess pieces on a board, a sequence of musical notes, or a schematic diagram of an electrical circuit (Simon, 1981). Most of us are experts in writing and speaking English: a typical college graduate knows roughly 50,000–100,000 words.

Third, we know that experts can process information very quickly: chessmasters are able to perform almost as well when they are allowed 30 seconds per move as when they are allowed 3 minutes per move (Simon and Gilmartin, 1973). This demonstrates that chessmasters—and experts in other areas—have organized information effectively, and thus can do a selective search through some 50,000 "chunks" to quickly zero in on a method, a move, or a solution to a problem.

How can these observations enable us to help our students move toward becoming experts? The first observation—that developing expertise takes a lot of time and effort—indicates that the hard work needed to achieve the status of expert is spent to a large degree in actively practicing the skills and techniques of the discipline. There are no short cuts to mastering material; only through time and effort invested in practice do students move along the novice-expert continuum. This means that the students must be motivated, and the teacher-student relationship is an important part of this effort. As a teacher, you need to develop this type of relationship with your students, providing assistance and encouragement as well as valuable corrective feedback.

In line with the second observation, experts have available for their use sizeable amounts of information: thousands of "chunks" are organized for flexible retrieval. As students become familiar with patterns in a discipline, you must help them recognize which pieces of information they need in solving a particular problem. You can assist this effort by identifying alternate ways to solve a problem and stating why they are more or less desirable. You can also mention what factors led you to choose the method presented in class as opposed to alternative methods.

Finally, the fact that experts solve problems quickly indicates that they process information essentially automatically. As a result, very few experts can explain the rapid mental processes by which they arrive at their answers. This is because they have created an efficient system of organizing and storing information in meaningful ways without always using a verbal rehearsal of the information. Such a system enables an individual to retrieve the stored information, generally through multiple, redundant paths. This has implications for teaching: you need to help the students identify multiple cues so they can organize newly acquired information for ready retrieval. For example, you can:

✦ provide examples which link new concepts to prior knowledge, either from earlier in the course or from other experiences

✦ present new concepts in more than one context or with more than one example to provide multiple cues

✦ mention explicitly the category of problem you are discussing

Teaching in this way will require substantial time for preparation since you are probably very familiar with the subject matter. You are accustomed to solving problems quickly in this domain, possibly skipping steps in working toward a solution, or collapsing several inferences into one without consciously realizing it. In contrast, your students will need enough guidance so that they think about each separate step in a problem solving effort.

Now let us examine some important characteristics of students that need to be taken into account for effective teaching.

Exercise: Consider explaining an activity with which you are very familiar to someone who has never done the activity before. Examples might include driving a car with a manual transmission, playing soccer, tennis, or another sport, or playing a card game such as poker or bridge. Why is it difficult to describe physical skills that you have developed over many years? Why is it difficult to describe intellectual skills? Now consider the types of skills needed in your area of expertise. What implications can you draw for the effort needed to teach these skills to your students?

KNOWING YOUR STUDENTS

Being an effective teacher requires that you understand—at least to some extent—the characteristics of students in your class. Achieving this is a real challenge: attempting to understand another individual is a highly complex task, and trying to understand what motivates an entire class of students is obviously much more difficult. Nevertheless, knowing certain things about your students is vital to successful teaching.

In this section, we first consider some examples of how student backgrounds can be taken into account as you plan a class. Then we discuss factors influencing motivation of students which impact your teaching. Next, we present examples of frameworks for identifying differences in the way students learn, and again provide suggestions on how you might accommodate these differences in the classroom. Finally, we discuss strategies that students can use to enhance their learning—strategies that you can discuss with individual students or with the entire class.

Note that in this section, we consider several examples of student characteristics that impact teaching in general. More specific applications of these ideas to planning a course, leading class discussions, and presenting lectures are given in the next three chapters.

Student Backgrounds

Among the most important student characteristics which influence learning are the knowledge and skills which they have acquired from prior experiences. Having information on this topic is vital to help you decide what to teach and how to teach it: repeating material the students already know will bore them, while starting at a level that is too advanced will frustrate them. Identifying where students currently are in terms of prior experience will enable you to start at an appropriate point and move on to new material.

In addition, classroom styles experienced previously by the students will affect their expectations. For example, individuals used to a structured lecture format may find classroom discussion or working in small groups intimidating at first. You may need to take special steps to encourage your students to participate in the types of activities you plan; in the above example, you might wish to begin with a more structured format and progress to less structure later in the semester.

Cultural backgrounds of the students can also have a marked effect. This is especially important for students from minority groups both within and outside the U.S., where cultural differences result in a variety of different ways in which learning takes place. For example, in some cultures students will never question or challenge authority, while in other cultures direct confrontations are the norm. Knowledge of these characteristics can thus help you interact more effectively with particular groups of students.

Factors Influencing Motivation

Just as students bring background knowledge and skills to the course, they also have interests and expectations which largely determine their motivation to learn. Effective teachers understand the factors affecting motivation that originate within the student (intrinsic) and know how to alter environmental factors that encourage learning (extrinsic). Intrinsic motivational factors focus on the attitudes and values of the students; extrinsic motivational factors focus on the actions of the instructor and others in the students' environment.

Most students will be motivated intrinsically if they feel they can be successful in performing an assigned task and if they value participating in the task. The extent to which students feel they can be successful is determined by factors such as:

+ their confidence level

+ the level of anxiety they feel associated with the task

+ their familiarity with the task

+ their perception of how challenging the task is

+ their feeling about the level of satisfaction that can be achieved by completing the task

Students' perceptions of the value of a task are based on how relevant they view the task in relation to the course goals, their career interests, or their personal goals. They may find satisfaction in the means (e.g., classroom activities, projects, or assignments) or they may be looking forward to the ends (e.g., their grade, potential job, or future financial rewards).

Extrinsic motivational factors can either strengthen or weaken the intrinsic factors discussed above. Some of the most important extrinsic factors include:

+ the enthusiasm of the instructor

+ the extent to which the learning activities go beyond simple memorization to apply and analyze concepts, e.g., through case studies, simulations, and laboratory exercises

+ the amount and type of student interaction with the material

+ the clarity of course goals and expectations for the students

The last of these implies that goals of the course should be stated in terms of what the students should be able to *do*, not simply what they are expected to know. Stating specific goals in this way helps to clarify course objectives and permits later evaluation of whether the objectives have been achieved, as discussed in later chapters.

Frameworks for Student Learning Preferences

Because students arrive in our classrooms with a variety of backgrounds and interests, they often respond differently to a common experience. This results in different "learning styles," or preferred ways in which students think, relate to each other, and relate to the classroom environment (Grasha, 1990). These learning styles are based on their personalities, and are reinforced by what has helped them to be successful in the past. To some extent, these styles are relatively constant across different situations, and they cannot be easily altered. However, with hard work, students *can* change their habits, and they can learn to adopt other styles in new situations. We therefore refer to these styles as "learning preferences" to emphasize that students have, to some extent, a choice in determining the way in which they learn. In fact, helping students to identify their own personal learning preferences and assisting them to use new preferences, when the situation warrants it, are important tasks for you as a teacher. These are ways in which you can make a real contribution in empowering your students to become successful lifelong learners.

A number of different frameworks have been developed to identify differences in the way students learn. Here we bring together a number of separate studies to arrive at four categories of learning preferences (see, for example, Canfield, 1980; Claxton and Murrell, 1987; Myers and Myers, 1980).

The first category includes basic personality traits that, for example, determine whether a person is introverted or extroverted, thinking-oriented or feeling-oriented, or reflective or impulsive. Such traits affect learning in a number of ways. As one example, reflective students need time to think about alternative solution possibilities and will probably not make an impulsive selection when asked. Thus you may wish to encourage the participation of these types of students by providing questions for them to consider quietly over several minutes, rather than orienting the discussion around quick answers. Or you can pause after you ask a question or pose a problem. Both of these strategies would benefit most students, but they are particularly helpful to reflective students.

A second category is based on the way an individual processes information. Some students prefer to study a subject from the "top down" by first examining the topic at the highest levels of complexity or abstraction; other students prefer the "bottom up" approach, beginning at the lowest levels and moving upward through logical, well-defined steps. Some students prefer concrete examples to help them understand abstract concepts; other students can easily conceptualize abstract information. To reach students who learn best when concepts are accompanied by concrete examples, you have two choices: you can match your teaching style to their learning preference, or you can purposely mismatch your teaching style to help the students expand their repertoire of learning preferences. If you choose the latter, be sensitive to the fact that students may feel threatened when confronted with a new way of learning: treat these situations carefully. There is a diversity of opinions on whether matching or mismatching teaching and learning styles results in more effective learning.

The third category focuses on social-interaction models which explain how students behave in the classroom. For example, a student may be dependent or independent, collaborative or competitive, participating or nonparticipating, or learning-oriented or grade-oriented. Once again, you may choose to reinforce existing student preferences or to encourage them to try alternative styles. If you choose to reinforce the existing preferences, you can provide a lot of structure to dependent students and let independent students work alone. You can encourage students eager to participate to do most of the talking in a discussion, allowing the others to sit quietly. On the other hand, if you see value in challenging preferences, you might prod the dependent student (who learns only what is required) to think about an issue that goes beyond the class material. Or you might assign a team project to help independent or competitive students learn to function in a group. Similarly, you might directly ask questions of nonparticipating students to engage them in classroom discussion. Whether you decide to match or mismatch teaching styles and learning preferences, an awareness of different learning preferences allows you to make deliberate choices in the way you teach.

The final category involves instructional preferences. Some students prefer at least occasional one-on-one interaction in order to perform well. Others may do best in a classroom environment. Many students prefer to learn by listening, while others prefer reading and still others thrive on direct experiences. Because students have different instructional preferences, you may want to provide variety in your classes. For example, you can provide some assignments with a lot of structure and others with less structure so that some students can impose their own structure on the material. You can allow opportunities for students who need personal interaction to meet with you individually. You can vary your explanations to include verbal, visual, and mathematical descriptions. And you can assign out-of-class work which includes readings, drawings, and experiments.

> *Exercise: Consider visiting a city for the first time. You have gotten together with a friend who lives there, and you are asking for directions on reaching several places in the city. Would you prefer that your friend draw a map for you? Provide a published city map for you to figure out? Explain in words how to get to each place? Describe landmarks that can help you find each place? Do you feel uncomfortable with all of these options and greatly prefer your friend to guide you personally as you travel through the city? Think about how your colleagues in engineering and science might answer these questions as well as friends who have chosen other disciplines of study. Can you identify any patterns?*

Learning Strategies

In contrast to *preferences* which describe the characteristics of learners, *strategies* are the specific actions which a student uses in order to learn, i.e., thinking or behaving in a certain way. These strategies are chosen on the basis of the individual's learning preferences (e.g., McKeachie et al., 1986).

Many strategies are intended specifically to help students acquire and organize new information. Some of these have been mentioned earlier in this chapter. For example, students can build links between new material and previous knowledge, providing multiple pathways to access the new information.

Other strategies can help students to plan, monitor, and regulate learning. Examples of planning strategies include skimming written material prior to careful reading, and setting overall goals for the amount of material to be studied. Generating questions about the material is another example. These planning strategies help to activate prior knowledge so that the reader may more easily build links to the new material. Strategies to monitor learning progress can help students to determine whether they should continue the present activities. For example, occasionally self-testing while reading a text can establish whether the student is indeed understanding the information. Strategies to regulate learning can insure that the pace is appropriate. If students realize that their reading comprehension is low because the material is difficult, they can adjust their reading speed accordingly.

Finally, there are strategies to manipulate the environment or available resources. McKeachie et al. (1986) describe several types:

1. *Environment strategies* involve determining the best place for serious studying, making sure that it is comfortable and devoid of distractions.

2. *Time management strategies* include setting a schedule for studying and establishing realistic goals based on the time available.

3. *Effort strategies* include being persistent in completing a task, knowing the right time for studying based on one's moods and feelings, and knowing how to reinforce accomplishments through self-defined rewards.

4. *Support strategies* involve knowing when to seek help from teachers, tutors, or other students.

All of these strategies can assist the learning process. You can thus help your students by informing them of the different strategies and making them aware of when such strategies can be of value.

It is clear that both learning preferences and learning strategies vary greatly from student to student, and that you can improve the success of your teaching by taking these into account. But how can you determine these characteristics for your students? A number of surveys and questionnaires exist specifically for this purpose. While we do not recommend any specific instrument, the following are commonly used for each of the four categories of learning preferences:

1. *Basic Personality Traits*—Myers-Briggs Type Indicators (MBTI) (Myers, 1976)

2. *Information Processing Preferences*—Learning Styles Inventory (LSI) (Kolb, 1976); Learning and Study Strategies Inventory (LASSI) (Weinstein et al., 1987)

3. *Social Interaction Preferences*—Grasha-Reichmann Learning Style Scale (Reichmann and Grasha, 1974)

4. *Instructional Preferences*—Canfield Learning Style Inventory (Canfield, 1980)

As an alternative to these instruments, you might simply ask your students on the first day of class to provide some information to help you learn about them. For example, you might list several examples of learning preferences and strategies, and then ask the students to write a paragraph describing the ones with which they feel most comfortable. This brief task will heighten students' awareness of their own preferences, and may help you to identify areas of the course where certain students might need a lot of direction.

We have just proposed that the way students process information will influence their success in learning new material. However, there are also other factors which directly affect student learning. Although you have little control over some of these, you nevertheless should be aware of them. Examples include student attitudes about learning, substance abuse, family problems, and personal disabilities. In some cases, you may be able to offer assistance, e.g., by suggesting counseling for students with personal problems. In other cases, you may be unable to help despite the best of intentions. Teaching can nevertheless be immensely rewarding: understanding how students learn is a vital step to enjoying these rewards.

Exercise: Consider the intellectual tasks that you find most challenging as a faculty member. Examples might be preparing lecture material, designing homework assignments and tests, designing research experiments, reading research papers written by your graduate students, or reading research papers of colleagues. Do you have a preferred time of day and location for working on these particularly challenging tasks? Have you developed specific procedures, such as skimming papers first before careful reading, or allowing a minimum amount of time between writing successive drafts of papers? How have these strategies changed with time since you were a student?

UNDERSTANDING THE LEARNING PROCESS

Early in this chapter, we considered characteristics of experts and proposed that you use this information to guide your students toward eventually developing their own expertise. We also identified factors that affect student learning and considered the different strategies by which learning can be enhanced. In this section, we explore *how* learning takes place, focusing on different conceptual models that attempt to explain how the human mind processes information. First, we consider the ways in which students organize and store knowledge. Then we discuss how students develop problem solving skills.

Organizing and Storing Knowledge

When students are exposed to new information, they have only a few seconds to make sense out of it before it is lost. This is because short-term memory is severely limited in the amount of storage space and duration. If the information can be made meaningful within these few seconds, it is transferred to the student's long-term memory. This transfer is a necessary condition but is not sufficient for later retrieval: some information may not be accessible even if it is in long-term memory because of the form in which it is stored.

How does a student find meaning in new information and store it in an appropriate form for later retrieval? As we have seen earlier in this chapter, new information must be linked to previously learned material. A current conceptual model contends that we have frameworks for existing knowledge, sometimes referred to as *schemas* (Anderson, 1990). For example, one type of schema may represent our knowledge about how features fit together to define an object, or how events fit together to form an episode. When people hear the word "lemon," they may immediately associate it as part of a food group "fruit" and subgroup "citrus fruit," with a distinct color, shape, and taste. They may also consider the various ways in which lemons can be used, e.g. for eating and cooking. Thus when people are told that a "citron" resembles a lemon but is slightly larger, they will readily make the connection, thereby taking the first step in storing this new information so it can be later retrieved. Choosing effective schemas is an important aspect of learning: problems may develop if a student does not choose appropriate schemas for the tasks at hand (Mayer, 1982; Bransford, 1979).

Creating links with existing information—which helps to make the information meaningful as well as retrievable—can be achieved in many ways (Weinstein, 1988; McKeachie et al., 1986). For example, students can elaborate on a concept by exploring the meaning behind apparently simple statements: a mathematical expression describing physical motion can be elaborated on by drawing a diagram representing the motion. Strengthening links can also be achieved by organizing information systematically; this may be done by clustering information around some shared characteristics (recalling earlier discussion, both the citron and the lemon are citrus fruits) or looking for relationships among the concepts (the citron is larger and less acidic than the lemon). Often the use of analogies and metaphors helps in establishing links with existing information.

Maintaining information in long term-term memory has been compared to creating an indexed and cross-referenced encyclopedia (Simon, 1976). The articles are arranged irregularly; all information must be accessed either directly through the index or indirectly through cross-references. The index entries are essentially familiar patterns recognized by the student that evoke retrieval of the information as a response. Like the difficulties of filing papers, knowing what index labels will be useful later is difficult in the beginning stages, so as a teacher you may want to clarify relationships between topics and sub-topics.

Once the information is stored in long-term memory in a useful way, students will be able to retrieve it and apply it to a variety of contexts if they occasionally revisit the material. The process of thinking about concepts learned earlier allows students to find new meaning in previously learned ideas and to establish new links to their prior experiences; this, in turn, can enhance their ability to learn new information. The success of retrieval also depends on how well the students have integrated and connected the new knowledge. If they have effectively integrated the information, and found redundant ways of organizing it, retrieval should be possible with a variety of prompts. Thus you may want to use periodic reviews in class to facilitate redundant, flexible organization of your students' knowledge.

> *Exercise: Consider the dynamics of a group meeting you are attending. Early on, you hear comments that trigger some thoughts of your own, and you make suggestions that spark ideas in the minds of others. Soon you find yourself caught up in a cascade of ideas, contributing to the group effort. Why do some meetings work well, while others never seem to get off the ground (as far as your participation is concerned)? How can these considerations help you to plan your classes so that your students are engaged in active learning?*

Developing Problem Solving Skills

The ability to solve problems is a joint function of domain-specific knowledge and general problem solving skills. Students enter your courses with a variety of these skills. For example, many students use means-ends analysis, where an individual applies three sets of information to solve a problem: what is given, what is desired (i.e., the form of the solution), and a set of operators or rules such as equations. The solver tries to reduce the difference between what is given and what is desired by applying various operators. Eventually, by successive application of operators, the desired solution is reached. A student's method of choosing the operators may be quite superficial. For example, an individual might not be selective but rather might choose equations in an attempt to solve the problem based merely on the fact that they contain the variables of interest. A more sophisticated search might select equations for further consideration based on the relevant principles involved in the problem.

Students sometimes have difficulty because their problem solving skills are rather general—in many cases, their skills are applicable to a wide variety of disciplines but not particularly suitable to any one domain. You want your students to strengthen these skills by developing them to suit the particular classes of problems in your course or discipline.

With practice and feedback, students begin to merge knowledge in their discipline with general problem solving strategies to form powerful condition-action rules, known in the field of artificial intelligence as "productions." One example of a production is a statement of the form "if p then q." To solve the equation $2x = 10$, one applicable production to solve for x is simply "if the variable x is multiplied by a constant and the goal is to solve for x, then divide both sides of the equation by this constant." Such productions become discipline-specific skills that can help students solve a variety of problems.

Productions represent more than mere facts—they include *processes* operating with a set of conditions describing when a particular problem solving step is appropriate. These processes are included in the condition-action pairs: when a condition is satisfied, then a process operates, namely an action is executed. The value of production systems in problem solving has been demonstrated in large artificial intelligence programs developed for specialized tasks (Simon, 1980). For example, DENDRAL uses data from mass spectrometry and nuclear magnetic resonance analyses to identify molecular species, while MYCIN uses symptoms to identify possible human diseases. In both of these programs, the key to solving the problem lies in recognizing familiar patterns, essentially identifying when the conditions of a condition-action pair are satisfied.

How do students acquire these productions? We all know that teaching and learning are not synonymous. Even when there is a teacher, the student must somehow internalize what the teacher is saying: the words of the teacher cannot be used directly by the student to solve problems. Rather, the teacher's statements must be converted by the student into the internal representation of the student's production system—resulting in changes in the mind of the student. Although we don't know the precise nature of these changes, we do know that such a conversion must take place, and this is what we call "understanding" of new material.

We have a better understanding of how such conversions occur in advanced computing systems. For example, Simon (1980) notes that the *adaptive production system* in artificial intelligence may simulate the human learning process. This type of system has the capability of modifying its own internal state by changing or adding condition-action rules based on feedback the system receives. If the adaptive production system is a reasonable model of human learning, it follows that formal instruction becomes less important, and practice—with feedback—becomes more important (Anderson, 1987).

Simon (1980) discusses two ways by which individuals can change their internal state. First, a person can internalize new information by studying example problems worked out by others. A student following the steps of an example problem in a textbook will try to translate these steps into condition-action rules that will enable him to solve another problem of the same type. Second, an individual can work through a new problem to find a solution. In this case, the student takes the given information and searches through her memory for a process that moves her closer to the desired state. There may be false starts, and she may have to backtrack. Once the solution is found, however, she will have internalized the rules and will be more efficient in solving similar problems in the future.

These models of human learning imply that students must be given discipline-specific problems to work out, and that there must be ample opportunities for them to develop their own internal rules for solving new problems. This is consistent with statements earlier in the chapter about the need for hard work and lots of practice to develop expertise: internalizing productions that can be used to solve problems is indeed difficult, but it is a necessary part of learning new information. Your job as a teacher is to facilitate this process.

> *Exercise: Consider different methods of solving integrals, such as integration by parts, substitution of variables, application of formulas for analytical solutions, and use of numerical techniques. How can you teach your students to recognize characteristics of integrals that enable them to choose the most appropriate method? Why is it necessary for the students to practice the various techniques after seeing them in class in order to really understand them?*

Considering Educational Goals

Up to this point, we have focused mainly on the process of learning: what we understand about how students learn, what factors influence their learning, and how you can help them improve their ability to learn new material. In closing this chapter, we would like to summarize a list of educational goals which will help you think about your expectations for student learning as we discuss many specific aspects of teaching in later chapters. The goals are taken from Benjamin Bloom's classic work *Taxonomy of Educational Objectives* (Bloom et al., 1956):

1. *Knowledge* involves simple recall of specific pieces of information, such as a pattern, structure, or sequence of events.

2. *Comprehension* is when an individual knows what is being communicated and can use the information without necessarily seeing its relationship to other material or recognizing its fullest implications. Examples include translation (the ability to paraphrase accurately), interpretation (the ability to state in words the meaning of a set of data, for example), and extrapolation (the ability to predict the continuation of a trend).

3. *Application* is the ability to use general ideas and rules in a specific situation.

4. *Analysis* involves dividing a problem into its component parts in order to clarify the relations among these parts.

5. *Synthesis* involves putting pieces of information together to form a whole. Examples include producing an original paper, generating a plan for conducting an experiment, or proposing a solution to a complex problem.

6. *Evaluation* involves making judgments about the extent to which a product satisfies stated criteria.

Although they did not consider information processing explicitly, Bloom and his associates set the stage for future work on the topic by proposing these six sets of goals for students to achieve in order of increasing sophistication.

This structure is still used to guide the creation of educational objectives and to help design learning experiences. We will refer to Bloom's taxonomy in the following several chapters as a way to help you think about your goals for student learning and to help you choose the best way to achieve them.

SUMMARY

In this chapter, we have discussed several aspects of student learning that provide a guide for effective teaching. First, we have seen that developing expertise takes considerable time and effort, no matter how bright the individual; the result of this effort is that experts can process information very rapidly through a system of efficient organization and retrieval. To help students progress along the path toward developing expertise, teachers must therefore provide opportunities for practice with feedback and a learning environment which motivates the students to work hard. Furthermore, teachers need to help students develop an organizational structure for learning new material so that the information is readily available for retrieval.

Second, we have seen that students' backgrounds, interests, and ways of learning vary greatly. Teachers must be aware of these differences in the classroom, occasionally altering teaching strategies to accommodate different types of learners, and be sensitive to the needs of individual students when working one-on-one or with small groups of students. In addition, teachers can suggest various learning strategies to the students to help them achieve the course objectives.

Third, we have explored the process of learning in terms of transferring information from short-term to long-term memory, and in terms of developing discipline-specific problem solving skills. We have also briefly reviewed current models emphasizing that students must internalize new information in order to be able to use it later in different applications. Two ways in which students can accomplish this are by studying example problems worked out by others and by working through new problems to reach solutions. Teachers need to offer learning activities that are consistent with both of these approaches.

Finally, we summarize educational goals which can help us to identify reasonable expectations of student learning and which are used as a basis for several issues on teaching in later chapters. In the next chapter, we turn to creating and implementing effective courses which take into consideration the various characteristics of student learning.

REFERENCES

Anderson, J.R., Skill acquisition: Compilation of weak-method problem solutions, *Psychological Review, Vol. 92, No. 2,* pp. 192–210, 1987.

Anderson, J.R., *Cognitive Psychology and its Implications,* New York, NY: W.H. Freeman, pp. 112–177, 1990.

Bloom, B.S., J.T. Hastings, and G.F. Madaus, *Taxonomy of Educational Objectives: The Classification of Educational Goals, Handbook 1, Cognitive Domain,* New York, NY: McCay, 1956.

Bransford, J.D., *Human Cognition,* Belmont, CA: Wadsworth, 1979.

Canfield, A., *Learning Styles Inventory Manual,* Ann Arbor, MI: Humanics Media, 1980.

Claxton, C.S. and P.H. Murrell, *Learning Styles: Implications for Improving Educational Practices,* Washington, DC: Association for the Study of Higher Education, 1987.

Grasha, A.F., Using traditional versus naturalistic approaches to assessing learning styles in college teaching, *Journal on Excellence in College Teaching, Vol. 1,* pp. 23–28, 1990.

Kolb, D.A., *Learning Style Inventory,* Boston, MA: McBer and Company, 1976.

Mayer, R.E., Instructional variables in text processing, in A. Flammer and W. Kintsch, editors, *Discourse Planning,* Amsterdam: North-Holland, 1982.

McKeachie, W.J., Improving lectures by understanding students' information processing, in W.J. McKeachie, editor, *Learning, Cognition, and College Teaching,* San Francisco, CA: Jossey-Bass, pp. 25–35, 1980.

McKeachie, W.J., P.R. Pintrich, Y. Lin, and D.A.F. Smith, *Teaching and Learning in the College Classroom: A Review of the Research Literature,* Ann Arbor, MI: National Center for Research to Improve Postsecondary Teaching and Learning, University of Michigan, pp. 30–35, 1986.

Myers, I.B. and D.B. Myers, *Gifts Differing,* Palo Alto, CA: Consulting Psychologist Press, 1980.

Myers, I.B., *Introduction to Type,* Gainesville, FL: Center for the Application of Psychological Type, 1976.

Reichmann, S. and A. Grasha, A rational approach to developing and assessing the construct validity of a student learning style scales instrument, *Journal of Psychology, Vol. 87,* pp. 213–223, 1974.

Simon, H.A., The information system called "human memory," in M.R. Rosenzweig and E.L. Bennett, editors, *Neural Mechanisms of Learning and Memory*, Cambridge, MA: MIT Press, 1976.

Simon, H.A., Problem solving and education, in D.T. Tuma and F. Reif, *Problem Solving and Education: Issues in Teaching and Research*, Hillsdale, NJ: Lawrence Erlbaum Associates, pp. 81–96, 1980.

Simon, H.A., *The Sciences of the Artificial*, Cambridge, MA: MIT Press, pp. 106–108, 1981.

Simon, H.A. and Gilmartin, K.A., A simulation of memory for chess positions, *Cognitive Psychology, Vol. 5*, pp. 29–46, 1973.

Weinstein, C.E., D.R. Palmer, and A.C. Shulte, *Learning and Study Strategies Inventory (LASSI)*, Clearwater, FL: Holt Publishing Co., 1987.

Weinstein, C.E., Assessment and training of student learning strategies, in R.R. Schmeck, editor, *Learning Strategies and Learning Styles,* New York NY: Plenum Press, pp. 291–316, 1988.

2

PLANNING
A COURSE

INTRODUCTION

In Chapter 1, we examined several characteristics of student learning. We considered ways in which individuals make the transition from novice to expert, and identified aspects of student backgrounds and interests which can impact learning. We also discussed models describing how the human mind processes information, and considered educational goals. How can you use this material as you plan a course? That is the subject of this chapter.

As a new faculty member with a recently completed Ph.D. thesis or postdoctoral work, you probably feel confident of your research skills. After all, you have devoted at least two or three years (or more) to your research project, and most of the interactions with your advisor have probably focused on research. You may also have had extended discussions on research questions with other graduate students, undergraduates, and staff members. In contrast to your experience in research, you probably feel much less confident about your ability to plan and teach a course. This is to be expected: few graduate students have as much experience in teaching as in research, and many have never taught by the time they receive their Ph.D.

Briggs and Wager (1981) define a course as "that organization of instructional activities, resources, and evaluation activities which leads to a prespecified directional change in the learners' behavior." This definition implies that many steps are involved in planning a course. In fact, developing a successful college-level course requires the same kind of effort as developing a successful research project. Although it *does* take a lot of work, there are many reasons why you should adopt a serious attitude toward your courses, even if you are at an institution that emphasizes research.

1. Education is a primary function of any college or university, and as a faculty member, you play an essential role in making sure this function is carried out in the best possible way. For this reason, many schools now require instructors to allow students to evaluate their courses; the results may be used in the promotion process.

2. Students expect and deserve high quality courses. Most of them pay a high price for their degree in time, energy, and money, and it simply isn't fair to shortchange them.

3. The development of courses can help you to develop a research program more easily (and vice versa) because there are many common tasks. Furthermore, exposure through coursework can introduce talented undergraduate and graduate students to your research interests and can thus serve as a means of attracting students into your research projects.

4. Careful course planning is time-efficient for faculty members inundated during a semester with the many responsibilities of faculty life.

5. Teaching can provide "intrinsic rewards" such as the opportunity to help others expand their knowledge and skills. These intrinsic rewards are the mainstay of an academic career.

In this chapter, we first present some general principles in undergraduate education upon which the next several chapters are based. Then we consider the analogy between planning a research project and planning a course. Next, we examine each of several steps in the process of planning a successful course. Finally, we summarize the process and mention ways to continually improve existing courses.

Helping Students Learn: Eight Principles of Undergraduate Education

Several educators have summarized principles for teaching at colleges and universities. In this section, we present a set that is a variation of the seven principles proposed by Chickering and Gamson (1987) but have been reordered and modified. Such principles have been used to develop teaching inventories and have provided a basis for continuing research in education (e.g., Sorcinelli, 1991). The principles listed below provide a foundation for the specific suggestions on planning a course and teaching that follow.

1. *Encourage active learning.* Students should be prepared to work hard when they enter a classroom, taking an active role in acquiring and maintaining new information during the class. They should continue their interest after

class hours as they work on their homework assignments. You can encourage active learning by keeping the material relevant and interesting to the students. For example, you can ask frequent questions to arouse their curiosity, present thought-provoking problems to encourage critical thinking, and provide them with concrete, real-life situations to analyze. Virtually all students are motivated about learning *some* things; you need to get the students to include your course material on their list.

Note: In the exercises which follow, the questions are phrased assuming some prior teaching experience. If you have not yet taught a course, imagine how you would answer the question in your future teaching responsibilities.

Exercise: In the last class session you taught, what questions did you ask and what examples did you use to stimulate interest in the course? How much "air time" did students have to question and comment? How many concrete examples did you use? Did the students have opportunities in class to apply the new concepts?

2. *Design effective learning experiences for students.* Most of the learning in a typical course takes place out of class. It is therefore important to design activities that will help the students learn after class hours, such as reading assignments, homework problems, group projects, laboratory experiments, and computer exercises. It is often helpful to prepare assignments that apply the class material to new contexts; this can establish multiple cues that aid in retrieving the material from long-term memory the next time it is needed, as discussed in Chapter 1. Furthermore, the assignments can force the students to recognize the conditions under which the class material is most useful for solving problems.

   Exercise: List the types of learning experiences you provided in the last course you taught. How did each experience contribute to achieving the goals of the course? Which were most successful and which were least successful?

3. *Provide prompt feedback.* Learning is an iterative process where students apply a new concept, discover errors in their application, and try again. Providing feedback to students is thus an essential part of teaching. Teachers should provide such feedback as promptly as possible, and it should be both corrective and supportive. Of course, feedback is distinct from evaluation: solution sheets for homework assignments and written comments on the students' papers can provide valuable feedback even when the assignments are not graded.

   Exercise: In the last course you taught, how many short classroom problems did you use to give immediate feedback to the students? How long did it take you to return graded assignments and tests? In what ways did your feedback provide support and encouragement as well as constructive criticism?

4. *Emphasize the importance of time and effort spent learning.* We saw in Chapter 1 that there is no substitute for hard work in learning a subject well. Students must make effective use of time both in the classroom and out of class in order to be successful. You need to emphasize that *everyone* who wants to learn a subject must put in the effort; you may also want to discuss effective study habits and time management strategies with your students. Obviously, you will need to plan all learning activities carefully to permit the best use of your time and your students' time.

   Exercise: In the last course you taught, did you ever discuss time management and related strategies, either with the class or with individual students? What did you do about students who did not appear to be spending the time needed to learn the material?

5. *Encourage student-faculty contact.* Interaction between students and faculty members is at the very heart of the educational process; recall in the previous chapter that every expert had a teacher who was also an expert in the same discipline. You need to interact effectively with your students in the classroom, displaying enthusiasm, sensitivity, and command of the subject matter. You also need to allow time for effective interaction out of class; this may be confined to tutoring during office hours, but may also extend to nonacademic affairs such as department social activities.

   Exercise: In the last course you taught, how many of the students did you know by name? How many times did students stop by your office to pursue course-related or non-course issues? In what ways did you show your students that you were receptive to helping them? Related to these issues, have you shown an interest in your students in other ways, such as by attending campus events sponsored by student groups?

6. *Encourage cooperation among students.* Promoting interactions among students in a class can have a marked positive effect. This type of cooperation can help students enhance their self-esteem, improve their collaborative skills, and develop personal responsibility. You can encourage these interactions in many ways. For example, you can organize cooperative in-class exercises such as group discussions, or you can assign group projects. The ultimate goal of such interactions is to help students learn from one another as well as on their own.

   Exercise: In the last course you taught, how many projects were assigned in which students were required to work together? In what ways did you encourage students to interact with each other during class discussions? Out of class?

7. *Communicate high expectations.* Contrary to popular belief, students often give their highest ratings to the most difficult classes they take. Attendance and class participation are also greatest in classes where students have to work hard. The message is clear: teachers who demand a lot of their students have the most successful classes in terms of both student enjoyment and learning. Therefore, to be an effective teacher, you need to set high but attainable goals. You also must make your expectations clear to the students, explaining that they will need to work hard and that their efforts will be rewarded. The personal "intrinsic" rewards should be emphasized—how mastery of the material can help the students in later pursuits.

Exercise: In the last course you taught, did you clearly define what you expected the students to be able to do after they completed the course? What did you do about students who had low self-confidence and were performing poorly?

8. *Respect diverse talents and ways of learning.* Each student brings a unique set of abilities, interests, and experiences into the classroom, resulting in different ways of learning as outlined in Chapter 1. You need to be responsive to these differences, varying your teaching style to reach the concrete thinkers and the abstract thinkers, the competitive and the noncompetitive, the dependent and the independent. You also need to encourage all students to voice their views on a topic while respecting the views of others. It may take a special effort to ensure that all students understand the material, such as by using language and examples that do not exclude students of certain cultures.

Exercise: In the last few class sessions you taught, what were the different strategies you used to reach students with various learning preferences? To what extent did you challenge students to develop new learning preferences? For students who never really "caught on," did you attempt to discover the reason and possibly alter your approach accordingly?

These eight principles provide a framework for the suggestions that follow, both in this chapter on planning a course and in the next several chapters that cover different aspects of teaching.

ANALOGY BETWEEN PLANNING A RESEARCH PROJECT AND PLANNING A COURSE

Successful faculty members must be adept in both research and teaching. Although these two roles are sometimes viewed as conflicting, many of the same skills are, in fact, involved in both categories. This is evident if we compare the major steps in planning a research project, particularly one that requires a proposal for funding, and planning a course. Such a comparison is illustrated in

Table 2-1. Although we present these steps in a linear fashion, we recognize that planning a research project or a course is an iterative process.

There are many differences in the details within each list, but there are also some important similarities. In particular, characterizing the audience, defining the objectives and scope of work, developing the work plan to achieve the objectives, and evaluating the results are common to both research and course planning. Note that Chapters 7 and 8 cover the steps in planning research and writing a proposal.

STEPS IN PLANNING A COURSE

Developing a course requires considerable effort. However, careful planning before the semester begins can save time in the long run, and can result in far better learning experiences for the students. Each of the steps listed in Table 2-1 is discussed below.

Assess the Backgrounds and Interests of Your Students

In Chapter 1, we presented some examples of student characteristics that influence learning. Such characteristics are vital in designing a course. For example, you must make sure that the learning activities in the course are appropriate for the backgrounds of the students; you don't want to spend a lot of time converting centimeters to meters or grams to kilograms in a senior physics class. On the other hand, you had better not assume that beginning freshmen can convert centipoises to slugs per foot per second. And remember from Chapter 1 that there is almost certain to be a spectrum of student backgrounds in your classes. Most students are probably used to working in metric units, but you may find students with more exposure to the English system—and some may actually *prefer* it! There will also be a variety of different groups represented—men and women, fast learners and slow learners, students from different ethnic groups and nationalities—and you will want to think about these groups as you plan the course. Suggestions on how to account for such different groups in discussion classes and lectures are presented in later chapters.

As emphasized in Chapter 1, the interests of the students—what motivates them—are also very important. Many engineering freshman want exposure to "real-world" engineering problems as soon as they arrive. Giving them lots of abstract mathematics before letting them see their first application to engineering is not likely to sit well. You will probably need to find creative compromises to satisfy their interest in problems that are beyond their current skills.

You can gather information about the students' backgrounds and interests through faculty colleagues who are familiar with the group of students you will be teaching. You also may want to use simple, anonymous questionnaires on the first day of the class. You can provide a number of topic areas where students can identify prior exposure, and you can ask them to list their interests and

TABLE 2-1

Steps in Planning a Research Project and Planning a Course

Planning a Research Project	*Planning a Course*
1. For a particular category of research, determine the possible funding agencies and their interests.	1. For each course, determine the backgrounds and interests of the students likely to enroll.
2. Choose the objectives of the research based on these interests as well as your interests and expertise.	2. Choose the objectives of the course based on these backgrounds and on the knowledge and skills which you deem appropriate to teach, as well as on your interest and expertise.
3. Choose the scope and content of the research based on time and money constraints.	3. Choose the scope and content of the course based on time and money constraints.
4. Develop a research plan to achieve the objectives, within the scope previously determined. The plan may include theoretical work, experimental work in the laboratory or field, survey questionnaires, etc. The experiments must be carefully designed, and appropriate data analysis and interpretation techniques must be chosen.	4. Develop the learning experiences to achieve the objectives, within the scope previously determined. These experiences may include in-class activities such as lectures, recitations, and group meetings, as well as out-of-class activities such as required readings and homework assignments.
5. Develop procedures to evaluate the success of the project, and disseminate the major findings through papers and presentations.	5. Plan feedback and evaluation of student learning through tests, written reports, and other assessment techniques.
6. Prepare a final proposal based on the considerations above.	6. Prepare a syllabus based on the considerations above.

expectations pertaining to the course. For certain courses, it may be appropriate to ask them to list their major and year in college. Some instructors also give a pre-test to determine the starting point for the course, including reviews of pre-requisite concepts.

All of this information-gathering underscores an important point: an instructor must take the characteristics of the students into account as the primary factor in deciding how and what to teach. And because it may be difficult to get the information you need and to know exactly how to use it, accounting for student backgrounds and interests requires experimentation. Few instructors are able to design a course that fulfills their expectations on the first try.

Exercise: Consider the last course you taught. What questions would have been appropriate to include on a pre-test for the first day of class? How would you use the responses to design the learning experiences of the course?

Choose the Course Objectives

Objectives serve different purposes for the teacher and the students. For the teacher, objectives provide a road map by which the class will travel: they can help you to plan effective learning experiences. Students, on the other hand, can use these objectives as instructional cues that indicate what they should learn. In some cases, the objectives can help students to understand why you have assigned certain readings and created the exams in a particular way (e.g., Levin and Long, 1981). Recall that one of the eight principles in the previous section was to communicate high expectations to your students; a clear set of objectives tells the students what you expect them to learn.

The objectives should indicate the expected knowledge and competence of the students by the end of the course. Each objective should state what the students should be able to do if they successfully complete the course; in this way, you can observe and measure the extent to which a student has satisfied an objective. Chapter 1 noted that specific statements of what a student is expected to do can provide motivation by clarifying the goals of a course. Consider the following examples:

+ The student will be able to identify the fundamental dimensions of force, momentum, energy, and other physical variables, and will be able to use relations involving these variables to solve simple problems in mechanics.

+ The student will be able to construct the pole-zero diagram of a transfer function and relate the location of the poles and zeros to the impulse and step resources.

+ The student will be able to make observations of a laboratory experiment and communicate these observations clearly in both written and verbal form.

✦ The student will be able to apply established engineering principles to solve problems in construction of a water distribution system.

✦ The student will be able to design and administer a questionnaire to determine public opinion on new designs for automobiles.

✦ The student will be able to argue effectively both sides of a debate on whether a natural wetlands area should be removed to construct a new shopping mall.

There is quite a bit of flexibility in choosing objectives. One course may be designed primarily to promote depth of knowledge in a particular topic, while another may focus on developing problem-solving skills. Nevertheless, the prudent instructor will consider a variety of objectives: students need a broad knowledge base and repertoire of skills to function effectively on-the-job, and they need to know when and how to use the information they have acquired. It is especially important that they understand how to continue learning independently once they leave college.

You may wish to consider the taxonomy of Bloom et al. (1956), discussed in Chapter 1, as you decide on course objectives. For example, you may determine that your students should be able to interpret a set of data (comprehension), use abstract information in a concrete situation (application), or state the underlying assumptions of a body of information (analysis).

Exercise: Consider the syllabus for the last course you taught. Were all your objectives stated in terms of what the students should be able to do by the end of the course? If not, how could the objectives be revised to indicate this?

Choose the Scope and Content of the Course

Here we come to a difficult issue: it seems that there is never enough time to cover all of the topics we feel are "essential" in a course. To solve this problem, some faculty will try to cram as much information as possible into a course, sacrificing depth. And the students learn very little, overall, except perhaps how not to teach a course. The truth of the matter is that *any* course could always cover more topics if we had infinite time—so let us admit that the best we can do is a "sampling" of topic areas within the broad subject of the course. As one of our colleagues often says: "Coverage is the enemy of teaching."

You should start at the level of understanding of the students as they enter your course. You then want to move forward at a pace that allows the students to learn the material thoroughly, getting as far as you can according to their backgrounds and abilities.

How can you make sure that the course will be of maximum usefulness, given the uncertainty in how far you can progress? One way is to begin your planning by listing topic areas that are candidates for the course. Then rank the topics in order of what you consider most important in the field and what you believe will interest the students. Based on rough estimates of the time needed to cover each topic, you can then make a tentative plan as to the content of the course. There obviously must be compromises in sequencing the material: on one hand, there must be a logical flow to the topic areas, but you also want to be sure to include at least some of the most important ones.

You may want to discuss with the students why you chose certain topics and omitted others. Content selection and sequencing decisions are strongly related to the way you view your academic discipline: by letting your students know how you put the course together, they may more effectively understand the flow of the course and its relation to the discipline (Lowther et al., 1989).

In Chapter 1 and earlier in this chapter, we emphasized the wide range in backgrounds, interests, and abilities among students. To accommodate this variability, you may wish to consider three categories of subject matter to include in the course: *basic* material which should be mastered by every student who passes the course, *recommended* material which should be mastered by those students seeking a thorough knowledge of the subject, and *optional* material which is intended only for those students with special interests who desire to learn more than what is offered in the course (Davis, 1992).

> *Exercise: Consider the last course you taught. Obtain syllabi for this course from other faculty members who taught it previously—either at your institution or others. Compare the various syllabi and explore the differences. Can you defend your choice of the topics you covered, and the structure of your course overall? What changes may be worth trying?*

Develop the Learning Experiences Within the Course

Keeping in mind the students' backgrounds and interests, the objectives, and the scope and content of the course, you must now attend to the specific learning activities that comprise the course. These may include lectures, recitation sessions, in-class problem solving exercises, tests, oral presentations, group projects, laboratory sessions, homework assignments, and other activities.

First, you must choose the textbooks or other reading material. If the course has been taught by others in previous semesters, you should examine the material they used—but don't adopt it without careful thought. You need to feel comfortable with the material: the way you teach the course is going to be somewhat different than the way others taught it. Consider factors such as the level of difficulty, the amount of detail, and the cost of the books. Note that the choice of reading material is a way to clarify objectives. For example, if you want to stress highly organized mastery of a body of information, a single text might be the best choice. If, on the other hand, you wish to have the students develop skills in comparing and evaluating disparate sources of information, a collection of materials may be justified. You need to think carefully about whether you want the reading material to elaborate on information presented in class, or whether you intend the readings to convey additional information. It is important that you don't choose a text intending to simply repeat information from the book in class. For one thing, reiterating reading material is not effective use of class time, which is far too limited to cover everything of importance in the text. Furthermore, students will realize that there is no need to come to class if they simply read the text—depriving themselves of the student-teacher contact that is so important for effective learning. This is discussed further in Chapter 4 on Lecturing.

Second, examine the reading material critically to determine where to place your emphasis and the logical order of coverage. It is usually inefficient simply to plan your course around textbook chapters in the order they were written: other authors would probably have ordered the chapters differently. A good instructor often needs to rearrange the order of chapters, delete certain material, and supplement the textbook with readings from other sources. Be sure that the reading material is well-integrated, and that the course flows logically from one topic to another. Make sure that you explain to your students the reasons for deviating from the text. In introductory courses, e.g., for freshmen, you may want to adhere to the textbook more closely than in advanced classes to help beginning students avoid confusion.

Third, determine the types of activities that will provide the students with opportunities to practice newly acquired skills, apply new information in different contexts, and ultimately achieve the course objectives. For example, if you want your students to develop skills in conducting engineering analysis, you will probably want to include quantitative homework problems. Group projects should be included if the course emphasizes working with others. Learning to communicate effectively is an element of some engineering and science courses; assigning written and oral reports will help students develop communication skills. In any course, such activities are at the heart of learning, so you need to choose them carefully. Chapter 5 on preparing activities for students covers this topic in more detail.

Fourth, create a course schedule based on the university calendar and on the amount of time needed to cover each topic adequately. Choose beginning and ending dates for major units to avoid conflicts with holiday periods. Allow time for correcting papers so that students get feedback before the next assignment is due. It is best to schedule class activities, homework assignments, and examinations in advance, to the extent possible, when you put together the calendar for the course. This will help students to manage their time more effectively.

Finally, examine all of the components of the course to make sure that they are consistent and complement each other in the manner intended. For example, your students are more likely to read assignments day by day if readings are pegged to particular lectures, or if the reading material is mentioned explicitly in class. This step is necessary to insure that all components of the course are coordinated, including lectures, recitations, reading materials, written assignments, projects, laboratory experiments, and examinations.

Exercise: Consider a course you are currently teaching. Are there a number of learning activities, or are students relying mainly on listening to lectures? If there are several types of learning activities, how does each activity contribute to achieving the objectives of the course?

Plan Feedback and Evaluation of Student Learning

After choosing the objectives, the scope and content of the course, and the learning experiences, you must plan methods of providing feedback to the students on their performance. This will enable them to determine how they should direct their future efforts in learning course material. You also need to consider how you will conduct evaluations, judging the "value" of the learning by each student. Recall that one of the eight principles was to provide prompt feedback; unfortunately, many new professors underestimate the difficulty of creating effective feedback and evaluation tools. Methods most commonly used include quizzes, examinations, formal student presentations, written reports, and problem sets given as homework. There are also a variety of classroom assessment techniques, essentially short in-class exercises, which can provide valuable feedback to both you and the students on the amount of learning taking place (Cross and Angelo, 1988). These exercises are discussed in Chapter 3.

College faculty too often base their choice of feedback and evaluation tools solely on personal preference, philosophical beliefs, time available, and habit (Lowman, 1984). It is important, however, to tailor your methods to the goals of the particular topic area. For example, testing the students on their creative problem-solving abilities may require you to develop open-ended problems. On the other hand, closed-form mathematical problems with unique solutions may be more appropriate for testing analytical skills. Written assignments may be best suited for testing synthesis and evaluation skills.

You should consider different ways in which you can provide feedback and evaluation. For example, you can use the results of a quiz to assign a grade or class rank, but you can also use the results as an indicator of where the student needs to place more effort or what topics need to be re-examined in lecture. To provide timely feedback, you may want to discuss the solutions to a quiz immediately after the students hand in their papers. Similarly, you may want to provide brief written comments on graded examinations and put together solution sheets to help students better understand their errors. Additional information on developing homework assignments and examinations is provided in Chapter 5.

Once you have chosen the individual components of the evaluation process, it is necessary to determine the appropriate weights in computing the final grade for the course. What fraction of the final grade will be based on performance on homework assignments? What fraction on the results of tests? The weighting scheme is a guide to students which indicates the relative importance attributed to each component. You should provide this scheme in writing at the beginning of the semester. Related to this issue are the criteria you use for grading, which also should be made clear to the students. Grading criteria are discussed in Chapter 5.

> *Exercise: Consider a course you are currently teaching. What types of evaluation tools are used? How is feedback given for each (solution sets, written comments on student papers, comments presented in class, etc.)? Do you lean more heavily to evaluation than feedback?*

Prepare a Syllabus for the Course

Just as a research proposal is the culmination of a considerable amount of preparatory work, writing the syllabus takes place only after you have attended to the many details of course organization. A syllabus tells students a lot about the instructor: a well-prepared syllabus can leave a lasting first impression which reflects the instructor's goals, direction, commitment, organization, and enthusiasm for the course. Furthermore, students learn more effectively when they understand the faculty member's intentions and expectations about a course.

Many faculty members and students view the syllabus as more than simply a list of information: they consider it a type of contract, presenting what students can expect from the instructor and, in turn, what the instructor can expect from the students. The students need to know where they are heading, why they are heading this way, and what requirements they must fulfill to be successful in the course.

The syllabus should explain the rationale, purpose, content, and procedures for the course. In a recent survey at our institution, we found that the following items were included in the most complete syllabi:

+ The name and number of the course, number of credits, the name of the University, the date by semester and year, the classroom meeting place, and a list of prerequisites.

+ The names, office locations, office hours, phone numbers and electronic mail addresses of the professor and teaching assistants.

+ A brief course description that provides an overview of the subject matter and a brief explanation of why students might want to take the course. The syllabus might also contain a brief explanation of how the parts of the course fit together.

+ A list of course objectives, stated in terms of what the students should be able to do by the end of the course.

+ Information about the learning experiences in the course, including in-class activities such as lectures and discussions, and out-of-class activities such as readings and homework assignments.

+ Information about policies established for the course, including attendance, late work, and make-up work.

+ A course calendar which includes (to the extent possible) a list of dates for homework assignments, readings, quizzes, tests, papers, projects, and other work.

+ Information about how grades will be determined, including the percentage of the grade for each major element of the course.

+ A caveat that indicates that parts of the course are subject to change to meet the needs of students in the course. This allows instructors to slow down or speed up the pace of the course if students show a need.

Some syllabi contain helpful hints to students on how to read certain material, take notes in class, or study for a particular type of test. These hints are particularly important for first year students who may not yet have adapted to the pace of university life or mastered effective study habits. Other syllabi provide study questions for students to think about as they read assignments outside of class; this technique is popular with faculty members who use case studies in class. Still other syllabi discuss issues of cheating and plagiarism, defining what constitutes each and outlining penalties for infractions.

A well-prepared syllabus can help both you and the students to achieve the course objectives. It is a necessary part of virtually any successful course.

Exercise: Look at one of your recent syllabi and compare it with the list above. Which items might you add to your syllabus to improve it? Are there items omitted from the list above that you feel should be included?

SUMMARY

This chapter has discussed the many issues related to planning a course. We begin by listing eight principles of undergraduate education as a foundation for future suggestions on course planning and teaching. Then we discuss similarities that exist between the steps in planning a research project and planning a course. Next, we discuss ways of determining the backgrounds and interests of students, provide examples of course objectives, and give suggestions for choosing the course content and learning activities. We also discuss ways of providing feedback to the students and evaluating their progress. Finally, we discuss the culmination of these efforts, namely preparing the course syllabus.

While the amount of work spent on planning a course is likely to be substantial, most faculty members report that they become more adept at the process with each new course. Also, as the course is taught in successive years, much of the groundwork will have already been laid. Nevertheless, a good instructor always re-evaluates a course based on feedback from students, changes in available information, and opportunities to implement new teaching strategies. Furthermore, each group of students is different and thus most courses require changes in scope and content. A successful course requires continual iteration.

REFERENCES

Bloom, B.S., J.T. Hastings, and G.F. Madaus, *Taxonomy of Educational Objectives: The Classification of Educational Goals, Handbook 1, Cognitive Domain,* New York, NY: McCay, 1956.

Briggs, L.J. and W.W. Wager, *Handbook of Procedures for the Design of Instruction,* Englewood Cliffs, NJ: Educational Technology Publications, p.77, 1981.

Chickering, A.W. and Z.F. Gamson, Seven principles for good practice in undergraduate education, *AAHE Bulletin, Vol. 39,* pp. 3–7, 1987.

Cross, K.P. and T.A. Angelo, *Classroom Assessment Techniques: A Handbook for Faculty,* Ann Arbor, MI : National Center for Research to Improve Postsecondary Teaching and Learning, The University of Michigan, 1988.

Davis, B.G., *Tools for Teaching,* San Francisco, CA: Jossey-Bass, p.5, 1993.

Levin, T. and R. Long, *Effective Instruction,* Alexandria, VA: Association for Supervision and Curriculum Development, pp. 27–28, 1981.

Lowman, J., *Mastering the Techniques of Teaching,* San Francisco, CA: Jossey-Bass, pp.184–209, 1984.

Lowther, M.S., J.S. Clark, and G.G. Martens, *Preparing Course Syllabi for Improved Communication,* Ann Arbor, MI: National Center for Research to Improve Postsecondary Teaching and Learning (NCRIPTAL), 1989.

Sorcinelli, M.D., Research findings on the seven principles, in A.W. Chickering and Z.F. Gamson, editors, *Applying the Seven Principles for Good Practice in Undergraduate Education,* San Francisco, CA: Jossey-Bass, pp. 13–25, 1991.

3

CONDUCTING DISCUSSIONS

INTRODUCTION

One of the joys of teaching is the personal interaction with students. It can be gratifying to see your students come up with a workable hypothesis, write a computer program that works, or figure out a mathematical proof. And it is especially gratifying to see them develop lifelong learning habits that get them started on a road to achieve their goals. Something *you* did is at least partly responsible for this positive change in behavior.

Up to this point, however, we have not addressed any details of student-teacher interactions. Now, having identified the foundation of how students learn and how courses may be structured, we are ready to delve into the art of classroom teaching. This chapter offers suggestions on how to lead class discussions, thereby helping students develop critical thinking and problem solving skills. Other methods of teaching are covered in successive chapters.

All faculty members lead discussions from time to time. These may be formal classroom discussions where students on opposing sides of an issue come prepared to voice their comments, or they may be impromptu discussions that develop naturally during class. Most of us develop the necessary skills simply by observing other discussion leaders. We adapt the techniques of others in our own discussions, using trial and error, and hope to improve over time. Here we attempt to make this process more efficient by offering a number of suggestions. Our claim is that *anyone* can become an effective discussion leader—with practice. In this chapter, we first suggest ways to prepare yourself prior to the discussion: we list information you need to obtain and how you can use it. Then we elaborate on your role during the discussion, focusing on how to provide effective leadership. Finally we present methods of evaluating the success of your discussion. Although we confine the chapter to discussions in the classroom, most of the issues also apply to other types of group meetings and thus are of rather general interest.

PREPARING FOR THE DISCUSSION

Assured that you have mastered the subject matter, you should now think about the upcoming discussion in terms of assessing the human element, evaluating the physical environment, planning the strategy which will influence the discussion, and preparing the students for the discussion. Let's consider each of these topics.

Assess the Human Element

Take a close look at your students as you prepare for the discussion. How big is the group? Do they include extroverts who won't want to stop talking, or are they mostly shy individuals who will need to be cajoled into contributing? What are their educational backgrounds? What is the gender ratio and mix of cultural backgrounds? Other factors may also be important, such as whether the students know each other well, and whether they have had prior experience with discussion groups.

Although a small group can have a productive discussion that is relatively unstructured, a larger group often needs more structure to keep the process orderly. All of us have been in group meetings where the discussion has gotten off track—no one is sure where the conversation is heading and everyone seems to have forgotten the reason for the meeting in the first place! A large group generally needs a strong discussion leader who can interrupt when necessary and steer the conversation back on course.

The educational backgrounds of the students are also important. If their backgrounds are varied and possibly weak, you may need to begin by asking some questions to establish a baseline for the class. Otherwise, the discussion may begin at a level that is too advanced, and many students will be lost from the start. Can you recall being a student in a group discussion and realizing that you don't have the vaguest idea of what's going on? The first thought is panic— you might be called on to comment. Then you look around and realize very few others know what's going on, but everyone is afraid to ask. Try to minimize the chance of that happening in *your* class. Find the right starting point.

Students who have never been involved in a discussion class before may need extra time to adjust to the somewhat altered role of the teacher and the students (MacGregor, 1990). If some are taking the course as an elective, their level of motivation may be much higher than that of students who are required to take the course. And if the students know each other well, the tension of talking in front of peers may be lessened under most circumstances. Give the students opportunities to get to know each other early in the semester, e.g., through group projects or small discussion groups.

Understanding the human element also includes recognition that diversity has many dimensions: race, gender, ethnicity, and disability, to name a few. Many people fear that discussing these issues simply reinforces stereotypes. However, if we carefully distinguish between images that are demeaning and those traits that help us to better understand certain groups, we are able to assist individuals in these groups. In particular, we can help them develop their strengths while they learn to work within a complex and sometimes biased educational system. A law student at the University of Michigan sums it up well: "Recognition of differences can serve to enforce and strengthen divisions or it can help to build and sustain a common understanding. For myself, although I cannot help but speak as an Asian American, I also hope to be heard and to listen, as an individual" (Wu, 1991). While there are no specific rules for responding to diversity in the classroom, you should be aware of your own biases and those which society imposes.

As an example, gender has received great attention in academe lately. Recent studies indicate that many faculty members (both male and female) treat women differently from men in the classroom, through overt or subtle actions. Some behaviors have been cited by women as particularly discomforting (Hall and Sandler, 1982; Tannen, 1990). Examples include:

+ Ignoring women while recognizing men, even when women clearly volunteer to participate in class
+ Calling directly on men but not on women
+ Calling men by name more often than women
+ Addressing the class as if no women were present
+ Waiting longer for men than for women to answer a question

As a discussion leader, you have a responsibility to insure that both men and women students in your classes feel comfortable—which can happen only by your developing a sensitivity to the issue of gender.

Members of another group have received increasing attention in the last decade: the "high risk" students (Jones and Watson, 1990). These include students of various ethnic backgrounds and races, disadvantaged students, the disabled, and students from socio-economic backgrounds whose probability of attrition is above average. All students do not receive equal preparation in their elementary and secondary schools, and high risk students are often at a disadvantage in the college classroom. Many of them come from low-income school districts where facilities and resources are inferior. In some school systems, these students are disproportionately placed in lower ability tracks. Moreover, the content of courses in these tracks is often different from that offered to students in other tracks; even instructional styles vary. As a result, bright but underprepared students—often with low self-esteem—arrive in our classrooms at an immediate disadvantage.

Although colleges and universities vary in their attention to the problem, most of them are beginning to identify the needs of high risk students. Many schools are implementing changes to help these students, such as hiring faculty and staff from nontraditional backgrounds, adding courses of particular interest to certain student groups, guaranteeing financial assistance, and creating social support networks.

Whatever the backgrounds of our students, we need to be careful not to judge them against expectations based predominantly on the performance of white males. As a leader in a discussion class, you can help students of various races and ethnic groups achieve their best by being sensitive to their needs. For example, in African-American culture, self-esteem is more peer-related, based not so much on academic success as on standing in a social group; traditional classroom discussions often ignore the importance of peer impressions (Collett, 1990; Guerriero, 1990). Thus you can help by allowing opportunities for students to test their opinions with peers as well as with the teacher. You can also acknowledge a student for taking a leadership position in the discussion.

As another example of cultural differences, Mexican-American students are often reared with the belief that one should not challenge authority (Cortes, 1978). These students may feel uncomfortable in class discussions that are posed as challenges between students and teachers. You can help by structuring some of your discussions to avoid direct confrontations; for those discussions where you wish to use provocative statements to elicit open disagreement, be sure to state your intentions up front. You may need to show particular sensitivity to certain students to help bring them into the discussion.

This need for sensitivity also extends to the increasing number of international students at many American colleges and universities. Faculty members must be prepared to help students from other countries become a part of the classroom discussion. For example, the Japanese emphasize indirectness to a much greater extent than Americans, taking care *not* to be too direct when communicating (Maurice, 1986). When responding to a Japanese student, you might need to ask several follow-up questions to what appears to be a superficial answer, instead of simply assuming that the student does not know the answer. Similarly, the Vietnamese culture emphasizes harmony, making it difficult for those students to contradict someone outright during a discussion (Garner, 1989). Consequently, you may need to intervene and reiterate what appears to be a subtly different perspective given by a Vietnamese student so that other students understand it as a new or opposing point of view. On the other hand, many European cultures emphasize direct and even argumentative language

(Maurice, 1986). Many specific traits and characteristics of different ethnic groups, and implications for classroom discussions, are now beginning to be published (e.g., Smith, 1989).

Conducting a discussion with students of different backgrounds can be an enriching experience in cultural awareness for the class. However, you do not want to put students on the spot by asking them to be representatives of a particular group. For example, you do not want to risk embarrassing a Jewish student by asking that individual how Jews on campus feel about a particular issue. Of course, a student may wish to volunteer an opinion for a group, which may be quite appropriate.

It is clear that planning a discussion requires consideration of the many human variables involved, and that learning how to account for these diverse backgrounds is a challenge. By recognizing the importance of the human element and developing a willingness to experiment, you are taking the first step to accepting this challenge.

Exercise: Think of the various descriptors you can use to categorize people as summarized above (gender, race, ethnic background, sexual preference, etc.), and consider the students you have in your current class in each of these categories. Now consider societal stereotypes for each category. How many examples can you think of where an individual does not fit a particular stereotype? Simply being aware of these stereotypes and identifying individuals who diverge from them can help sensitize us to the diversity of our students.

Evaluate the Physical Environment

The physical environment of the classroom can have a marked impact on the discussion. The size of the room, the seating arrangement within the room, and the teaching aids available (chalkboard, flip charts, overhead projectors) are important. Comfort factors which affect all of us, such as temperature, lighting, background noise, and air quality, cannot be overlooked. While faculty members usually can make only limited changes in most of the categories, we generally do have control over one of the most important determinants of a successful discussion—the seating arrangement within the room.

A poor seating arrangement can cause a lack of interaction within the group, thereby hindering what otherwise might have been a fruitful discussion. The best seating is one in which all participants can see each other. You may want to request a room with movable desks or chairs which can be placed in a circle, or a conference room which contains tables that can be placed in a U-shape.

You can also improve comfort in the classroom in some cases. For example, you can arrive early in a room which is sometimes uncomfortably hot and open the windows before the students arrive. If the room is located in a noisy area, you can open the windows and doors before class begins and then shut them when the noise level elevates. The point here is simply to make the classroom comfortable to avoid distractions that might hinder the discussion.

Plan the Strategy for the Discussion

Planning the discussion strategy begins with choosing the goals of the discussion as they relate to the course objectives. These objectives were defined in Chapter 2. You also need to decide how tightly structured the discussion should be, and how the material should be organized to best achieve your goals.

A common complaint from students about discussion classes is that the goals are often unclear or unattainable (Tiberius, 1990). To avoid this problem, you can use the same idea discussed in Chapter 2 regarding course objectives: the goals should be stated in terms of desired behavior of the students by the end of the discussion. Perhaps you want them to be able to argue effectively for deregulation of the airline industry. Or perhaps they should be able to come up with alternative solutions to a traffic intersection that always gets snarled during rush hours. In all cases, the goals need to be realistic in terms of the amount of time available, and they must be relevant to students' interests and expectations. Suggesting ways to minimize traffic congestion throughout a large urban area may be too ambitious for a one-hour class; choosing one or two intersections is more reasonable. It only takes a few minutes at the beginning of each discussion to tell the students what you expect to accomplish that day. Remember that a well-stated goal permits evaluation of the success of the discussion based on the performance of the students.

The next step in planning the strategy is to decide the appropriate level of structure which you will impose on the discussion. The spectrum runs from highly structured, e.g., with narrowly defined discussion topics and strict time limits for each speaker, to virtually unstructured, depending on your personal interests, the course material, and the group itself. For example, a group of senior electrical engineers in a circuit design class will need less structure than freshmen who have not yet chosen their majors in an introductory chemistry course. You need to decide on the amount of authority and control you would like to maintain during the class.

Finally, you need to organize the material with respect to the goals previously chosen. Welty (1989) suggests several steps which discussion leaders should go through during this planning phase:

+ Read the assignment carefully, anticipating any nuances which the students might discover.

+ Decide on important concepts and subconcepts, perhaps developing these into an outline that reflects priorities. In the middle of a good discussion, you can then quickly discard the less important concepts if time is a factor.

Experienced leaders know that discussions often go where comments lead, which may or may not be in the direction of the core concepts. You need to be ready to redirect the flow of ideas, if necessary.

✦ Create an outline of questions to match the concepts, thinking of questions that promote discussion rather than ones that have simple answers. Although you will need to ask unplanned questions in response to the direction the discussion takes, it is helpful to think in advance about higher-level inquiries that challenge the students intellectually (Bloom et al., 1956; see Chapter 1). For example, you may want to think about questions which will force the students to synthesize and evaluate the material. The best discussions evolve out of questions which students find intellectually stimulating, challenging, and exciting.

One option in planning discussions is to apply the case study method. Although traditionally used in business and law schools, case studies may be quite useful in engineering and science courses. This technique enables students to address real-world, complex problems, illustrating that such problems have no set formulas. Students learn to use their own intellect and judgment. They also have an opportunity to exercise a variety of skills, as they must determine the problem to be solved, identify background data, apply analytical tools, generate alternative solutions, evaluate their solutions, and finally recommend a course of action. Furthermore, the related roles of personal experience and learning often become clear to the students in discussions of case studies: experience provides valid data for learning, while learning organizes experience (Erskine et al., 1981).

Exercise: Consider a previous discussion you attended, either as a leader or a participant. If there were clearly stated goals, were there times when the conversation began to stray from these goals? What was done to redirect the flow of ideas? How successful was the overall discussion in meeting its goals and, in hindsight, what could have been done to have a more successful discussion?

Prepare the Students for the Discussion

The final step is to prepare the students for active participation in the discussion. Simply assigning reading material is rarely enough. Students need to read with a purpose in mind so that they can analyze, synthesize, or evaluate the information in the context of the discussion. To help students achieve this, you might try the following:

✦ Provide the students with a list of questions about the material to focus their thinking as they read. Beginning questions might ask for a recall of important facts. Later questions could then progress to higher-level thought processes to force the students into more sophisticated thinking even before the discussion begins. In this way, the students are no longer passive readers: they are now actively engaged with the material.

✦ Assign other tasks which force the students into active thought. For example, you might require the students to prepare a brief written statement on the reading. For first-year students not yet used to college-level material, this could simply be a summary of the information. For more advanced students, you might assign them to write a comparison between the author's arguments and previous class material, or an illustrative example using concepts in the reading.

✦ Ask the students to generate questions for the class discussion based on the reading material.

All of these suggestions involve writing tasks as a means of forcing the students into deeper thought. Furthermore, getting the students to think in advance about the topic may be especially valuable for reflective learners who take a bit more time to master new material, as mentioned in Chapter 1. You might use the assignment as a way to begin the discussion: ask several students to paraphrase their summaries in class, or generate a list of questions on the board from those written by the students.

There is another reason for assigning writing tasks. All academic disciplines have their own traditions, including conventions for acceptable writing. These conventions sometimes differ from what the students may have learned in English classes (Maimon, 1979). Consequently, you have the opportunity to introduce students to what constitutes acceptable writing practice in your discipline.

Exercise: Look at the same discussion you considered in the exercise in the previous section. What type of preparation was given to the students ahead of time? What specific reading and writing assignments could have been made that would have helped the students perform better in the discussion?

Providing Effective Leadership During the Discussion

The preparation which we just summarized is necessary, but not sufficient to set the stage for a successful discussion: you also need to develop an ability to lead the group effectively. This part of the process is by no means simple; it is a balancing act which takes time to perfect. In this section, we first consider the various functions of a discussion leader. Then we summarize desirable characteristics of the leader that can contribute to effective discussions. Finally, we discuss ways of dealing with participants whose behavior may impede the progress of the group.

Functions of a Discussion Leader

As leader, you need to be concerned with both the content and the process of the discussion. In terms of content, you need to introduce the issues that serve as a starting point and to make sure that these issues are being addressed in the discussion. Cooper and Heenan (1980) note that a discussion leader must serve as a *teacher* (communicating information), *synthesizer* (abstracting and condensing information), *clarifier* (providing examples and elaborating on confusing concepts), *timekeeper* (monitoring time in relation to the goals of the discussion), and *evaluator* (assessing progress towards the goals and students' reactions to the material).

In terms of process, you need to guide the group as the conversation develops by dealing with the interactions, behaviors, and feelings of the students. In this context, Cooper and Heenan (1980) note that the leader must play the role of *facilitator* (making sure all participants who wish to speak are heard), *mediator* (helping to resolve differences among group members), *climate setter* (establishing rules, procedures, norms, and behaviors), *pulse taker* (determining how participants are reacting to the discussion), and *encourager* (being warm, friendly, and responsive to encourage risk-taking). Your goal is to involve as many students as possible in the discussion—including the most passive individuals. It is particularly important that the discussion does not degenerate into a "knowledge-giving monologue" in the form of a lecture or a dialogue *between* you and the students. You need to encourage interaction *among* the students, perhaps by asking them to respond to each other's comments, or by initiating small group interactions like panel discussions or debates. Faculty members often find this part of the process difficult because many students do not believe that they can learn from their peers. Nevertheless, promoting interactions among students is one of the key functions of a discussion leader: the importance of encouraging students to learn from each other was emphasized in Chapter 2.

> *Exercise: In the last discussion you led, how many of the functions listed above applied at various times during the class? What were your functions during times that the discussion was going well? What were your functions during times that the discussion was going poorly?*

Characteristics of Discussion Leadership: Effective Behaviors

Balancing the content and process functions is a vital part of leading a discussion. In this section, we present specific behaviors that enable a leader to be effective in both of these roles, based on Cooper and Heenan (1980) and Welty (1989).

1. *Effective Questioning*: the ability to ask different types of questions, including those that demand higher level thought processes (e.g. analysis, synthesis, and evaluation from Bloom's taxonomy), those that help students to extend their thinking, and those that stimulate student-to-student interaction. As discussed in Chapter 1, some students need more time than others to reflect on questions. Thus it is important to pause and allow time for

thought after posing a question in order to bring a greater number of students into the discussion.

2. *Active Listening:* the ability to hear not only what a person is stating, but also the underlying feelings about a subject. The choice of words and the way they are communicated reveal what is important to the speaker. It is essential to communicate back to the speaker that you understand what was said through your body language, words, or use of the chalkboard.

3. *Peripheral Vision:* the ability to see, hear, and intuit the group process, and to use this ability to understand what each group member is experiencing. This task involves paying attention to non-verbal cues that indicate the level of each student's self-esteem, since self-esteem plays a major role in making students feel valued by the instructor and by the rest of the group. Students who feel valued through their contributions are better learners, so discussion leaders must recognize when to provide more direct guidance, and when to use encouragement, reinforcing words, and actions.

4. *Empathy:* the ability to see issues from another's perspective in order to make students feel comfortable discussing the non-majority view.

5. *Sense of Timing:* the knowledge of when to intervene with a question, summary, or bridge from an earlier remark, and when to remain silent.

6. *Clarity:* the sense of how to convey information in a way that is easy to understand, e.g., by restating muffled prose or using the chalkboard to clarify issues.

7. *Differentiation:* the ability of the leader to separate himself or herself from the students to facilitate the group process without becoming totally absorbed in the subject matter.

8. *Variability:* the sense of when to be serious or light, confrontive or supportive, depending on circumstances.

9. *Connecting with the Group:* the ability to reach each participant in the discussion, accounting for the emotional, intellectual, and physical state of the individual. This task includes knowing which students need help, which need stroking, and which need quieting. This task becomes easier as you become better acquainted with members of the group. Once you can recognize individual strengths, weaknesses, and interests, you will know whom to address during certain times in the discussion.

10. *Self-Disclosure:* the willingness of the leader to share feelings, thoughts, and appropriate personal information with the group.

11. *Flexibility:* the willingness of the leader to make changes in the discussion

format and content if necessary. Welty calls this "controlled spontaneity" — maintaining a balance between free wheeling discussion and control.

How can an individual learn these behaviors? One way is by watching experienced discussion leaders and taking careful note of their actions at key points in the discussion. Another way is to videotape your own discussion classes and observe how you reacted to various situations. Or you can have a colleague or teaching assistant join your class and comment afterwards. With practice and hard work, virtually any individual can develop these qualities.

Exercise: Attend a colleague's discussion class, or make arrangements to have your discussion class videotaped. How many of the above leadership behaviors can you identify? Were there times in the discussion when some of these behaviors were not practiced but would have been useful?

Dealing with Difficult Behaviors

Because you will be dealing with individuals of widely differing personalities and backgrounds, you will need to respond to a range of difficult behaviors. It is helpful to prepare yourself for some of the most common behavioral problems before the discussion occurs. Examples of such problems and appropriate responses are given in Table 3-1, adapted from Cooper and Heenan (1980).

If a *monopolizer* continually usurps the discussion, you can deflect the attention from this student by indicating your appreciation of his or her comments and then suggesting that the class hear other perspectives on the subject. Interrupting a monopolizer requires finesse and careful timing, and you run the risk of hurting the student's feelings, but there is sometimes no alternative to an interruption if things are getting out of control.

Distractors and *intellectualizers* sometimes elicit laughter from the other students. Depending on the tone of the discussion, you may be able to enjoy the remarks along with everyone else. If the student is likely to be hurt, however, your best policy may be to politely change the direction of the discussion.

Apologizers often have low self-esteem. Building or expanding on the ideas of these students during the discussion can help boost their confidence level and make them more productive members of the group.

Questioners and *Know-It-Alls* can take up a lot of class time. Be prepared to step in, politely of course, to redirect the flow of ideas.

Finally, *Pollyannas* may have low self-esteem and as a result be unwilling to commit themselves to an opinion that might require a strong defense. You may be able to provide some support for these students if a defense is needed, thereby encouraging them to take a stance.

Cooper and Heenan (1980) discuss other problem behaviors, such as Fighters, Complainers, and Rescuers. Getting to know your students—their individual strengths and weaknesses, their goals and aspirations—can help you to

TABLE 3-1

Managing Difficult Behaviors

Behavior	Strategy
The *Monopolizer* takes up a great deal of "air time."	Say something like "we have been primarily hearing from one or two people. I'm interested in hearing from the rest of you," or "You have made some interesting comments and now I would like to give some other people the opportunity to speak."
The *Distractor* often asks questions or makes comments that have nothing to do with the material currently being discussed.	Respond by saying "That question is interesting but not directly related to the material which we are discussing. Perhaps you and I can discuss that issue after class."
The *Intellectualizer* translates even simple thoughts and ideas into complex theories.	Respond by saying "Try to express the idea in one sentence."
The *Apologizer* tends to preface questions or statements with an apology. For example, "Maybe I should not say this, but..." or "Maybe this is not what you're asking but..."	Say "You have made some very interesting points. You do not need to apologize for speaking."
The *Questioner* repeatedly asks questions.	Suggest that the student "Take a guess as to what I meant by that statement," or say "We only have a limited amount of time and that question will be addressed later on."
The *Know-It-All* is an expert on everything and always adds something or corrects what you have said.	Respond by saying "It seems as if you have opinions very different from mine. Would you like to present an opposing point of view?" or implement a strategy similar to that which you would use for the monopolizer.
The *Pollyanna* will avoid conflict or disharmony at any cost.	Gently insist that "You must make a decision," or "You must make a critical comment."

choose the most appropriate response when these problems surface. Choosing the response that is best for both the student and for the group as a whole will eventually become easier as your teaching skills develop.

But besides these concerns, more mundane problems occasionally occur. For example, some students habitually come late to class. Or you might have students who read the newspaper, talk with students around them, pass notes, or fall asleep in class. There is no unique way to deal with these problems. Faculty at our institution have a wide range of responses, from ignoring the problem to throwing the student out of class. In any case, thinking in advance about how you might react is worthwhile. Faculty members forced to make a decision on the spur of the moment don't always choose the response they would have liked if they had had more time to think about it.

Some instructors have come up with rather extreme ways to deal with these types of problems. We heard of one individual who encouraged his students to arrive on time by locking the door when class started. Late students had to suffer the embarrassment of waiting until the professor unlocked the door to let them in, usually several minutes later. On one occasion, a tardy student in this class mistakenly thought there was an exam and resorted to passing a note under the door, pleading with the professor to let him in. (He was allowed to enter.) We don't advocate this approach!

Exercise: Consider some student behaviors that you find most irritating. What are possible reasons why the students are behaving in these ways? How would you alleviate the problem in each case?

EVALUATING THE SUCCESS OF THE DISCUSSION

The discussion you prepared for seemed to go well. Sure, there were some rough spots, but overall the students seemed satisfied and probably learned a few things. How can you best evaluate the discussion and use the experience to prepare for the next one?

You can use *formative evaluation* to help you become more adept in your role as discussion leader. This method can improve a person's skills, a course, or a program by identifying strengths and weaknesses in individual components of the process while it is still being developed (Davis et al., 1981). You can implement formative evaluation by receiving feedback on your performance as a discussion leader and by determining what your students are learning in the discussion. Let's consider each of these categories.

Feedback on Your Performance

Students can provide valuable information on how well you are leading in-class discussions. Research on the validity of student evaluations has been encouraging (e.g., Cohen, 1981); we believe that anonymous student comments on some aspects of a course—a month after it begins, at mid-term, or at its end—can help you to improve your skills in leading discussions. For example, within the first few weeks you may want to ask students to identify the strengths and weaknesses of the class and to suggest ways to improve it. You might also ask if the pace of the course is appropriate. Your questions should be somewhat open-ended so that students feel free to respond with any concerns that strike them. Student evaluations are even more effective if faculty members evaluate their own performance using the same instrument and then compare the results with student responses. Discussing the results with a colleague or trained consultant, e.g. from a college or university Teaching Center, may also result in new ideas and improvement of the course (Cohen and McKeachie, 1980).

Another powerful assessment technique mentioned briefly above involves the use of audiotapes or videotapes. These tools can help to identify differences between what you perceive is happening during the discussion and your actual behavior. Most people have selective memories, and teachers are no exception; we tend to recall classroom highlights or disasters, and a tape can fill in important but forgotten details (Seldin, 1980). You can use the tape by yourself, along with guidelines for self-evaluation, or you can ask a colleague or consultant to review the tape with you (Braskamp, 1978).

> *Exercise: For your next discussion class, write several questions that could be used on student evaluation forms to help you gather information to improve your abilities as discussion leader. How can you word the questions to encourage your students to be as frank and open as possible?*

Feedback on Student Learning as a Result of the Discussion

In Chapter 2, we discussed the importance of providing feedback to students and teachers in a variety of forms, and mentioned brief in-class exercises as one important method. These exercises are particularly appropriate for discussion classes.

Many of the techniques take very little time but provide concrete feedback about the level and quality of student learning. For example, you can take five minutes at the end of class and simply ask the students to list several concepts which applied to the central theme of the discussion, perhaps in order of importance. You can also ask the students to use this list to identify relations among the various concepts—for example, which concepts are subsets of others, and which are independent. Several ideas for in-class exercises are provided by Cross and Angelo (1988).

> *Exercise: For your next discussion class, create a list of questions for the students to answer that will help you identify how well the students are learning the material. Consider questions that could be used as brief in-*

class exercises, as well as questions that could be assigned as homework problems. How might you use the results of these assessments to make changes in the class?

SUMMARY

In this chapter, we have provided a number of tips on how to lead discussions in the classroom. These suggestions fall into three categories. First, it is essential to gather information prior to the discussion to help plan an appropriate agenda. Information on the size of the class and backgrounds of the students is needed, as well as knowledge of the classroom environment. Second, the quality of leadership during the discussion is important. The leader must perform well in two capacities, as a provider of information upon which the discussion is based, and as a guide to interactions among the group members. Finally, it is worthwhile to evaluate the success of the discussion. This involves getting feedback on the effectiveness of the leadership as well as the success of student learning.

Leading a discussion, just as working with groups of people in any capacity, is an extremely complex task. The task may even be viewed as intimidating in the sense that one cannot predict audience responses—and therefore it is difficult to plan ahead of time *how* to lead the group. Nevertheless, a new faculty member can do well as a discussion leader: the skills developed in graduate school for discussing research results can be adapted readily into the classroom. With practice, anyone can lead a discussion. And it is precisely the uncertainty in audience responses that makes leading a discussion exciting and rewarding.

REFERENCES

Bloom, B.S., J.T. Hastings, and G.F. Madaus, *Taxonomy of Educational Objectives: The Classification of Educational Goals, Handbook 1, Cognitive Domain*, New York, NY: McCay, 1956.

Braskamp, L.A., Colleague evaluation of instruction, *Faculty Development and Evaluation in Higher Education, Vol. 4*, pp. 1–9, 1978.

Cohen, P.A., Student ratings of instruction and student achievement: a meta-analysis of multisection validity studies, *Review of Educational Research, Vol. 51*, pp. 281–309, 1981.

Cohen, P.A. and W.J. McKeachie, The role of colleagues in the evaluation of college teaching, *Improving College and University Teaching, Vol. 28*, pp. 147–154, 1980.

Collett, J., Reaching African-American students in the classroom, in L. Hilsen, editor, *To Improve the Academy, Vol. 9*, Stillwater, OK: New Forums Press, Inc., pp. 177–188, 1990.

Cooper, S. and C. Heenan, *Preparing, Designing, and Leading Workshops: A Humanistic Approach,* New York, NY: Van Nostrand Reinhold Company, pp. 56–103, 1980.

Cortes, C. Chicano culture, experience, and learning: extracting learning styles from social/cultural diversity, *Studies of Five American Minorities,* Southwest Teachers Corps Network, ERIC Document No. 158 952.

Cross, K.P. and T.A. Angelo, *Classroom Assessment Techniques: A Handbook for Faculty,* Ann Arbor, MI: National Center for Research to Improve Postsecondary Teaching and Learning, The University of Michigan, 1988.

Davis, B.G., M. Scriven, and S. Thomas, *The Evaluation of Composition Instruction,* Inverness, CA: Edgepress, p.7, 1981.

Erskine, J.A., M.R. Leenders, and L.A. Mauffette-Leenders, *Teaching with Cases,* London, Ontario: School of Business Administration, University of Western Ontario, 1981.

Garner, B., Southeast Asian culture and classroom culture. *College Teaching, Vol. 37,* pp. 127–130, 1989.

Guerriero, S.J., Multicultural awareness in the classroom, *The Journal of Staff, Program, and Organization Development, Vol. 8,* pp. 167–173, 1990.

Hall, R.M. and B.R. Sandler, The classroom climate: a chilly one for women, *Project on the Status and Education of Women,* Washington, DC: Association of American Colleges, 1982.

Jones, D.J. and B.C. Watson, *"High Risk" Students in Higher Education: Future Trends,* ASHE-ERIC Higher Education Report 3, Washington, DC: The George Washington University, 1990.

MacGregor, J., Collaborative learning: shared inquiry as a process of reform, *The Changing Face of College Teaching, Vol. 42,* pp. 19–30, 1990.

Maimon, E.P., Talking to strangers, *College Composition and Communication, Vol. 30,* pp. 364–369, 1979.

Maurice, K., Cultural styles of thinking and speaking in the classroom, *Teaching Across Cultures in the University ESL Program,* ed. P. Byrd, Washington, DC: National Association for Foreign Student Affairs, pp. 39–50, 1986.

Seldin, P., *Successful Faculty Evaluation Programs,* New York, NY: Coventry Press, pp. 82–95, 1980.

Smith, D., *The Challenge of Diversity: Involvement or Alienation in the Academy?* Report No. 5. Washington, DC: School of Education and Human Development, The George Washington University, 1989.

Tannen, D., *You Just Don't Understand: Women in Conversation*, New York, NY: Morrow, 1990.

Tiberius, R.G., *Small Group Teaching: A Trouble Shooting Guide*, Toronto, Ont.: Ontario Institute for Studies in Education Press, 1990.

Welty, W.M., Discussion method teaching: a practical guide, in S. Kahn, editor, *To Improve the Academy, Vol. 8,* Stillwater, OK: New Forums Press, Inc., pp. 197–216, 1989.

Wu, F.W., The trouble with universities' interest in diversity is, they've embraced it as a panacea for racial tension, *Chronicle of Higher Education, Vol. 37,* p. 26, 1991.

4

LECTURING

INTRODUCTION

In Chapter 3, we addressed techniques for leading successful discussion classes. We emphasized the need to know your students as individuals, to interact with them in response to their specific needs. We discussed the need to promote interactions among students. In contrast, lecturing involves a very different type of interaction. The flow of information is primarily from instructor to the students. In many large classes, it is virtually impossible to know all of the students as individuals and to respond to them individually. Yet lecturing reaches large numbers of students and remains a dominant form of teaching at most colleges and universities.

Promoting active learning in lectures may be difficult at times; the challenge is to find ways to actively engage students in the material during the lecture. Effective lecturing requires the talents of scholar, writer, producer, comedian, showman, and teacher (McKeachie, 1980).

In this chapter, we begin by discussing preparations for the lecture. Then we discuss the delivery, highlighting ways to capture student attention and interest. Finally, we address ways to evaluate the success of the lecture. This chapter focuses on lectures for courses at the college level, although much of this information also applies to teaching of other types. The extension of this material to presentations of research results (e.g., at conferences) is included in Chapter 11.

PREPARING THE LECTURE

There is no substitute for adequate preparation; even a superb delivery will do little to hide the weaknesses of a hastily prepared presentation. Let's discuss preparing the lecture in terms of choosing the objectives, assessing the audience, organizing the presentation, and preparing the necessary visual aids.

Determine Your Objectives

In the most general sense, every presentation serves the same function: to affect individuals by getting them to respond or change in some way (Mambert, 1968). But what is this response in the case of a course lecture? Essentially, you want to introduce the students to new information which they will use both to satisfy the course objectives and to use in their personal and professional lives. We have seen in Chapter 1 that new information can be learned in a way that makes it useful mainly if there are strong connections to material previously learned. The objectives of each lecture, therefore, should be chosen considering what the students already know, and should be linked to the objectives of the course.

Many beginning faculty members design overly ambitious lectures. All of us have been in lectures where the instructor was trying to cover a dozen topic areas—speaking as quickly as possible to get through all of the material—and no one learned much of anything. Don't fall into this trap. Choose at most three or four major points for a fifty minute class. Remember that lectures should not carry the major responsibility for transmitting information—reading assignments achieve this much more efficiently. Lectures can, however, elaborate on material in the text and bring together material from a variety of printed sources.

The specific objectives of a lecture should thus be modest. We suggest that you express them in terms of desired student behavior, as was done in Chapter 2 for choosing course objectives. What is it that you want the students to be able to do after the lecture? For example, a faculty member presenting a lecture in a fluid mechanics course might decide that students should be able to compute energy losses for water flowing through pipes of different materials. Clearly, students will know at the end of the lecture whether or not they can complete this task.

Stating the purpose of the lecture—and presenting a brief outline of the material—helps the students to know where they're heading and how to organize the new ideas. Furthermore, both you and the students will have a way to evaluate the lecture.

> *Exercise: Examine the notes from your last few lectures. Did you have clear objectives in mind when you wrote these notes? Did you share these objectives with the students? How did these particular lectures contribute to the overall goals of the course?*

Assess the Audience

Achieving your stated goals requires that you know your audience. Many lectures fail because the instructor underestimates or overestimates the abilities of the students. In other cases, the instructor is insensitive to the needs of the students or is not aware of their expectations. A good lecturer treads a fine line, challenging students while not overwhelming them, and giving them what they need in an accessible form.

You already should have obtained some information about the audience before the first class. Recall Chapter 2, where we stated that you could determine the students' backgrounds and interests through discussions with faculty colleagues who have taught the group before. We also stated that designing the course is an iterative process, since the design may change as more information about the students becomes available. Such information about the students is also valuable in writing each lecture. You will want to use the course objectives to plan your lectures, but you will most likely modify the lectures as you get to know the students better. Repeated contact with the students offers a distinct advantage over a one-time lecture presentation (e.g., a guest lecture for a colleague's class): you have an opportunity to experiment and to modify your objectives and lecturing style to better match the audience. Flexibility is the key.

What do you need to know about the audience to help you plan effective lectures? To some extent, the information about students useful in planning discussion classes (Chapter 3) is also helpful here. In large lecture classes, you may want to use questionnaires for some of the items. The following information is useful:

+ How large is the group?

+ What are the backgrounds of the students? (e.g., year in school, major, previous education and work experience)

+ Is ability expected to be evenly distributed, or might there be a skewed or bimodal distribution?

+ Are the students required to take this course or have they elected to do so?

+ What do the students hope to gain from the course?

+ What prerequisites or other related courses have the students had?

+ What was included in these related courses? (It would be helpful to obtain a syllabus or talk with the instructors.)

+ Will students be taking related courses simultaneous to this one?

Clearly, the answers to these questions can help you to plan your lectures. For example, if the material is completely new to most of the students, you will want to lecture at a slower pace: remember from Chapter 1 that individuals require time to learn material which is completely new to them. Similarly, a large group will probably require a slower pace than a smaller lecture class due to the diversity of learning styles. You also may need to make a greater effort to insure that most of the students in a large class are keeping up with the ideas you are presenting. Chapter 2 emphasized that covering material is not synonymous with learning it, a point sometimes ignored by lecturers.

Exercise: Consider a lecture that you recently gave. How would you change the objectives of the lecture if your assessment of students showed that the class as a whole was very highly motivated and willing to put in extra effort? How would you change the objectives if your assessment showed that most of the students were not particularly interested in the material? What would you do to motivate the second group?

Organize the Lecture

The basic outline for any talk is straightforward: first you tell them what you're going to say, then you say it, then you tell them what you've said. Let's consider each of these in the context of a class lecture.

Introduction

As students come into the classroom, they are probably thinking and talking about everything except the subject matter at hand. Your first task is to draw students' attention to your lecture. One way to accomplish this is simply by beginning to write on the board, or by asking a question about material in the previous lecture. Another way is to begin with a provocative comment or a question that arouses audience interest.

Once the students are listening, you should state the purpose of the lecture and present a brief outline of how you will proceed. In Chapter 1, we noted that students learn more if they know what they are expected to learn. You also may want to link this lecture with past or future classes since students do not often make the connections themselves. Because the students' level of attention deteriorates early in the lecture, reaching a low point after about fifteen minutes (McKeachie, 1986), the first few minutes are critical and you should maximize their use.

Body

The body of the lecture should be organized to include a few key points arranged in a logical scheme. Carlile and Daniel (1987) discuss five schemes which are commonly used to structure a talk:

+ *Chronological Scheme:* orders events in the sequence of their occurrence in history.

+ *Spatial Scheme:* orders things as they occur in space.

+ *Problem-Solution Scheme:* arranges a speech in two parts—the presentation of a problem and its solution.

+ *Causal Scheme:* presents the causes of a problem or event and then presents the effects that result; this scheme can also be inverted to show an effect and then prove its cause.

+ *Topical Scheme:* divides the subject matter into a series of subtopics that derive naturally from the general topic area.

Other structures are also possible. For example, McKeachie (1980) suggests that a lecture can move from the familiar to the unfamiliar, from concept to application, or from phenomena to theory to evidence. Regardless of the structure you choose, students are better able to retain information covered in lecture if it is carefully organized.

Despite the careful organization of many lectures, students often have difficulty perceiving the structure. It is therefore usually a good idea to transmit literally and visually the structure of the lecture and perhaps even the reasoning behind it to the class. For example, you can communicate the structure of the lecture by creating an outline, listing major points to be covered, or drawing a diagram on the board. Note that understanding the structure can help the students distinguish between the essential information and what is of secondary importance.

For any of these schemes, the nature of the subject matter and the backgrounds of the students will determine the amount of information you can comfortably present in a lecture. Consequently, you need to think carefully about the material you will use to support the major topics. Of critical importance in explaining your points is the use of examples and the use of comparisons (Arthur, 1984).

Examples help a speaker to clarify important concepts. You can use real examples of events that have occurred, hypothetical examples which have the possibility of occurring, or anecdotes which offer a hypothetical story, perhaps to simplify a complex, real-world problem.

Comparisons can help to explain difficult or unfamiliar concepts: they allow you to establish a link between the new information you are presenting and information that the students already possess. Analogies and metaphors often function effectively in this regard because most audiences are accustomed to these types of comparisons.

The choice of appropriate supporting material must also account for the diversity of student backgrounds and cultures in the class. Chapter 3 emphasized the need to be sensitive to different groups of students in discussion classes, and the same is true in lectures. For example, faculty members often do not realize how culturally-based examples are; they may forget that examples which clarify a concept for white middle class American students may not necessarily do so for students of other cultures. Recently, a foreign student told us that she responded to a question assuming that a "cable company" meant a telephone company which, in her experience, is a monopoly. Because the faculty member meant cable company in the American sense of the word, he used it as an example of a competitive industry. Responding to this example did not enhance the student's understanding of the concept of competitiveness in American industry, which was the faculty member's point. We may need to rethink examples as we open our classrooms to students of other cultures.

We also need to consider how the language we use in lectures will be perceived by students of diverse backgrounds. It is prudent to avoid rhetoric that reinforces stereotypes and is otherwise degrading of particular groups. Referring to a scientist or doctor as "he" and to a laboratory assistant or secretary as "she" is no longer acceptable in most scholarly writing and speaking. A considerable literature, some of which is summarized in Chapter 3, is emerging on diversity and how teachers can account for differences among students.

Finally, the body of the lecture should include periodic summaries which reinforce and link the main concepts. For example, you probably want to refer to assigned reading material which supplements the lecture. This will help students to make connections which they might not make on their own, and may provide a sense of continuity among the various aspects of the course. Furthermore, referring to the assigned reading indicates that this material is important in understanding the lecture.

Conclusion

Like the introduction, the conclusion plays a number of important roles. It provides an opportunity to summarize the key points, to show the links among these points, and to tie the concepts to other knowledge. If you began the class with a question or item of curiosity, you might resolve the issue at the end to tie together the entire lecture. Or you might conclude by posing unanswered questions to be treated in a reading assignment or in a future lecture to pique student interest. Because the learning curve indicates that students' attention rises at the end of the lecture, you should consider using the last few minutes to emphasize key points you want them to remember.

> *Exercise: Consider one of your recent lectures. Can you identify the organizational scheme used for the body of the lecture? What types of material did you use to support the main points? How was your lecture linked to the previous lecture, and to the next one? Consider asking one or two students to see their notes—this can help you determine if the students are understanding the organization and key points of the lecture.*

Prepare Visual Aids

Because many students learn by visual reinforcement as well as by listening, it is helpful to use visual aids during a lecture. Chalkboards and overhead transparency projectors are most commonly used, and these can be quite effective. A chalkboard has the advantage of spontaneity: although you should decide ahead of time what to write on the board, you have the flexibility of adding or deleting material on-the-spot based on class responses. Overhead transparencies are useful when there is a particularly large class—some lecture halls are so large that a chalkboard cannot be easily read from the back of the room. You can prepare transparencies in advance that look quite professional, or you can write on them during the lecture with the advantage of facing the class as you write.

Transparencies are also useful for illustrating complex diagrams that would take too long to draw on the board. However, be careful here—don't use transparencies as a means to increase the amount of written material you present in a lecture. We have attended lectures that degenerate into a race: the students try to copy what is on each transparency before it is replaced with the next one. That hardly promotes active learning!

Other visual aids may also be useful in lectures. Examples include slides, videos, computers (perhaps connected to a large screen), written handouts, items passed around the class, and laboratory demonstrations. Whatever visuals you choose, be sure to prepare them effectively. Mambert (1968) outlines seven rules:

1. *Form Follows Function:* Be sure that the content, picture, shape, color, and lettering style serve a specific, identifiable purpose.

2. *Simplicity:* Do not make "busy" visual aids that try to say too much for the time and space allotted. Aids should be brief and well-structured.

3. *Clarity:* Design the visual aid to be understandable on a purely sensory level, without requiring detailed explanations.

4. *Visibility:* Be sure that the entire audience can see the visual from anywhere in the room; use appropriate size lettering.

5. *Unity and Consistency:* Do not make abrupt changes in style or format of the visual aids (the same way you should not make abrupt changes in the language or pace of the lecture).

6. *Appropriateness:* Make sure that the visual aids are proper and consistent with the speech and the occasion.

7. *Multidimensionalism:* Many visuals will activate thoughts that influence sound, smell, taste, and touch. Your visuals should activate these other senses, if appropriate.

As you prepare your visuals, keep in mind that the choice of medium is far less important than the content and the way that you convey it. Faculty members who plan lectures with the use of visual aids often plan much more carefully than lectures without any visual aids: it is the planning and organizing—including things like the explicit structure—that makes a difference, not only the visual aid itself (Fenton, 1990).

> *Exercise: Consider the visual aids you used in your last few lectures. If you used the chalkboard, how much of the writing on the board was planned? How much was decided on-the-spot, based on your interactions with students during the lecture? If you used transparencies, how much writing was*

included on each one? Did you write directly on the transparencies during the lecture to emphasize certain points? Good visual aids are well-planned but can be changed during the lecture as need arises.

MAKING AN EFFECTIVE DELIVERY

You have now completed your preparations. You have a captivating introduction, a well-organized set of material for the body of the lecture, and succinct concluding remarks. You have interesting examples and other supporting information. Your visual aids are planned. All of this is necessary—but not enough. Many faculty members have given what could have been an outstanding lecture in a monotone voice, never leaving the podium or looking at the students. Obviously, delivery plays an important role in how students receive what you say.

A number of simple rules can go a long way in contributing to an effective delivery. *Never* read the lecture; instead, talk to the students from your outline. Use a conversational tone somewhat resembling the way you would talk to one or two students informally—only louder. Speak with short sentences, personal pronouns, and verb and pronoun contractions (Dickinson, 1991). Try to maintain a voice that is clear and relaxed, and avoid irritating mannerisms that often result from nervousness. (Some students enjoy counting the number of times a lecturer says "oh well" or other nervous habit, not paying the slightest attention to the lecture!) Look at your students often to show your interest in them; watch their eyes to see if they're understanding you. And most important, be aware of your overall lecturing style so that you can work at improving it. All of us have experienced particularly good lecturers—think of them as role models.

As you plan an effective delivery, think about how you can get the students to actively listen to the lecture. One of our colleagues has observed that only a very small fraction of all students are good note-takers; many simply copy what is on the board. To encourage active listening, he doesn't allow his students to use more than one page for taking notes, forcing them to be discriminating about what they write. Other faculty members provide a brief outline of their lecture on the board; we have seen earlier that students can learn new material better if they understand the structure of the presentation. Still other instructors distribute copies of their transparencies or slides as handouts. This strategy enables students to spend less time writing during the lecture and more time listening. However, some students may feel that they can rely on the handouts rather than pay attention in class; for this reason, it is probably better to use only a skeletal outline with space for annotation as a handout. Depending on the nature of the handout and how you will make use of it, you might also consider distributing material at the end of class.

You can use other techniques to maintain student interest. For example, you can ask rhetorical questions which get the students to think about a topic without requiring a verbal response. You can also ask a question at the beginning of the lecture which forces students to take a side by show of hands, thus giving them a stake in the lecture and providing an incentive for them to listen. We have a colleague who begins one of his lectures by asking how many students believe that the government should subsidize the arts. This grabs the students' attention and helps to maintain their interest through a lecture about government intervention in an open market economy. Another one of our colleagues asks a question to elicit responses which are then put on the board. For example, he once asked a freshman class to state attributes of individuals who have chosen careers in engineering; he then used the responses to identify characteristics of successful engineers.

As another technique to promote active learning, you can temporarily halt the lecture for an in-class activity. Some of our colleagues occasionally interrupt their lectures to ask students to work in groups of two or three to discuss a particular problem. Although the task itself lasts only a few minutes, there is a substantial payoff: the passive mode is broken, and students remain attentive for the next fifteen or twenty minutes. Others have interrupted their lectures for a brief in-class writing task on the lecture material, perhaps for less than five minutes. The lecturer then asks for volunteers to read their responses as a summary of the topic.

The importance of in-class activities by students is demonstrated by a commonly observed situation: it almost always takes students much longer to work an example in class than it does for the instructor to put an example on the board and explain it. Many students simply fall behind when the instructor is working such example problems, and they would be lost if they were not forced to take the time to work the examples themselves.

There is clearly no unique "best" way to deliver a lecture; you need to practice and experiment to find the most appropriate strategy. More information on delivering presentations in contexts other than a classroom setting is presented in Chapter 11.

> *Exercise: Videotape one of your lectures, with the camera directed at the students (they may feel uncomfortable at first, but will soon forget about the camera). During the lecture, watch the students to see if they are actively listening, and respond appropriately by asking questions, clarifying points, and possibly getting the students to interact with one another. Then view the tape. Were your impressions during the lecture accurate, or do you notice new reactions among the students? Exercises such as this can help you to become more aware of how the audience is reacting to your lectures.*

EVALUATING THE LECTURE

Working toward the goal of excellence in lecturing requires feedback. In order to improve your skills, you will need feedback on your lecturing style as well as on the success of student learning. You may want to include both internal reviewers (you and your students) and external evaluators (colleagues and trained consultants, e.g., from a college or university Teaching Center). Internal evaluators have ringside seats to the regular classroom lecture, although external evaluators can bring a fresh outlook and an unbiased perspective to the evaluation process.

Many of the feedback procedures discussed in Chapter 3 on leading discussions apply directly to lectures. For example, you can solicit student comments using appropriate survey forms both during the semester and at the end of the term. You might ask students which aspects of the lecture helped them and which hindered their learning. You can also invite colleagues to attend your classes, or arrange to have your lectures audiotaped or videotaped.

As suggested for discussion classes, you can use in-class student performance to help evaluate your lectures: you don't need to wait for a test to find out how much the class is learning. Simply take a few minutes at the end of class and ask the students to write down the three or four main points of the day's lecture. If you want to know whether students understand the relationships between the major ideas, ask them to diagram these relationships. This exercise will indicate whether the students have grasped the ideas but not the relationships among them. There are many similar classroom assessment techniques you can use—for more information, consult Cross and Angelo (1988).

Overall, lecturing is a skill which you can perfect. An excellent lecture is not an accident, but rather the result of lots of preparation, careful thought about delivery, and repeated evaluations for fine-tuning. Students appreciate good lectures; unfortunately, they get far too few of them. You can help change that— and earn the respect of both students and colleagues. Additional information on lecturing is presented in many references, e.g., Brown and Atkins (1988), Eble (1976), Eison (1990), McKeachie (1994), and Gibbs et al. (1987).

SUMMARY

In this chapter, we have discussed techniques for successful lecturing in a classroom setting. To prepare for the lecture, you need to consider the objectives of your presentation, which are related to the objectives of the course, and also the backgrounds and interests of the students. You then can organize the lecture to capture and maintain the students' attention. Preparing appropriate visual aids is an important part of the process, whether you use the chalkboard, overhead transparencies, or other media.

You must carefully plan the delivery. Rules for public speaking, such as appropriate appearance and an effective speaking style are obviously important. However, other considerations are important, such as maintaining active learning and providing links between the lecture material and other knowledge which the students possess.

Finally, you should evaluate your lectures to enable continual improvement. The use of audiotapes and videotapes permit self-evaluation. Additional feedback by students, faculty colleagues, and trained consultants from your institution's Teaching Center can also provide valuable suggestions.

Lecturing remains the principal teaching method at most colleges and universities. It should be considered both a privilege and a responsibility to lecture; give your students the best experiences you can provide.

REFERENCES

Arthur, R.H., *The Engineer's Guide to Better Communication,* Glenview, IL: Scott Foresman, 1984.

Brown, G. and M. Atkins, *Effective Teaching in Higher Education,* London: Routledge, pp. 7–49, 1988.

Carlile, C.S. and A.V. Daniel, *Project Text for Public Speaking,* New York, NY: Harper and Row, pp. 14–15, 1987.

Cross, K.P. and T.A. Angelo, *Classroom Assessment Techniques: A Handbook for Faculty,* Ann Arbor, MI: National Center for Research to Improve Postsecondary Teaching and Learning, The University of Michigan, 1988.

Dickinson, L., Credibility, *The Teaching Professor, Vol. 5,* pp. 3–4, 1991.

Eison, J., Confidence in the classroom: Ten maxims for new teachers, *College Teaching, Vol. 38,* pp. 21–25, 1990.

Eble, K.E., *The Craft of Teaching,* San Francisco, CA: Jossey-Bass, pp. 42–53, 1976.

Fenton, E., *In Most Cases It's the Message That Counts, Not the Medium: An Analysis of Research About the Use of Media in Education,* Pittsburgh, PA: Carnegie Mellon, The University Teaching Center, 1990.

Gibbs, G., S. Habeshaw, and T. Habeshaw, *53 Interesting Things To Do In Your Lectures,* Bristol, England: Technical and Educational Services Ltd., 1987.

Mambert, W.A., *Presenting Technical Ideas: A Guide to Audience Communication,* New York, NY: John Wiley and Sons, Inc., pp. 118–140, 1968.

McKeachie, W.J., Improving lectures by understanding students' information processing, in W. J. McKeachie, editor, *Learning, Cognition, and College Teaching,* San Francisco, CA: Jossey-Bass, pp. 69–85, 1980.

McKeachie, W.J., *Teaching Tips: Strategies, Research, and Theory for College and University Teachers. 9th ed.,* Lexington, MA: D.C. Heath, 1994.

5

PREPARING ACTIVITIES FOR STUDENTS: EXAMS AND ASSIGNMENTS

INTRODUCTION

When we think of student learning in courses, the picture that comes to mind for many people is a group of students sitting attentively in a lecture. We often assume that most of the learning in a course takes place in class, at least for the best students. The homework assignment given at the end of class evaluates whether the students understand what they learned in that lecture, and the test given next week will evaluate whether students understand the sum total of several lectures.

Is this a reasonable model of student behavior in a course? Good teachers know that it isn't. Even for the very best students, the bulk of the real learning in a course can't take place during lectures—there simply isn't enough time. Information can be *introduced* in class. However, the real learning takes place after hours, when students are struggling with assignments that extend the classroom material to new applications, or when they are studying for an exam. A more accurate picture of learning in a course would consider students in their dormitory rooms working individually on a difficult problem, or testing each other in a study group in preparation for the next test. Assignments and exams are thus more than merely evaluation tools; they are a vital part of student learning.

Most of us develop the ability as faculty members to prepare exams and assignments in the same way we develop other teaching proficiencies—by adapting the techniques of others. These are usually chosen on the basis of what worked well for us as students, since most of us teach in the way we ourselves learned. However, students learn in many different ways, as we discussed in Chapter 1, and some of your students may not be as motivated as you were. There is thus a good deal of trial and error in preparing tests and assignments for a course. This chapter attempts to make the process more efficient by pointing out a number of options that have worked for others.

The chapter is divided into several parts. First, we consider possible objectives of exams and assignments. Then we discuss the design of these educational tools, focusing on the most common types of test questions. Next we consider how tests and assignments can be administered to a class. Finally, we discuss ways of interpreting students' grades in these activities to help us evaluate learning and teaching. Throughout this chapter, we use the term "assignments" to mean homework problems, individual projects, group projects, or other activities in which the students must complete an assigned task. "Projects" refer to assignments that are more involved than brief homework problems, for example, open-ended problems that require written reports, detailed literature surveys, laboratory work, and numerous other possibilities.

OBJECTIVES OF EXAMS AND ASSIGNMENTS

In general, goals of examinations fall into several categories:

1. To provide an indication of what the students have learned

2. To motivate students to learn

3. To help students think about concepts in new ways

4. To provide an indication of the effectiveness of teaching

5. To assign grades

The first objective—to measure what students have learned—is perhaps the most commonly cited reason for giving exams. Student learning occurs in a number of categories, for which several models have been developed. Chapter 1 refers to the hierarchical model of Bloom et al. (1956) which includes knowledge, comprehension, application, analysis, synthesis, and evaluation. You can create exams to test any or all of these. For example, you can test comprehension by asking students to identify relations between specific instances and more general ideas. If you want to test for application of what they have learned, you might provide a situation where students must determine the approach to a task themselves. Analysis, synthesis, and evaluation involve more complex thought processes that can be tested through relatively open-ended problems without unique solutions. Examples of appropriate questions for testing student learning according to Bloom's taxonomy are shown in Table 5-1. Note that the use of exams to evaluate student learning can provide information valuable to both students and faculty: ways of using test results to provide feedback to students are discussed later in this chapter.

The second objective is to motivate students to learn new material. In the introduction to this chapter, we emphasized that classroom activities represent only a small portion of learning time; the way students spend their time outside of class is much more important to total learning. Unfortunately, many students review class material only when it becomes an absolute necessity, such as just before an exam. This argues for occasional testing to encourage students to study. Of course, it is necessary to find the right balance. Too many tests mean less class time for lecture and discussion, more teacher time for grading, and perhaps a signal to the students that testing is more important than learning. Nevertheless, tests should be considered as an important motivation for study.

The third objective of exams is to provide a learning experience: you can pose questions in such a way that students are required to think about concepts in a new light or to notice new relationships. Such tests may force some students to learn on-the-spot, and student performance can provide a measure of true understanding rather than the extent of rote memorization. However, it takes some students longer than others to apply a concept to a new situation, and therefore you should allow plenty of time. A 1:4 rule is used by some faculty members: if you can do a problem in 10 minutes, give the students 40. We assume here that you will work through all problems before giving the test to the class—this is a must! If you decide to use exams as learning experiences, be sure that the test questions are consistent with your style of teaching. For example, you can lead discussions in which you encourage your students to apply their knowledge to new contexts in class; you can then reinforce this through homework assignments and exams which require students to apply their knowledge to yet other contexts. It is dangerous to teach one way and then test another way, since student performance is likely to be poor—and relatively meaningless—in that situation (Hatten, 1989).

The fourth objective is to provide you, as course instructor, with feedback on the effectiveness of your teaching. Testing can help you to determine which topics you taught well and which you did not teach adequately. This information allows you to re-explain the problem area for the students, and it enables you to alter your presentation in future classes.

The last objective of examinations is to enable you to assign grades. This is perhaps the weakest of the objectives because performance on a test may be a poor indicator of what the students have learned. Tests can provide, at best, a measure of student understanding for a very limited number of questions. Furthermore, the use of tests for grading has a number of potential side effects: it

TABLE 5-1

Examples of Questions to Test Student Learning at Different Levels

Statement of the Problem: A rural mountain village in a developing country has never had electricity. Assume you are a member of a United Nations team to study possible electrification of the village.

Level of Bloom's Taxonomy	Example Questions and Answers
Knowledge	What is the population of the village? What are some characteristics of the housing stock?
	(The population is 300. The houses are built of stone, mud, and wood, with thatched roofs. Most houses contain only one or two rooms. The houses are lit simply by candles.)
Comprehension	Observe the activities of the people in the village and summarize a few aspects of their lifestyle.
	(The people are mostly farmers. Because there is no plumbing, water for drinking, cooking, and washing must be carried from a nearby river. Trees in the area are cut as fuel for heating and cooking, which has caused deforestation. Because of these chores, the people have little time for leisure.)
Application	Using your knowledge of ways in which electrical energy can be converted to heat and mechanical energy, identify aspects of their lifestyle that could be improved by electrification.
	(The time and effort needed to carry water from the river would be virtually eliminated if electric water pumps were installed. Electric stoves could replace indoor wood fires, and indoor lighting could be installed.)
Analysis	Calculate the electric power needed to deliver 5000 gallons/day of water to the village, and to provide each house with an electric stove and two 100-watt light bulbs.
	(Determine the power needed in each category, then sum to obtain the total power requirements of the village.)
Synthesis	Develop alternative designs for hydroelectric plants to produce the electricity needed by the village.
	(Several designs are possible.)
Evaluation	Based on a set of criteria which include capital costs, operating costs, reliability, and other considerations, choose the best design for the hydroelectric plant.
	(Choice is dependent upon the specific situation.)

may encourage cheating, promote conformity in learning, and create an unhealthy competitive atmosphere (Eble, 1976). Because tests may not be the best measure, many faculty members use test scores as merely one component of grading—they also include performance on homework assignments, class participation, and results of written or oral reports to determine the final grade.

Let us now turn to the goals of assignments. For the most part, these can serve the same functions as examinations. However, there is usually more emphasis on learning than on evaluation. This is partly because the students have more time to learn the material—we noted earlier that the learning process cannot be rushed. Recall from Chapter 1 that one model for learning involves internalizing new information so that it can be used to solve problems, and this can occur in two ways: learning by studying worked-out example problems, and learning by working out new problems (Simon, 1980). Students don't have time to do substantial amounts of either in class, but they can take the time to learn in both ways from out-of-class assignments, provided that the assignments are appropriately designed.

Assignments are also more useful for learning than for evaluation because it is sometimes difficult to know whether the solutions represent individual efforts. Indeed, it may be beneficial to encourage students to work together on their assignments so that they can develop a habit of learning from each other, as emphasized in Chapter 2.

Although homework sets and projects can be valuable learning tools, it takes considerable effort to design effective problems. The assignments must be creative and interesting, and should promote learning in such a way that the students will be able to apply what they've learned to new contexts. Furthermore, the students must see tangible benefits in doing the assignments, for example to help them learn material they find intellectually challenging, to promote personal interests, and to help their final grade. You may be able to use some of the homework problems from the text as class assignments, but make sure you choose problems that are consistent with the course objectives.

One final point about goals of exams and assignments: be sure that you share these goals with your students. In Chapter 2 we emphasized that a syllabus should include a clear statement of the goals of the course, since students learn more when they know what they're expected to learn. The same applies to the goals of assignments and tests. Furthermore, the types of exams and assignments you give send messages to the students about what you consider to be important. If you request regurgitation of formulas on exams, that encourages students simply to memorize information. On the other hand, if you demand that students apply what they've learned, you encourage them to think more elaborately about the course material. So tell students what they should learn from the exams and assignments and why it's important. They will almost certainly take a greater interest in the course.

Exercise: Consider the last class you taught. Were there opportunities—in the assignments, in class notes, or in the text—for the students to learn from worked-out examples? How did you encourage your students to take advantage of these opportunities? Now consider the exams and assignments you gave in that course. To what extent did these activities satisfy each of the five goals outlined at the beginning of this section? Did you share the goals of your exams and assignments with the students?

DESIGNING APPROPRIATE PROBLEMS

Designing an effective exam is a difficult task. You need to tread a fine line between too easy and too challenging, considering the time allotted for the exam. The problems must be interesting and perhaps even intriguing: a good test arouses curiosity. Completing the test successfully should provide the students with a sense of accomplishment, not simply because they have earned a good grade but also because they have learned something new. Furthermore, your tests must account for the differences in abilities and learning styles in your students. This can be accomplished by including a variety of testing methods, either within a single exam or from one test to the next. You can usually provide variability without compromising your objectives, particularly if you test for a number of skills such as comprehension of concepts and application of ideas to different situations.

Your choice of the type of exam question must also be based on class size and availability of teaching assistants. In many cases, there are tradeoffs between the time it takes to create an exam and the time it takes to grade it. Most experienced teachers have at least one frightful story about writing an exam in a hurry—and not realizing that one of the questions could have several possible meanings. The penalty in these cases is that the graders must consider all possible interpretations of the problem, making it tedious to correct the exam. In addition, the objectives of the test are likely to be compromised, and the students may be upset about the possibility of losing points. A good test, in contrast, can be designed so that the grading is straightforward, and so that information can be useful to both you and your students.

Test questions can be categorized in a number of ways. In this section, we discuss the advantages and limitations of four types of exam problems: multiple choice, short answer, unstructured (often quantitative), and essays. Any of these types of problems can be used on closed-book or open-book tests; similarly, any of these types can be given on in-class tests or on take-home exams. The best choice depends on your particular objectives and institutional traditions, as well as characteristics of your students. For more information on each type of test question, refer to Lowman (1984), Gronlund (1985), Hopkins and Stanley (1990), and Erickson and Strommer (1991). A recent review of the literature on testing students at the college level is given by Fenton (1992).

Multiple Choice Questions

This category is often used to evaluate a student's recall ability. Nevertheless, it is possible to design such questions to test higher levels of thinking. You can test skills such as analysis, synthesis, and evaluation, although it may be time-consuming to anticipate several possible answers to each question that match common student misunderstandings (Clegg and Cashin, 1986). Multiple choice tests are sometimes used in very large classes where time spent grading is significant.

The following recommendations regarding multiple choice questions have been adapted from the sources cited above:

✦ Start to write your questions during the first week of the course; constructing questions soon after you've discussed the topic in class is much easier than doing so several weeks later.

✦ Include several options (the experts recommend four) for each question, and vary the position of the correct answer in a random manner to reduce the role of chance.

✦ Make the wrong choices plausible and attractive to the uninformed, although you should avoid trick questions and answers.

✦ Make all choices approximately the same length and grammatically consistent with the question being posed.

✦ Avoid words, grammar, and sentence construction that will cue test-wise students to correct or incorrect responses; avoid words such as always, never, all, none, or only.

✦ Avoid negative wording where possible.

Multiple choice tests are not often used in upper-level engineering and science classes since it is frequently important to evaluate the students on their approach to solving a problem. This requires short answer or unstructured problems.

Short Answer Problems

Like multiple choice questions, short answer problems can test many different levels of learning. For example, you can ask students to compare concepts, establish a relation between seemingly unrelated ideas, or apply a theory to a new situation. This type of question may take less time to create than multiple choice questions, but may require more time to grade. The short answer format may be particularly useful for testing students where you do not want to provide as much structure as in a multiple choice question. In designing this type of problem, be sure to indicate the maximum allowable length for the response so that students don't turn each question into an essay. You also need to determine how many points to assign to each item, and what is required for full or partial credit.

Unstructured Problems

This category is most useful when you want to determine whether students can provide a workable framework for a problem. Because there are usually a number of ways to solve unstructured problems, it is especially important to establish your objectives clearly and to communicate them to the students. For example, you'll need to let the class know if you're testing them on the specific problem solving methods you used in class, or if you'll allow other methods. For some problems, you must decide whether you want the students to synthesize a number of different approaches, pulling together class material in a new way. If so, you need to prepare the class for this type of exercise, perhaps through examples.

Grading an unstructured problem is more difficult. You'll need to establish a grading system consistent with your objectives and consistent with what you presented in class. This means determining ahead of time what is required for full or partial credit. However, it is difficult to anticipate how each student will respond, and considerable judgment in applying your grading criteria may be necessary. For example, a calculus exam at our institution included a question on how long it would take for bacteria in a culture to reach a population of several million, given the initial population and its time for doubling. Rather than simply using an exponential equation for the population as a function of time, one student filled an entire page by successively doubling the population and keeping track of the number of time steps! It was tedious, but it worked. You need to decide if such an approach merits full or partial credit.

Essay Questions

Essays are particularly useful for revealing the students' ability to think critically, independently, and originally. As the least structured of the various types of questions, essays can also be used to determine whether a student understands overall contextual issues as well as detailed knowledge, and to evaluate how the student approaches a problem.

Nevertheless, there are a number of difficulties with essay exams. In-class essays are written under time pressure, which may make it difficult for some students to organize their thoughts carefully. While essays allow students the opportunity to express themselves, this type of exam places a heavy emphasis on their writing skills. Thus the students are being tested on their ability to communicate as well as on their understanding of the course material. Furthermore, essays are time-consuming to grade. There is no unique way to evaluate them; some faculty members use an analytic scoring method where points are given for each correct component of the answer, while others use a holistic system in which the essay is graded in its entirety. Finally, it is essential to write the questions with extreme care to insure that the students know what constitutes a good answer. Be specific about the problem to be tackled; if you simply ask the students to write about a "topic area," you run a greater risk of getting "core dump" from those who decide to put down everything they know. You may also want to put limits on the length of each essay to give the students an idea of how much information you expect.

Any of these four types of questions can be used for homework assignments. However, there are usually no severe time constraints on completing homework problems as there are for an in-class exam. Furthermore, while exams can be open-book or closed-book, students are usually allowed to use any available material for homework problems. This may include library reference material, computer tools, videotapes, and other sources. All of these issues point toward more elaborate and richer problems for homework assignments than are feasible for exams. For example, we know of one faculty member at another institution who assigned a homework problem on statistical treatment of air pollution data from across the U.S.: he made available to the students the air quality databank of the Environmental Protection Agency, consisting of several million data points, to enable the students to compute actual trends in pollution levels over several years. The software was written in such a way that the students did not have to spend a lot of time manipulating enormous datasets: much of the background work was done for them. Yet they were working with real data and arriving at highly relevant conclusions. A prudent instructor will take advantage of such opportunities to come up with meaningful problems.

All exam or homework questions that you create should satisfy certain criteria. The following criteria for tests are often cited (e.g., Johnson, 1979; Mehrens and Lehman, 1984):

1. The test should be *valid* in that it accomplishes its design objectives, e.g., it measures the extent to which a student has learned certain material and skills.

2. The test should be *objective* in the sense that experts agree on what constitutes a correct answer for each question.

3. The test should be *reliable* such that a student would achieve the same score upon repeated attempts.

4. The test should be *practical* in terms of the time it takes to create, administer, and grade.

To some extent, these criteria also apply to homework assignments and certain types of projects. Of course, not all criteria will apply equally well to all types of exams. For example, it may be difficult to create an "objective" essay exam on which experts would agree about the correct answer. Criteria for essay tests may include internal consistency of the argument, adequate evidence to support the argument, and use of relevant factual information. Because the various categories of exam questions provide different types of information about what students have learned, you may wish to use a mixture of types of questions on some of your tests. This will also allow students with different strengths to demonstrate their abilities; e.g., the ability to focus on the details of problems versus looking at a problem holistically. Let us now consider ways in which exams and assignments can be given to a class.

ADMINISTERING EXAMS AND ASSIGNMENTS

Assignments that parallel material presented in class or in a text are necessary learning tools in an engineering or science course. Weekly assignments are typical. However, homework problems and projects by themselves are not always sufficient to keep students alert and interested; you may also want to establish a regular testing schedule.

Be sure that you are consistent in the messages you give students in class, in assignments, and on tests. Your reasons for giving each problem in an assignment and each test problem should be apparent to the class, and the objectives of each should also reflect the goals of the course. Repeating the same messages in these different contexts is an important part of the learning process. In particular, this repetition helps students to organize and store information for use in multiple contexts.

One important part of teaching a class is making sure the students are honest in their work. It is sad but true that cheating is widespread at many of our colleges and universities. We heard about a professor in a class of sixty who saw two students copying answers during an exam. Rather than yank the students out of the room, he tried another approach: he announced to the class that he saw two students cheating, without giving a hint as to their identity. He explained that if these two students were to stop by his office during the following week and admit their offense, he would lessen the penalty. To his surprise, seven pairs of students showed up! Protecting the honest ones in the class demands that you don't give scofflaws an opportunity. That generally means allowing plenty of space between seats during an exam, with one or more individuals present to keep an eye on the class.

In another instance, the professor of a large lecture saw a student, whose name he didn't know, copying from his neighbor during the final exam. Rather than interrupt the student, he waited until the end of the exam. As the student walked to the front of the room to turn in his paper, the professor stopped him and mentioned that he had seen him cheating. The student, aware that the professor didn't know his name, suddenly threw his final exam into the middle of the stack of some 200 final exams being turned in and raced out! They never found out who he was.

Some faculty members request that students work individually on their homework assignments; in these classes, collaboration on the assignments is sometimes a widespread problem. A number of schools have honor codes in which a tradition of trust between students and faculty offers a sense of pride. Some honor codes are so strong that take-home examinations as well as homework assignments are the norm. However, virtually all schools have established strict disciplinary rules, often stated in a Student Handbook or other publication, and it is important that your students know these rules. It is also important that they know your specific policies. This issue was stressed in Chapter 2; some course syllabi include a policy on cheating and plagiarism. Many instructors use the same homework problems year after year, and this works with varying degrees of success depending on the situation. Under most circumstances, however, it is usually not wise to repeat test questions for subsequent classes.

One technique to minimize cheating has worked well in some classes at our institution. On each day that a homework assignment is due, a brief in-class quiz is given. The objective of the quiz is to determine whether students understand the homework problems at the time the assignment is due. Students are encouraged to work together on their homework problems—as long as all of them understand the material by the due date. This approach is intended to put an emphasis on student learning rather than on insuring individual efforts in the completion of specific homework problems. A difficulty with this approach is that the method favors students who thrive on working in groups, while students who prefer to work individually may be at a disadvantage.

There are compelling reasons why you should encourage students to work together in learning material for your course. Promoting collaboration is consistent with one of the eight principles for undergraduate education in Chapter 2, which emphasized the importance of cooperation among students. Indeed, a considerable amount of research has shown that students working in groups often gain a deeper understanding of the subject matter than those working individually (Light, 1990; MacGregor, 1990; Slavin, 1989). This is especially true in project courses, where there are a number of tasks to be shared among the group. The mutual search for understanding helps students to develop both intellectual and social skills. Of course, students must take responsibility for gaining at least a minimum level of understanding about each task performed by coworkers in the group.

You will need to decide whether to give open-book or closed-book tests. In part, the choice depends on your objectives. Some faculty members allow students to bring only certain items to the exam, e.g. their textbook, their class notes, or perhaps a single sheet with formulas and other essential information. We heard of one faculty member who announced that each student could bring whatever he or she could carry into the exam; one student carried in his roommate!

As a final issue, feedback on exams and assignments is a vital part of the process. The importance of feedback was emphasized as one of the eight principles of undergraduate education in Chapter 2, and was discussed further as part of planning a course (end of Chapter 2) and helping students in discussion classes (end of Chapter 3). To assist students in assessing their performance on exams, homework assignments, and projects, you can distribute solution sets to the class along with the graded papers, or you can go over the problems in class. One method that has worked well is for students to put their correct solutions on the board. This provides an added incentive for doing the work. Another technique is for you or your teaching assistants to hold an extra class to cover results of exams or assignments. Whatever method of feedback you choose, make sure it is prompt, corrective, and supportive.

Let us now consider how we can use the results of tests and assignments to evaluate the success of learning and teaching.

INTERPRETING THE RESULTS OF EXAMS AND ASSIGNMENTS

Graded exams and assignments can play an important role in evaluating the performance of individuals and also the performance of the class as a whole. We consider each of these topics in turn.

Evaluating the Performance of Individual Students

The two most common schemes for evaluating individual performance are the absolute grading system and the class curve. The absolute grading system measures a student's achievement with respect to a specified standard. The standard is based on a continuum of knowledge or skills from zero proficiency to perfect performance (Hammons and Barnsley, 1992). The student's grade is assigned independent of other students' performance. This form of grading has many advantages. For example, it clearly indicates whether a student can perform a task at a certain level of competence. This can identify which students have not mastered the material and thus may need help before going on to more advanced parts of the course. Absolute grading can also motivate students since there are no predetermined limits on the number of students who can earn high grades.

The class curve system compares the performance of one student against the performance of others, thus indicating the student's relative position within the class. We believe this approach is undesirable for a number of reasons. It does not indicate whether a student is proficient with the material, but rather only indicates whether one student is more or less proficient than another. It can undermine cooperation among students because their grades depend on the performance of their classmates. Furthermore, students who are below the class average may view themselves—and be viewed by others—as incompetent, even though they may be quite able (Hammons and Barnsley, 1992). Nevertheless, the curve is sometimes favored by students as well as teachers if there is concern that grades will be lower than warranted due to difficult tests.

Other grading schemes are also used in certain situations. For example, a pass/fail system is sometimes appropriate. As you grapple with any grading scheme, keep in mind that the goal is to obtain a fair evaluation of how well the students have learned the material. Grades have important implications for future employment, graduate school, scholarships, and other pursuits; make sure you establish and apply a fair grading policy. Further information on grading is provided by Milton et al. (1986) and by Fenton (1992).

> *Exercise: If you used absolute grading in the last course you taught, how did you choose the percentage levels that defined each grade? Did the fraction of students earning each grade change significantly from previous years, if you taught the course before? Assuming your grading is consistent, these variations may indicate why it is important to alter one's teaching to fit the class—planning to cover predetermined amounts of material may result in moving too fast or too slowly for a particular class.*

Evaluating the Performance of the Class

Cross and Angelo (1988) describe a method known as "classroom research" for evaluating the performance of learning by an entire class, and for evaluating teaching by the instructor. They note that information collected for these purposes must be used differently than information collected to evaluate individual students. There are three distinct differences. First, the motivation for collecting the information is not to grade students; rather, the motivation is personal, based on the teacher's desire to increase the overall level of student learning. Second, the performance of individual students is not as important as the performance of the class as a whole. Finally, the criteria for success are not the letter grades assigned to the students. Rather, the criteria must be chosen by the teacher; for example, analyzing the *process* by which a student arrived at the answer, rather than the correctness of the answer, may be appropriate. The following list of questions may be useful when using test and homework scores to evaluate the success of a class:

1. Questions about students

   a. How many students are learning the material well and how many aren't?

   b. Which students are learning well and which aren't?

   c. What are successful learners doing that others in the class are not?

2. Questions about course content

   a. How much of the course material are students learning?

   b. Which elements of the course are students learning?

   c. How well are students learning the material?

3. Questions about teaching

    a. How does the teaching style used in the course affect student learning, both positively and negatively?

    b. What specifically can be changed about the teaching style to promote optimal learning?

Exercise: Consider how you would answer the questions above for the class you are currently teaching. How can you use the answers to make changes in your teaching that would improve the class?

    The information presented in this chapter suggests that you need to take seriously the tasks of preparing exams and assignments. As you make your preparations, you may wish to consult with more experienced faculty colleagues. After all, you wouldn't hesitate to discuss a research question with them—why not an exam problem? In addition, if you have teaching assistants, you will probably want to provide copies of the problems to them in advance. Have them work out the problems—they may have good suggestions for improvements. All faculty members, and most students, recognize the difficulty of preparing effective exams and assignments. Don't hesitate to ask for help.

SUMMARY

    In this chapter, we have discussed examinations and class assignments as vital components of a college course. We have presented several objectives for both student and teacher. For the student, exam questions and assignments can provide motivation to learn new material and indications of how well the material is being learned; for the teacher, they can provide opportunities to present new concepts and to evaluate the success of teaching. Exams and assignments are also important for establishing grades.

    Several types of exams can be used, ranging from highly structured multiple choice tests to relatively unstructured essay examinations. In all cases, however, you should design the exam to meet specific objectives, and you should communicate these objectives to the students.

    Preparing acceptable examination questions and problems on assignments is a difficult task. However, good students appreciate a good exam or homework set, and that appreciation will show in terms of class attendance, performance, and overall interest in your class. It is a part of teaching a course that, like delivering a good lecture or leading an active discussion, can be rewarding.

REFERENCES

Bloom, B.S., J.T. Hastings, and G.F. Madaus, *Taxonomy of Educational Objectives: The Classification of Educational Goals, Handbook 1, Cognitive Domain,* New York, NY: McCay, 1956.

Clegg, V.L. and W.E. Cashin, *Improving Multiple Choice Tests,* Idea Paper Number 16, Kansas: Center for Faculty Evaluation and Development, Kansas State University, 1986.

Cross, K.P. and T.A. Angelo, *Classroom Assessment Techniques: A Handbook for Faculty,* Ann Arbor, MI: National Center for Research to Improve Postsecondary Teaching and Learning, The University of Michigan, 1988.

Eble, K.E., *The Craft of Teaching,* San Francisco, CA: Jossey-Bass, pp. 110–119, 1976.

Erickson, B.L. and D.W. Strommer, *Teaching College Freshmen,* San Francisco, CA: Jossey-Bass, pp. 135–149, 1991.

Fenton, E., Evaluation: Writing Problem Sets, Quizzes, Examinations, and Paper Assignments (Chapter 8), and Grades and Grading (Chapter 9), unpublished manuscript on Teaching in Colleges and Universities, Carnegie Mellon University, 1992.

Gronlund, N.E., *Measurement and Evaluation in Teaching, 5th edition,* New York, NY: Macmillan, pp. 169–228, 1985.

Hammons, J.O. and J.R. Barnsley, Everything you need to know about developing a grading plan for your course (well, almost), *Journal on Excellence in College Teaching, Vol. 3,* pp. 51–68, 1992.

Hatten, J., Why do students fail?, *The Teaching Professor, Vol. 3,* pp. 1–2, 1989.

Hopkins, K.D. and J.C. Stanley, *Educational and Psychological Measurement and Evaluation,* 7th edition, Englewood Cliffs, NJ: Prentice-Hall, pp. 200–319, 1990.

Johnson, D.W., *Educational Psychology,* Englewood Cliffs, NJ: Prentice-Hall, pp. 463–465, 1979.

Light, R.J., *The Harvard Assessment Seminars: Explorations with Students and Faculty About Teaching, Learning, and Student Life,* First Report, Cambridge, MA: Harvard University Graduate School of Education and Kennedy School of Government, 1990.

Lowman, J., *Mastering the Techniques of Teaching,* San Francisco, CA: Jossey-Bass, pp. 184–209, 1984.

MacGregor, J., Collaborative learning: Shared inquiry as a process of reform, in M.D. Svinicki, editor, *The Changing Face of College Teaching*, Number 42 in the series *New Directions for Teaching and Learning*, San Francisco, CA: Jossey-Bass, pp. 19–30, 1990.

Mehrens, W.A. and I.J. Lehman, *Measurement and Evaluation in Education and Psychology, 3rd edition,* New York, NY: Holt, Rinehart, and Winston, pp. 266–310, 1984.

Milton, O., H.R. Pollio, and J.A. Eison, *Making Sense of College Grades*, San Francisco, CA: Jossey-Bass, 1986.

Simon, H.A., Problem solving and education, in D.T. Tuma and F. Reif, *Problem Solving and Education: Issues in Teaching and Research,* Hillsdale, NJ: Lawrence Erlbaum Associates, pp. 81–96, 1980.

Slavin, R.E., Research and cooperative learning: consensus and controversy, *Educational Leadership, Vol. 47,* pp. 52–54, Dec. 1989/Jan. 1990.

6

WORKING WITH TEACHING ASSISTANTS

INTRODUCTION

Many colleges and universities employ graduate students as teaching assistants (TAs) to help with course instruction. Some faculty members welcome the use of TAs and use the opportunity to nurture future colleagues, while others cringe at yet another responsibility of faculty life. Indeed, supervising TAs can be time-consuming, but the benefits can far outweigh the costs. If done effectively, you, the teaching assistants, and the undergraduate students can all gain from the TA experience.

Some of these benefits become clear if we consider the principles for undergraduate education outlined in Chapter 2. For example, one of the principles emphasized prompt feedback on student performance in the class; TAs who grade papers accurately and promptly can help provide this feedback. Another principle stressed the importance of productive faculty-student interactions. TAs can help here, too, by improving your understanding of the needs of students in the class.

In this chapter, we explore ways in which you can help to make the TA experience work for all involved. We begin by discussing the professor-TA relationship, considering the attitudes of each group. Next we provide examples of typical teaching assistant responsibilities. We then discuss specific ways in which you can help your TAs meet their obligations. Finally, we discuss special considerations in working with TAs from outside the United States.

ATTITUDES: THE PROFESSOR-TEACHING ASSISTANT RELATIONSHIP

Faculty members and teaching assistants have a wide variety of attitudes about their respective roles in the relationship. Clearly, your own attitudes will greatly influence the way your TAs will perform their responsibilities. Negative feelings, even when partially masked, can undermine the system and cause frustration; in contrast, a positive attitude can contribute greatly to the success of a course. Let us consider some of the typical faculty attitudes:

+ The primary role of the teaching assistant is simply to make your life easier by transferring much of the menial teaching-related tasks to someone else. TAs pick up on this attitude quickly. Those who view their role differently will resent this attitude, while others will accept this message as an affirmation that research is important while teaching is not. In either case, it's a losing proposition.

+ The TA is a valuable source of help for your course, not only by sharing the work load but also by providing information. For example, a TA can identify students who may need extra help and relate feedback from students who may be reluctant to talk with you directly. TAs also pick up on this attitude, and most will respond positively by asking what they can do to help.

+ The TA is a potential future colleague, and thus it is desirable to develop an effective working relationship in which you and your TA can learn from each other's experiences. This attitude has perhaps the greatest long-term benefits. After all, you can serve in a multiplicity of roles: as an *advisor* who shares knowledge, a *supporter* who provides emotional encouragement, a *tutor* who gives specific feedback on performance, and a *role model* who effectively balances the various responsibilities of faculty life (after Cusanovich and Gilliland, 1991). Most TAs quickly recognize this attitude and appreciate it.

The attitudes of your teaching assistants are also important in determining how they approach their responsibilities. Consider the following contrasting attitudes of TAs:

+ The teaching assistantship is a necessary burden because it is required by the department or because it provides a stipend. This attitude may be well-founded. After all, graduate students attempting to complete their theses have to deal with a diversion of time and energy away from their research. However, you can help your TAs to develop a more positive outlook since the TA experience can help them in ways they might not have considered.

+ The teaching assistantship provides help to both the instructor and the students in a course. The TA can help the instructor by providing feedback on where students are having difficulty, and by suggesting alternative methods and examples. On the other hand, the TA can help the students by providing clarification or missing information.

✦ The teaching assistantship is an opportunity to develop skills useful for a variety of professions. Clearly, the experience in working with students is valuable for those pursuing academic careers. However, working with people in different roles can help in virtually any profession, and graduate students who recognize this will naturally put a greater effort into their work.

These attitudes depend on the career goals of the individual TA, the messages sent by you as course instructor, and the attitudes of other faculty members and graduate students in the department. It is important for both you and your TAs to understand each other's beliefs and attitudes and to work within (or sometimes around) these views. Overall, the message is clear: the TA experience will be far more successful for all involved if you can motivate your teaching assistants to do the best job they can.

Exercise: Consider your first responsibility as a TA when you were a graduate student. Which of the above attitudes was displayed by the faculty member for whom you worked? How did that influence your attitudes? Now consider the first time you supervised a TA in one of the courses you taught. Which attitude did you display? the TA?

RESPONSIBILITIES OF TEACHING ASSISTANTS

The specific responsibilities of TAs can vary greatly from department to department within a college and even from one instructor to another within a department. For this reason, you should communicate your expectations to your TAs as explicitly as possible. The following list is intended merely to provide suggestions which can help you and your TAs agree upon their responsibilities.

Conduct Recitation Sessions

Some faculty members expect TAs to review lecture material and to provide more detail on important concepts which were only touched upon in lecture. Other faculty members want their TAs simply to cover example problems during the recitation. Still others view recitation as a time for students to raise questions. No doubt, the TAs also have thoughts on how to spend time in recitation, perhaps based on their own experiences as undergraduates or as TAs in other classes. Be sure to let your TAs know what you expect in recitation sessions and make an effort to solicit their suggestions. Be willing to discuss differences of opinion and work to reach agreement with them.

Conduct Laboratory Sessions

If your course includes laboratory work, you may want your TAs to circulate around the lab to discuss the experiment with the students. This can prompt the students to think through the underlying concepts involved in the experiment, and thus process the information at a deeper level of understanding. Encourage your TAs to perform the experiment themselves in advance so that they can more readily help the students. Finally, you may want the TAs to reinforce how a particular lab fits into the more general course material because students often do not make these connections on their own. More detailed information on how to plan and conduct laboratory sessions is provided by Boud et al. (1986).

Write Exams and Homework Assignments

Some faculty members request assistance from their TAs in creating test and homework problems. If you want your teaching assistants to do so, you can help them by providing previous exams and homework assignments as examples, and by communicating your specific objectives for each exam and assignment as discussed in Chapter 5. Also discuss grading criteria with them, since they will probably be responsible for correcting the problems. Be sure there is enough time for you to carefully work through each problem and to suggest revisions before distribution to the class.

Create Solution Sets for Quizzes, Exams, and Homework Assignments

Whether you or your TAs create the test and homework problems, you may still want your TAs to write the solution sets. Provide guidelines and examples of these, along with specific dates and enough revision time so that you can suggest changes. Make sure that the solution sets do not skip or collapse steps, a potential problem "experts" sometimes experience as we discussed in Chapter 1.

Proctor Examinations

If you ask your TAs to proctor exams, stress the importance of beginning and ending on time, seating students in a way to minimize the temptation to cheat, and staying alert by periodically strolling around the room. It would be best if the TAs have worked through the exam problems so that they can respond to questions. You may wish to provide some guidance on how to answer questions (e.g., whether you will allow the TA to provide certain information if asked, and whether the TA should announce the question and answer to the entire class so that everyone has the same information).

Grade Exams and Homework Assignments

This task should be easier if solution sets have been created. You will need to reach agreement with your TAs on the number of points to award for each component of the problem, and on whether you expect the TA to provide written feedback on each paper while grading. You may want to establish a policy on grading disputes so that the students know when it is appropriate to approach a TA and when it is appropriate to approach you with a problem. In cases where you are assigned multiple TAs, do your best to maintain consistency in grading. For example, each TA can grade one problem across an entire class, passing the full set of papers from one TA to another for grading the next problem. This is more effective than dividing the papers among several TAs who are likely to have different grading criteria for a single problem. It is always important for the TAs to communicate with each other regarding grading criteria, perhaps by having them spot check each other's work. One approach that has worked on occasion at our institution is to have all of the TAs grade exams together in a single room where they can ask each other questions about partial credit and other issues.

Schedule Office Hours for Tutoring

Your teaching assistants need to be aware of customs in the department regarding office hours, as well as your expectations about their availability and accessibility. If you require them to hold office hours, let them know how many hours per week to schedule. Suggest that they stagger the times because of students' class schedules. You may wish to make arrangements for your TAs to schedule extra hours immediately before an exam. You may also wish to suggest ways in which they can be effective tutors. For example, a TA should refrain from simply solving problems when a student seeks help. Instead, the TA should ask questions to identify the source of the confusion, then provide cues and suggestions to enable the student to work out the problem. In many cases, the student can solve the problem right then and there. Be sure your TAs understand that students develop problem-solving skills by practicing them, as we discussed in Chapter 1, not by watching someone else repeatedly solve problems. Also let your TAs know that their role during office hours is to help students with academic-related problems, not personal or psychological problems. Because issues like these sometimes arise during office hours, you may wish to provide your teaching assistants with a list of the appropriate support systems on campus to deal with these problems, or have them refer the student to you.

Conduct Review Sessions

Many faculty members wish to help students review material prior to an exam without taking class time. If you want your TAs to conduct a review session for this purpose, provide them with your thoughts on how to organize the session; the ideas presented above for recitation sessions may be appropriate here. However, because the review is likely to address particular topics to be covered on a test, the session may need to be more narrowly focused. For example, you might provide an exam on the same material given in the course in a previous year. The TAs and students can then work through this exam in the review session. Or perhaps the students will want to set their own agenda, e.g., by preparing questions on topics that are still confusing to them. Recall from Chapter 1 that students maintain knowledge, and thus are able to use it at future times, when they revisit it frequently and develop multiple links with other information. Thus review sessions can serve a vital role in the learning process.

Attend Lectures

You may want your TAs to attend lectures you give so that they hear the same presentation as the students. This is particularly important if you are covering material not readily available in a textbook, or if the TAs are unfamiliar with the material. However, you might relieve your TAs of this responsibility under certain circumstances. For example, this may be appropriate if they have been a TA for the course before and you feel there is little to be gained from attending the lectures. Be sure you make this decision carefully; you want your TAs to have all the necessary information, yet you don't want to waste their time. After all, they are undoubtedly over-committed just as you are.

You may expect your TAs to be responsible for any of the above functions. Some faculty members divide all of the responsibilities equally among TAs, while others may ask their TAs to rotate responsibilities or to specialize in some of the tasks. In any case, you need to discuss with your teaching assistants which responsibilities you expect them to perform and, if possible, how much time they should spend on each task.

> *Exercise: Consider the last course you taught for which you had TAs. Which of the above responsibilities were applicable? How did you make sure your TAs understood their responsibilities and your expectations of them?*

WAYS OF HELPING YOUR TEACHING ASSISTANTS TO MEET THEIR RESPONSIBILITIES

One of the most common complaints of TAs over the years has been the resentment of a system that expects too much of them without providing any real training. In many cases, TAs are thrown into a classroom without the benefit of training as a teacher. In other cases, they are handed piles of papers to correct without guidance on how to grade or provide feedback. This may sound familiar—many new faculty members find themselves in the same situation. However, the problem is worse for TAs because they are younger, having just finished their baccalaureate in some cases. Graduate students who are TAs for the first time often express considerable self-doubt and are in particular need of guidance, while experienced TAs who have moved past this survival stage are able to concentrate on the impact of their instruction (Sprague and Nyquist, 1991). Those graduate students who learn the ropes only by trial and error lament the cost in terms of time, effort, and self-esteem. Don't let this happen to your TAs. If your department or college offers a teaching assistant training program, require your TAs to attend. If not, you may wish to pursue channels to have such a program set up. One model which has worked well at our institution is outlined in Table 6-1, for use in a department where TA responsibilities are limited to grading, tutoring, and conducting review sessions.

Even if your TAs have access to a TA training program, you still need to provide information and support. In this section, we consider ways in which you can help your teaching assistants before the semester begins, during the semester, and after the course is completed.

Before the Semester

It is desirable for departments to assign TAs well before the semester begins. Unfortunately, however, this is often not the case, and new faculty members rarely have control over the timing or the process. Despite when appointments are made, you will want to meet with your TAs prior to the first class to define the course objectives. You will also need to discuss the schedule for homework assignments, projects, tests, and other parts of the course. Be explicit about your expectations for the TA role for each of these, and indicate that you are open to suggestions on ways to improve the course. Be sure to give each TA a course syllabus, textbook, solutions manual for the text if available, and other relevant written material. Also provide as much information as possible on the backgrounds of the students. You may want to share your experiences in planning the course, as discussed in Chapter 2, with your TAs. This may provide them with further insight.

For courses in which your TAs will lead recitation sections, you will want to discuss what to do on the first day of class. TAs often find this a very intimidating session. You might suggest that they begin by introducing themselves and their backgrounds, asking the students to do the same. Then they can discuss the course objectives, grading procedures, and their role as a teaching assistant. Have them spend a few minutes delving into the material to give the students an idea of what the class will be like.

TAs who are leading recitation sections may also appreciate ideas on teaching methods. You might suggest that they observe your classes, or the classes of faculty colleagues or other recitation instructors. Talk with them about teaching and learning strategies (Chapters 1–5). If your institution has a teaching center, suggest that they attend some of the programs appropriate for their needs.

During the Semester

It is necessary to hold regular meetings with your TAs—perhaps weekly— to exchange papers for grading, discuss new assignments, and attend to problems that inevitably arise. You can use these meetings to keep track of overall progress in the course; TAs can share their experiences with you and with each

TABLE 6-1

Example of a Teaching Assistant Seminar Program at Carnegie Mellon

Topic of Seminar	Objectives and Learning Experiences
Seminar 1: *Grading*	Seminar participants will be able to identify different grading practices, set up criteria for grading, and begin to develop skills for grading a variety of types of problems Learning experiences include the following: 1. Discussion of grading practices and grading criteria 2. Participation in a grading exercise: copies of an undergraduate exam with problems worked out (to demonstrate a variety of errors) are graded individually by each TA during the seminar 3. Comparison of results: TAs in the seminar discuss the scores they selected and their reasons
Seminar 2: *Tutoring*	Seminar participants will be able to identify the types of problems that students may have when seeking assistance of TAs, and will be able to apply effective techniques to help those students. The participants will also understand when they need to refer students to other individuals, such as the faculty member in charge of the course. Learning experiences include the following: 1. Discussion of tutoring methods 2. Presentation of a videotape showing one-on-one tutoring sessions within the department for TAs to identify issues 3. Use of a questionnaire containing typical questions from students seeking assistance; the questionnaires are completed individually by each participant during the seminar to determine how they would respond in different situations 4. Discussion of the videotape and questionnaire responses, illustrating effective as well as ineffective tutoring methods
Seminar 3: *Conducting Review* *Sessions*	Seminar participants will be able to identify the different ways of conducting review sessions in preparation for an exam or major project, and will be able to organize and run a review session while serving as a TA for a class. Learning experiences include the following: 1. Discussion of techniques used in review sessions 2. Presentation of a videotape showing typical review sessions run by TAs 3. Discussion of the advantages and disadvantages of each method of conducting a review session, based on the videotape and personal experiences

Note: published information on the topic is distributed to the participants at each seminar for later reference.

other. You may also want to administer evaluation forms for the students to complete after the first three or four weeks of classes, allowing them to comment on your teaching as well as on the performance of the TAs; you can then discuss these responses with your TAs to enable mid-course corrections. You will also want to use evaluation forms at the end of the semester.

For TAs who are recitation instructors, you might assist by attending an occasional recitation class to provide feedback on their teaching style. You might also suggest that they have some of their sessions videotaped for review by themselves or by trained consultants, e.g. from your institution's teaching center. Methods of improving teaching skills by using these techniques are discussed by Bennett et al. (1987) and Levinson-Rose and Menges (1981).

There are special considerations for large lecture classes with several recitation sections. Of utmost importance is well-established communication. Frequent meetings between you and all of the recitation instructors are essential; each instructor must know what the others are doing and you need to keep track of the whole works. Exchanging ideas on which activities are working and which aren't can help you to rapidly implement good ideas across the sections. You also need to make sure that policies of the instructors are consistent so that no section is particularly advantaged or disadvantaged. There always seems to be one section that lags behind the rest, often through no fault of the recitation instructor. You will need to make an effort to help students in that section and to help the recitation instructor cope with the problem.

You should remember not to equate a teaching assistant's knowledge of the material with the ability to teach it. TAs usually need advice on developing skills such as how to actively involve students in problem solving, how to interact with students during office hours to assure maximum learning, and how to deal with classroom behavior problems or cheating situations. Most TAs will appreciate your help in these matters.

A few words are also appropriate on personal relations. The teaching assistantship may be the first time your TAs have been in a supervisory role, and some of them may need considerable guidance in developing interpersonal skills. For example, under certain circumstances you may need to advise your TAs of the following rules of normal conduct:

+ Respect confidentiality by refraining from discussing private matters of students with other TAs.

+ Refrain from criticizing you when talking with the students.

+ Treat students with respect and treat them fairly and equally, despite personal feelings about particular individuals.

+ Be careful about touching students or closing an office door when only you and the student are present in the office.

✦ Refrain from dating a student in the current class; wait until the semester is over to establish these types of personal relationships.

After the Semester

Asking your students to evaluate the class at the end of the semester can provide valuable feedback on how your TAs performed. You should provide a copy of these responses to the TAs and discuss the results with them. Because TAs often have close associations with the students, they can usually provide information you could not otherwise get—perhaps details a student would be hesitant to put in writing on an evaluation form. Be sure to take advantage of this: ask your TAs to comment on the strengths and weaknesses of the course as the students perceive them. You might also get suggestions on new topics of particular interest to the students that could be added to next year's course. Use of TAs for this purpose is discussed in detail by Boehrer and Chevrier (1991).

Overall, teaching assistants and faculty members can help to strengthen each other's teaching as well as management skills. Therefore, you want to encourage your TAs to reflect on their experience for professional development (Allen, 1991). You can greatly assist your TAs in this; for example, if you observed your TAs in their recitation sections throughout the semester, let them know how their teaching has progressed. The same applies to developing skills in creating exams or in grading them. Offer suggestions on ways they can continue to grow.

Exercise: Consider the last class you taught for which you had TAs. Did you meet with your TAs both before and during the semester? In what ways did these meetings help the course run more smoothly? Did you hold a meeting after the semester was completed to provide feedback to each other? Think about special problems that developed during the semester; how could these problems be better handled next time, now that you have the experience of dealing with them?

SPECIAL CONSIDERATIONS FOR INTERNATIONAL TEACHING ASSISTANTS

International TAs bring different perspectives and backgrounds which can add a lot to a course. However, they may also bring culturally related problems such as communication difficulties and possible misunderstandings in the roles of student and teacher. Many colleges and universities have become sensitized to the issue of international TAs in recent years, providing special classes for TAs from other countries. These programs usually promote learning in several areas, such as developing instructional skills and fluency in English, as well as acquiring cultural information (Civikly and Muchisky, 1991). You should encourage or even require your international TAs to attend any of these programs that seem appropriate.

TAs from other countries often arrive with assumptions about the students, the teachers, and the classroom environment in general. These assumptions may or may not be correct; you can ward off potential problems by correcting any misunderstandings early in the semester. Let us consider each of these categories (adapted from Sarkisian, 1990).

Assumptions about Students

Many countries have a standard national curriculum which provides a common background to all students in an undergraduate discipline. Furthermore, getting into such a program is often highly competitive; unlike most American colleges, only a few percent of the students desiring admission may be accepted. Thus many of our international graduate students who serve as TAs are unprepared for the variety of backgrounds they will encounter in the classroom, and they may not be aware of the wide range of abilities and levels of motivation that are characteristic of our undergraduate classes. You can help your TAs make the adjustment by discussing these issues with them. You might also encourage them to talk with other TAs, particularly those from the same country who have already made the adjustment.

Assumptions about Teachers

Many international TAs come from educational systems where the instructor is viewed as an absolute authority who is never questioned. Imagine the surprise of a new international TA, serving as a recitation instructor, when an undergraduate student openly disagrees with the method of problem solving the TA is presenting. Clearly, the TA needs to understand that the student is not showing disrespect, but rather is simply exercising the right to question.

There are numerous other differences in teacher behavior and in teacher-student relations. For example, we have discussed the importance of actively involving students in the learning process and in providing frequent and specific feedback. These practices differ widely from those in countries where professors lecture, students never speak in class, and testing occurs only once per year. While your international TAs may not be comfortable with the American style of teaching, they nevertheless must accept these practices and learn to adapt to them.

Assumptions about the Classroom Environment

Many international TAs are unaccustomed to the informality of the American classroom. Most of us are used to students who arrive late for class, wear informal (or even inappropriate) dress, or eat during the class. Furthermore, our students occasionally sleep in class, or use the time to read the campus newspaper. Sometimes we tolerate these behaviors and sometimes we don't, but such informality is rarely a surprise. It is important that your TAs understand that these behaviors are widespread. You can help by letting them know the appropriate actions under different circumstances.

International TAs, like all TAs, can greatly benefit from information you provide on how to perform their responsibilities effectively. Make sure that your suggestions are specific, and that cultural differences are not a major impairment. In extreme circumstances, if you have done everything you can, it may be necessary to replace a TA so that students in a recitation section are not handicapped. After all, some international graduate students may not be able to perform certain roles due to language or cultural problems, just as many American graduate students discover late that they are inappropriate as teachers or researchers. However, most cases of language and cultural differences can be dealt with adequately with proper guidance.

> *Exercise: If you have worked with international TAs, how have you informed them about cultural differences that may influence their TA role? Are you familiar with programs on your campus to help international graduate students adapt to our system? (Examples include special programs in English as a second language and in TA training for international students.)*

SUMMARY

In this chapter, we suggest that you and your TAs build a sense of shared responsibility as you teach and learn together. We discuss how different attitudes can impair or assist a TA in completing certain responsibilities.

These responsibilities can vary greatly among departments and even within a single department. For example, TAs may run review sessions and laboratories, proctor exams, grade papers of all types, write exam questions and homework problems, conduct private tutoring, and lead a recitation section. You need to discuss with your TAs what you expect of them and provide information to help them achieve these expectations. Programs for helping teaching assistants with their responsibilities have been set up at a number of colleges; encourage your TAs to attend. Note that it is always a good idea to solicit suggestions from your TAs on how they can best help and on what you can do to improve the course overall.

Finally, international TAs can bring new and interesting perspectives to a course, but they may need special guidance from you to overcome language and cultural barriers. Many colleges now offer training programs specifically geared to non-American teaching assistants, and it is usually a good idea for your international TAs to take advantage of these.

For many graduate students, the TA role is one of the best opportunities to receive supervision that prepares them for academia. Thus helping your TAs not only provides you with coursework assistance, but also helps many striving graduate students to prepare for their future careers.

REFERENCES

Allen, R.R., Encouraging reflection in teaching assistants, in Nyquist, J.D., R.D. Abbott, D.H. Wulff, and J. Sprague, editors, *Preparing the Professoriate of Tomorrow to Teach*, Dubuque, IA: Kendall/Hunt Publishing, pp. 313–317, 1991.

Bennett, B., B. Joyce, and B. Showers, Synthesis of research on staff development: A future study and a state-of-the-art analysis, *Educational Leadership, Vol. 45*, pp. 77–87, 1987.

Boehrer, J. and M. Chevrier, Professor and teaching assistant: Making the most of a working relationship, in Nyquist, J.D., R.D. Abbott, D.H. Wulff, and J. Sprague, editors, *Preparing the Professoriate of Tomorrow to Teach*, Dubuque, IA: Kendall/Hunt Publishing, pp. 326–330, 1991.

Boud, D., J. Dunn, and E. Hegarty-Hazel, *Teaching in Laboratories*, Surrey, England: The Society for Research into Higher Education and NFER-NELSON, The University, Guildford, 1986.

Civikly, J.M. and D.M. Muchisky, A collaborative approach to ITA training, in Nyquist, J.D., R.D. Abbott, D.H. Wulff, and J. Sprague, editors, *Preparing the Professoriate of Tomorrow to Teach*, Dubuque, IA: Kendall/Hunt Publishing, pp. 356–360, 1991.

Cusanovich, M. and M. Gilliland, Mentoring: The faculty-graduate student relationship, *Communicator, Vol. 24*, pp. 1–3, 1991.

Levinson-Rose, J.L. and R.J. Menges, Improving college teaching: A critical review of research, *Review of Educational Research, Vol. 51*, pp. 403–434, 1981.

Sarkisian, E., *Teaching American Students: A Guide for International Faculty and Teaching Fellows*, Cambridge, MA: Danforth Center for Teaching and Learning, Harvard University, 1990.

Sprague, J. and J.D. Nyquist, A developmental perspective on the TA role, in Nyquist, J.D., R.D. Abbott, D.H. Wulff, and J. Sprague, editors, *Preparing the Professoriate of Tomorrow to Teach*, Dubuque, IA: Kendall/Hunt Publishing, pp. 295–312, 1991.

7

SUPERVISING GRADUATE RESEARCH

INTRODUCTION

The second half of this book focuses on issues in research: working with graduate students, writing and reviewing research proposals and technical papers, delivering presentations, and conducting graduate seminars. To some extent, all of these topics involve educating various audiences. Thus the material presented in the remaining six chapters builds upon many of the concepts in the first half of the book.

This chapter discusses a key element of a successful faculty research program, namely the supervision of graduate students in their research. Although you conducted research as a graduate student, you probably did not have the opportunity to supervise the research of others. Supervision of research is a complex task that requires teaching others how to do a difficult job. Proper supervision requires just the right amount of guidance—too little can allow the student to flounder, while too much can prevent the student from developing independence. As in any type of teaching, it is important for you to know your students well—their strengths and weaknesses, their likes and dislikes, their personal goals.

Many aspects of classroom teaching are relevant in graduate supervision. For example, you have to know the subject matter well, and you must be able to communicate that knowledge clearly. However, the concepts in research are much more difficult to grasp than those in formal coursework. Research takes place at the cutting edge of a discipline and thus involves concepts that are new and often untested. In addition, graduate student supervision includes teaching the *process* of conducting research as well as technical issues. The relation between graduate student and advisor can be considered analogous to the guild relationship between apprentice and master. The outcome of the process is an individual qualified to practice the trade of research (Connell, 1985).

In this chapter, we present several ideas that can help you supervise your graduate students effectively. First, we discuss the graduate school environment from the perspectives of both student and advisor. Then we present the steps in graduate research leading to a completed thesis. Finally, we present problems resulting in graduate student dropout, focusing on "ABDs" (All But Dissertation). Throughout this chapter, we discuss only Ph.D. research. The motivations of the student pursuing an M.S. or M.A. degree may be quite different from those pursuing a Ph.D., and this will influence your role as advisor. However, many of the issues for Ph.D. research discussed here will be relevant to supervising Masters theses. Some of the issues will also be relevant to undergraduate research.

THE GRADUATE SCHOOL ENVIRONMENT

The attitudes of graduate students in a research program can be quite different from those of faculty members, and these differences may cause misunderstandings throughout a graduate student's term of study. The key to avoiding these types of problems is to strive to understand the respective viewpoints early enough to correct the situation.

Perceptions of the Students

Most graduate students arrive at their new department without a thorough knowledge of the environment. In many cases, they have not visited the school prior to their decision to attend; they may not have talked with any of the faculty members or other students. Even in cases where an applicant visited the school, their conversations with faculty members and current graduate students are likely to have been brief, perhaps focusing on logistical issues such as financial support and housing. Incoming students are not likely to be familiar with current research areas in any detail, and they may not appreciate the need to develop a good working relation with a faculty advisor. Most important, new graduate students are not likely to have an adequate understanding of the way faculty conduct research.

Because of this lack of understanding, many incoming graduate students have developed preconceived ideas about their path to the Ph.D. For example, many students envision the process as a somewhat lonely experience, where one secedes from the outside world to focus all energies on a single important question. In their minds, the discomfort of this existence is well worth the expected outcome: a nearly flawless and definitive work on an important topic. In fact, some students do conduct their dissertation research in a relative vacuum. Furthermore, some theses are indeed landmarks in their field. But these are not the usual case; very few theses are definitive works, and most students would benefit by maintaining outside interests during their stay in graduate school. For students who continue in academia, the thesis may merely be a stepping stone to more sophisticated projects that they will someday supervise. It is the responsibility of the faculty advisor to correct misconceptions such as these.

Hartnett (1976) has summarized the most important expectations of graduate students in evaluating the environment of graduate programs. First and foremost, students expect the faculty to be accessible and interested in helping them with their research. Second, there should be a sense of community, a way to overcome the feeling of isolation when a student becomes engrossed in a narrow dissertation topic. Third, students expect the faculty to have a positive attitude toward teaching. Fourth, they expect faculty to be fair and accurate in their evaluation of student performance. Finally, the students expect the curriculum to be sufficiently flexible to accommodate their individual needs. Hartnett claims that although these elements are important to graduate students, they may not be regarded in the same way by the faculty.

Perceptions of the Faculty

Most faculty engaged in research genuinely enjoy working with graduate students. After all, it is exciting to participate in the creative process with another individual having similar interests, and it is gratifying to help a student mature and become a successful researcher. Nevertheless, there are some students whose personalities or backgrounds simply make graduate supervision unpleasant. Furthermore, many faculty members are under severe time constraints and must limit the amount of time they spend supervising their students. This means that faculty guidance sometimes focuses on specific technical questions about the research project and excludes important issues related to the overall intellectual growth of the student. For example, graduate students must learn to take responsibility, set priorities, organize time effectively, manage conflict, and evaluate their own performance (Clark, 1980). University administrators generally expect their faculty to put in time for supervising research, but rarely show a sensitivity to the time required for other types of graduate student supervision.

Effective teaching of research methods requires an environment that enhances creativity. This implies that a faculty advisor should allow a certain level of ambiguity as the student begins to understand the research process (Seeman, 1977): the topic should be kept fairly broad and the research questions somewhat open. Such an environment is not always created by well-meaning faculty. In many cases, pressures to produce research results, particularly by young faculty members seeking tenure, may result in a less flexible and less free-form research environment than would be optimal for development of the graduate student.

The differences between faculty expectations and student expectations are often the root of recurring problems in graduate supervision. Overall intellectual growth rather than acquisition of research skills may be most important to the future careers of the students, while production of research results are sometimes most important to the faculty. Thus a faculty advisor can help by keeping in mind issues important to the graduate student's development.

Maintaining a Healthy Environment

Conflicts between advisor and student that arise due to differences in perceptions are difficult to resolve. Students may be victim to a faculty member's inattentiveness or insensitivity to their problems; on the other hand, some students may be unable to fulfill reasonable expectations of the advisor. A healthy environment which fosters open communication may alleviate both of these problems. A faculty member can contribute to this environment by interacting with students on a social as well as academic level, and by being approachable and receptive to student ideas. Getting to know the students as individuals can also help the educational process. It is particularly important for a faculty member not to abuse the inequity built into the system; students have little recourse if their advisor is too busy to provide a reasonable level of guidance. Proper graduate supervision requires ethical behavior by both faculty members and students, as cited in the ethics statement of the American Association of University Professors (1977) regarding responsibilities of professors (Brown and Krager, 1985).

Faculty members can help to create a healthy environment for graduate students in many ways. For example, Katz (1976) states that a faculty advisor should:

+ Attend to the needs of the students, e.g. by insuring adequate office and laboratory space, computer facilities, and a reasonable stipend.

+ Show an interest in the personal development of the students, taking the initiative to provide guidance and to give recognition for student progress.

+ Facilitate exchange of ideas between the student and other members of the research group, perhaps in part through weekly seminars.

+ Encourage cooperation rather than competition.

+ Foster imagination and creative pursuits through exposure to disciplines outside of the dissertation topic.

+ Help students to satisfy their curiosity, e.g. by staying after class to allow students to probe a particular topic in depth.

✦ Encourage students to take a variety of courses to promote a broad knowledge base.

The graduate school experience should be a combination of "grind and creativity" (Trivett, 1977), where students have opportunities to express originality but also understand the need for disciplined and occasionally repetitive hard work. The importance of these conditions for overall personal development should not be underestimated. After all, many students pursue interests other than their dissertation topic soon after they leave graduate school; it may be more important for them to develop their intellect than to develop skills in a particular research effort. Thus creating an environment where graduate students can develop in many ways is important to the overall success of a graduate program. Additional information on creating a healthy environment for graduate students is presented by Toombs (1974) and Reisman (1976).

In the next section, we consider ways in which these developmental issues and the perceptions of the student and faculty advisor are related to the overall goal of the student in graduate research: completion of the thesis.

Exercise: Consider your role as an interviewer of a graduate applicant who is visiting your department. What questions would you ask the student to help you make a decision about whether to admit her into the department? What would you ask her to help you make a decision about whether you would be willing to supervise her thesis? Conversely, what information would you provide to help her decide whether to accept your offer? Interviews such as this, along with opportunities for the applicant to talk with other graduate students, can minimize chances of later misunderstandings.

CONDUCTING GRADUATE RESEARCH AND COMPLETING THE THESIS

A graduate research project normally involves several steps. For example, consider the following list of tasks which all Ph.D. students must complete:

✦ Determine the research topic and identify specific objectives.

✦ Design the experimental and/or theoretical work needed to achieve the objectives.

✦ Conduct the work, e.g., collect and analyze the data.

✦ Write the thesis and disseminate the research findings through a variety of ways: conference presentations, journal articles, research reports.

✦ Complete the final examination and submit the thesis.

In this section, we discuss these steps in turn, describing your role as faculty advisor in each instance. In addition, we consider the relationship between you and your graduates after completion of their Ph.D.'s.

Some of the information presented here is taken from the survey of graduate research in the U.S. by Berelson (1960), and from more recent work by Balian (1988), Madsen (1990), Ziolkowski (1990), and Fenton (1992). Faculty members may also find it useful to consult guides published by individual colleges and universities about how to prepare theses (e.g., Hart and Lawler, 1989).

Determine the Research Topic

Nobel Laureate Herbert Simon once said "...having a good question, a fundamental question, and having some tools of inquiry that allow you to take the first step toward an answer—those are the conditions that make for exciting science" (Harte, 1988). Without the fundamental question and the tools, an idea is not a viable research topic. But there is always a complexity of inspirational and mundane factors, beyond these important principles, that make choosing a thesis topic a real challenge.

The most desirable projects are challenging, intriguing, and important (e.g., the results can contribute to improving our quality of life in some way or are intellectually interesting). They also must be feasible within time and money constraints. Obviously, these qualities are very much a function of individual perceptions. Some students want to work on practical problems with immediate, tangible benefits, while others prefer abstract research whose benefits are more obscure or of a different kind. The desires of the student are obviously a top priority in choosing the topic of the dissertation.

Many other factors may also influence the choice of research topic. Three potentially important categories include the availability of funding, the availability of facilities to conduct the work, and the interests of the faculty. The role of each of these factors is highly variable from one discipline to another and even from one department to another within a discipline.

The availability of funding has a major bearing on choice of research topics in science and engineering. In most departments, faculty members are expected to provide their graduate students with financial support, often from grants and contracts. Nevertheless, because of limited available funds, many students are self-supporting. Note that self-supporting students may have considerable flexibility in choosing a research topic. For students receiving financial assistance from the department, on the other hand, the sources of funds are likely to influence the research topics available. For example, financial assistance may come from a fellowship or other source that requires the student to conduct research within a broadly defined area; in this case, there is usually some flexibility within the topic area. There may also be flexibility in choosing a research topic if the funding is linked to a teaching assistantship. However, the student is expected to devote a considerable effort to coursework in this case, and funds may not be available for laboratory equipment or supplies. When student financial awards are linked to research grants or contracts, there are often specific deliverables required. This may limit the choice of research topics available, although there are a number of advantages such as continued financial support for the student in future semesters as well as purchase of equipment and supplies to conduct the research. An intangible but important benefit of contract research is that the relevance of the project is usually spelled out ahead of time, which may satisfy the student's desire for a meaningful thesis.

The availability of facilities can also be a major determining factor in the case of experimental research. Laboratory space, analytical equipment, and computer systems can have an impact on the choice of research topics. Many graduate applicants have obtained some information about available facilities before accepting an offer to enroll in a graduate program. However, this information may be incomplete. For example, the incoming students may be unaware of facilities in other departments that they can use in their research, and hence you may need to give them this additional information.

The interests of the faculty represent another primary force in determining research topics. In some departments, students are free to choose their faculty advisor after they arrive at the beginning of the semester; the students may search out those faculty members who have interests and projects that most appeal to them. In other departments, students formally indicate their top choices of advisor, while faculty members indicate their top choices of new graduate students. A group of faculty then attempts to make optimal matches. Sometimes the matching of graduate students and faculty advisors takes place during the application process, and the freedom to change advisor after arrival may depend on the availability of projects. For any of these systems, you might need to "sell" your research interests to get the best graduate students. Consider what motivates you about the project—your enthusiasm just might be contagious.

Aside from funding, facilities, and faculty interests, there are some general issues about helping your students choose a thesis topic. You will most certainly need to suggest possible research topics and reading material, and it may be helpful to introduce your student to other individuals with appropriate expertise. Furthermore, you need to act as a sounding board for ideas that the student may have. Frequent meetings between you and the student may be necessary—keep criticism to a minimum at this point to encourage creative discussion. It is important for the student to recognize that defining the research topic is an evolving process that may continue through much of the project. Results of early experiments often dictate the direction of later work.

The most successful research topics are narrowly focused and carefully defined, but are important parts of a broad-ranging, complex problem. You can play a key role in helping to identify such topics based on your experience in the field. Research topics tend to broaden with time, so beginning with a narrow project can help the student focus energy on a particular manageable problem.

Although helpful, sharing your knowledge of current research topics is not always sufficient: many articles from years back identify unsolved problems that may have been long forgotten but are nevertheless interesting and relevant. If you haven't already done so, it may well be worth reading some of the classics in your field—you will almost certainly get some fresh insights that you can share with your graduate students.

A student often finds these early discussions frustrating, because he may spend considerable amounts of time exploring possible research ideas only to discover that the topic is infeasible or uninteresting. Plenty of understanding from you—as well as reassurance that frustration is normal at this stage—is the best advice. However, if a number of fruitful projects are explored but the student is never satisfied, you may have to push him toward a decision.

Additional information on choosing research topics is presented in Chapter 8 on writing research proposals.

Design the Research Plan to Achieve the Objectives

Once the student has identified the research topic, your role is to provide guidance in determining which experiments to conduct and which data to collect. You may also need to prod the student to begin thinking about the data analysis and interpretation techniques so that the research results will be of maximum use to others. The plan is merely a best guess at this point, a rough road map—subject to change—for the student to follow. Be sure to establish a time schedule for the initial phases of work, as this will enable the student to begin estimating the amount of time necessary to conduct a piece of the research. The complexity of thesis research requires an appreciation for staying on schedule; too many academicians have stories about theses that took years longer than expected. Put the plan in writing so it can serve as a form of contract between you and the student. There should be sufficient detail so that the student feels comfortable using the plan as a guide, but not so detailed that it becomes difficult to modify the plan as need arises.

This design phase of the research requires the student to shift thought processes. While the first step in a project involves a literature review, i.e., a summary of what has been done, the design phase demands a critical look at the work of others. Your role as advisor also changes during this phase—while previously you encouraged creative and divergent thinking, you now need to provide thoughtful criticisms of the student's experimental design (Blanton, 1977; Connell, 1985).

An important part of the design phase of the program is that the student must prepare a thesis proposal and take a qualifying examination. In many programs, this is an oral exam which may cover coursework as well as the thesis proposal. The committee members who participate in this exam are usually chosen by the advisor. Note that the membership may be different from the final thesis examination committee, although many of the same individuals are often present on both committees. The main purpose of the qualifying exam is to determine if the candidate has the necessary background and preparation to proceed with plans for Ph.D. research. Therefore, the committee should include individuals who have had the student in classes relevant to the proposed research. It is also desirable to determine if the student has breadth in technical areas other than those directly related to the research, so faculty members from other areas are usually represented on the committee. In some departments, there is a requirement that at least one member of the committee be outside of the candidate's home department in order to serve this purpose. Besides examining the student's qualifications, members of the committee may also assist the student throughout the research work. The student should be aware that these additional resource persons are available.

Conduct the Work: Collect and Analyze the Data

You need to insure that a viable research plan is in order before the work begins. When the student is finally given the OK, she will usually need little encouragement to begin the work planned for so long.

The specific tasks will, of course, vary greatly from one project to another. Many engineering and science projects require laboratory work, and this may involve the purchase or construction of specialized equipment. Projects involving field work may require considerable attention to logistical details. Research that includes computer modeling needs software as well as databases. Some projects require recruitment of human subjects, or acquisition of laboratory animals. In many types of projects, coordination with other research groups may be necessary. This is particularly true of some projects in the sciences, where groups of several dozen researchers working on a single problem is not uncommon.

Your supervisory role at this point is obviously dependent on the nature of the project. However, some general guidelines may be useful. First and most important, maintain a strong interest in the project by participating in an appropriate way. A complex field or laboratory project, for example, may require an experienced pair of hands; you may be working one-on-one with your students in this situation. Other projects may be best conducted by the student with only occasional input from the advisor, particularly if the student shows a lot of maturity in acquiring the necessary skills and conducting the research tasks. Skills of another individual may be needed, such as a member of the student's qualifier committee or a laboratory technician. Undergraduates may be brought in to assist with certain tasks, a procedure that has become more popular in recent years. By appropriately participating in the project, you need to provide enough guidance to enable the student to get the work done while still allowing him to feel ownership of the project. This will normally require you to make occasional observations of the student in action in the laboratory or at a field site, if feasible, even in those projects where a student is working somewhat independently.

Second, let your students know that you are available to help in times of crisis. Virtually every graduate project has emergencies, and these may be devastating to the student. Examples include equipment breakdowns, loss of computer files, the discovery that another research group has already solved the problem, and personal difficulties. In some cases, the tools used to conduct the work prove to be inadequate, such as equipment that does not perform to specifications. In other cases, the original premise of the research may be at fault. The student usually needs someone to turn to at these times; there is little substitute for an understanding and capable advisor.

Third, maintain close contact with your students to insure that the work is progressing toward the long-term goal. It is difficult for anyone involved in research—students and faculty alike—to keep the ultimate objectives of the research in mind while simultaneously attending to day-to-day problems that develop. You can help to insure that the direction of the work is consistent with the objectives. This is best achieved through regular, frequent meetings scheduled in advance. It is a good idea to take notes at these meetings so that you have a running record of the student's progress as well as written agreements about what work the student will complete. Or you might consider having the student take notes and provide you with a copy. In cases where you are not working closely with the student in field or laboratory projects, it is also important for you to examine samples of the raw data in order to identify possible problems that the student may not see.

Finally, be particularly attentive when the data acquisition phases of the project are winding down and the data interpretation becomes the main focus. Most graduate students lack experience in analyzing and interpreting data. For example, many use the available statistical procedures somewhat mechanically and without careful thought: they should be encouraged to sit back and think about their data before plowing into detailed computer analysis. After all, some of the most important scientific discoveries have been surprises that came about when individuals thought carefully about what they observed. We can attribute Fleming's discovery of penicillin, the Curies' success in isolating radioactive elements, and Goodyear's invention of vulcanized rubber to careful observations of patterns whose importance was not previously recognized. Effective data interpretation thus requires creativity and confidence; many students may be unable to interpret meaningful patterns in the data simply because they do not have the confidence to acknowledge that what they see is indeed important (Blanton, 1977).

Furthermore, many students are unaware of the great amount of effort needed to analyze and interpret data; this process usually takes much longer than the data acquisition. As a result, they may have the impression that their thesis work is closer to completion than it really is. Frequent conversations with the student during this part of the work can minimize unpleasant surprises.

Write the Thesis and Disseminate Research Findings

The student should consider writing the Ph.D. thesis as an integral part of the research program, and thus should not wait until the experimental work is completed before organizing the results. Most thesis research consists of a number of component projects, each with its own objectives and findings. You should encourage your student to write each component as it is completed. The written statements may take several forms, such as conference papers, journal articles, or research reports for funding agencies; the process of transferring the findings to writing will help the student to think about the major points to address in the thesis. And in some cases, the student can modify these written pieces and use them directly as sections of the thesis. In fact, a number of universities are now accepting sets of published articles in lieu of a conventional Ph.D. thesis (Monaghan, 1989).

Many graduate students identify the writing of a thesis as the most difficult task in their graduate education. Young faculty members will identify with this observation; effective writing is difficult and time consuming. Besides, the student may find it difficult to organize voluminous research results into a logical framework. The sheer size of a typical Ph.D. thesis is enough to frighten many otherwise steadfast graduate students. Nevertheless, the skills and discipline gained by a student preparing a thesis are valuable preparation for a career in research or in management.

There are many things you can do to ease the anxiety associated with writing the thesis. Most important, you can encourage your student to begin writing early, perhaps for publication. You might also provide examples of good writing by others in topics related to the research. Throughout the entire process, be prepared to review documents written by the student and to provide ample comments. This may require you to rewrite portions of the document at first; eventually, there should be enough examples of revisions and other feedback to enable the student to make substantial improvements in writing style. A short turnaround time in providing written comments is important.

Many pitfalls can develop during the writing phases of a research project (Connell, 1985). One common problem is that the student may not know the appropriate level of detail in describing experimental procedures. A general guideline suggests that there should be sufficient information in a thesis to enable the reader to repeat the experiment. However, this level of detail is generally not desirable for other forms of publication, such as a journal article. Another pitfall is that the student may want to delay providing you with early drafts of written material, intending instead to deliver highly polished prose; you might want to discourage this, since it is more important to determine first whether the technical content is appropriate. The goal of early drafts should be to make the research findings clear to you as the advisor, while later drafts should attempt to make the statement clear to the outside world. Finally, the student may be disappointed that the research findings are not more conclusive, and thus she may be tempted to halt the writing and go back into the data collection phase. You may need to intervene, depending on the circumstances.

The Final Steps: Complete the Final Examination and Submit the Thesis

This last phase of the Ph.D. may be exhilarating but at the same time exhausting to the student. The last-minute time pressures of getting the thesis out to the committee prior to the examination, the anxieties about the oral examination, and the possibility of major revisions in the thesis can be extremely stressful. You can help by making sure the thesis meets the required standards for acceptability before it is distributed and by making the student aware of the steps in the process of thesis defense.

The members of the thesis examination committee are usually chosen by agreement between the student and advisor. Details of selecting the members are important; you should consider several criteria (Connell, 1985). Some of the faculty members who served on the qualifying examination committee may be appropriate for this committee as well. However, other individuals who are familiar with the research area and can offer useful feedback are most desirable. The committee members should have stature in their field so that the results of the final exam will carry some weight. Furthermore, it may be useful to have committee members who are able to assist the student after completion of the doctorate, perhaps by helping with job placement. Although individuals hostile to the student's perspectives should be avoided, it is nevertheless important to include critical but knowledgeable faculty members on the committee. Avoid choosing committee members simply because they are sympathetic with the student.

Even if they are carefully chosen, not all committee members are likely to take the time needed to read and understand your student's thesis in depth. In his autobiography, Herbert Simon (1991) states that two out of four members of his thesis committee were unwilling to claim that they knew what he was doing. Perhaps 50% is reasonable for a Ph.D. committee.

You can also assist in the final phase of the process by preparing carefully for the examination. For example, there may be particular aspects of the student's work about which a member of the committee feels skeptical, or there may be extenuating circumstances such as problems with equipment that affected the quality of a portion of the thesis work. Be aware of these and other potential problems; where appropriate, discuss the problems with the student. Also be prepared to offer assistance during the examination, e.g., by explaining your views on a controversial aspect of the work. Besides these issues, the student may be confused about certain points raised by the committee during the defense; it is your responsibility to make sure these points are clarified. If there are necessary revisions, you may need to offer technical as well as moral support. In cases where there are substantial disagreements among the committee members, try to determine those points for which there is a consensus and suggest compromises for the other issues. Obviously, these are situations which call for a considerable amount of finesse; success at this comes with experience.

Finally, you need to be aware of the department and university rules regarding completion of all degree requirements. It is the responsibility of the student to make sure everything gets done, but you can assist by providing information.

After the Ph.D.

Your relationship with the recent Ph.D. graduate will not end on the day the thesis is signed. In fact, you can continue to be of great help once the graduate begins work; this is particularly true if the new position is in academia. You are likely to be reviewing the graduate's proposals and journal articles, and you may be in a position to provide recommendations for government committee memberships and consulting jobs. It is almost a certainty that you will be asked to write letters concerning promotion and tenure for the graduate.

For these reasons, it is important for you to stay in touch with the student. It is, after all, to your credit (whether warranted or not) if the student achieves success in her own career.

A set of heuristic rules about graduate supervision has been created by one of our colleagues. These are given in Table 7-1 (kindly provided by Professor S.J. Fenves, Carnegie Mellon).

Exercise: Give an explanation for each of the heuristic rules on supervising graduate students in Table 7-1. What do your explanations imply about how to evaluate graduate applicants? About how to provide guidance to graduate students once they are in your program?

TABLE 7-1

Some heuristic rules about supervising graduate research.

On relation with advisees

Rule 1:	Your relation with your advisor is a very weak predictor of your relation with your advisees.
Rule 2:	Your relation with advisee x is a weak predictor of your relation with advisee x + 1.

On advisee's expected research performance

Rule 3:	A student's classroom performance is a weak predictor of his/her research performance.
Rule 4:	A student's M.S. thesis performance (under any advisor) is a very strong predictor of Ph.D. research performance (Corollary: beware of non-thesis M.S. programs).

On research conduct

Rule 5:	Your funded research grant is a mildly strong predictor of what will actually be the advisee's thesis contents and results.
Counter-rule 5a:	Open-ended, unrestricted grants are harder to deal with than funded contracts: you do not have the luxury of having thought out the problem by writing the proposal.
Counter-rule 5b:	Research of self-supporting or externally funded students is the hardest to deal with: you don't have an a priori plan, and the initiative comes from the student, not you.
Rule 6:	By the time the advisee's thesis is nearing completion, you will have lost the global picture (Corollary: you do need that first paper based on the thesis to recover your own understanding).

On personal growth

Rule 7:	Notwithstanding Rules 1 and 2, you have "bonded" with your advisor and advisees for life.
Rule 8:	Don't worry about technological obsolescence: your advisees will keep you learning.

GRADUATE STUDENT DROPOUTS:
THE "ALL BUT DISSERTATION" PHENOMENON

If you spend enough time at any university, you will probably hear stories about graduate students who were well along on their Ph.D. research, but for some reason never finished their theses. Most of these students leave the university without intending to return. Some students, however, fully intend to finish their thesis, and they may keep this desire alive for years. We know of one graduate student who stopped his Ph.D. research "temporarily" to take a full-time job; although *in absentia* for over 15 years, he has continued to pay tuition every year, not willing to give up the idea of completing his thesis! Minimizing graduate student dropouts is important to your research program as well as to your students; you may have responsibilities to a funding agency that are jeopardized if a student leaves.

A brief look at the experiences of ABDs can provide insight that may help you minimize dropouts. Jacks et al. (1981) interviewed 25 former students in various fields of humanities, science, and engineering who left their graduate programs before completion of their theses. The overall findings of this study can be divided into reasons for leaving the program and the students' perceptions of the impact of leaving.

Reasons for Leaving the Program

The two most common reasons cited for leaving graduate programs were financial problems and an inability to get along with the advisor and/or the committee. Financial problems were particularly severe for those students attempting to raise a family while attending graduate school; in many cases, the student not only had a family but also outside employment. It is clearly important for the advisor to understand these external pressures when working with the student to plan schedules for completing the research. In some cases, the advisor may need to alert the student of an over-commitment problem; some students are unaware of the level of effort needed to see the doctorate through to completion.

The problems of poor working relationships with advisor and/or committee varied greatly among the ABD students interviewed. Some of the students reported that their advisors were inaccessible, incompetent, or had little interest in their topic. In some cases, the advisor originally assigned had left the program, and responsibility for advising the student was changed to another faculty member with little interest. In other cases, the students acknowledged that their advisors had warned them of projects that were potentially unmanageable, but they decided to take the risk. Many students admitted not knowing what to expect in a Ph.D. program, discovering too late that it was inappropriate for them.

Students' Perceptions of the Impact of Leaving the Program

The ABD students in the study offered a variety of opinions regarding the impact of leaving a graduate program. Some felt that the lack of a Ph.D. was a detriment to their careers, while others felt it was not. There was an overall feeling that lack of a Ph.D. made a difference in terms of finding employment, but that a person's performance was an overriding factor in promotions on the job. Of course, there are differences in the types of jobs available to the two groups; university teaching positions and many other research positions are open primarily to Ph.D.'s. The lack of a Ph.D. may also have impaired the mobility of ABDs as evidenced by the fact that most of the group of 25 have remained at the same job since leaving the Ph.D. program. In contrast, more than half of a group of over 600 individuals who graduated with Ph.D.'s over the same time period changed jobs at least once.

Overall, the message from these former students is that clear and open communication between advisor and student is of paramount importance in preventing dropout from graduate programs. This takes time and effort from both parties.

SUMMARY

In this chapter, we have summarized the process of supervising graduate students in thesis research. We have considered this supervision to be an educational process, distinct from conducting the research.

At each step in supervising a graduate research project, there are certain roles which you must play. Determining the research topic usually requires you to help the student generate ideas through free and open discussion. These discussions are then replaced by thoughtful criticisms which lead to a research plan. Conducting the research involves a variety of tasks depending on the nature of the research; in all cases, frequent meetings with the student can help you follow the progress of the research and enables you to step in quickly when the need arises. Preparation of the thesis requires your help with the organization of results and writing style. Finally, you need to help the student to prepare for the thesis defense and to complete the Ph.D. process.

You will probably want to remain in contact with former Ph.D. students after graduation to assist them as they begin their own careers, particularly if they embark on careers in research. Speaking on behalf of former students can be a significant help in the competitive research arena.

Overall, you can be of most help to your graduate students by maintaining an active interest in their research and by providing the benefit of experience without dominating their work. Perhaps your most important long-term goal as advisor is to impart an understanding of *quality* in evaluating research and to communicate both the joy and the satisfaction that comes with supervising a successful research project.

REFERENCES

American Association of University Professors, *AAUP Policy Documents and Reports*, Washington, DC: 1977.

Balian, E.S., *How to Design, Analyze, and Write Doctoral and Masters Research*, 2nd edition, Lanham, MD: University Press of America, 1988.

Berelson, B. *Graduate Education in the United States*. New York, NY: McGraw-Hill, 1960.

Blanton, J.S., Midwifing the dissertation, *Teaching of Psychology*, *Vol. 10*, pp. 16–19, 1977.

Brown, R.D. and L.A. Krager, Ethical issues in graduate education: Faculty and student responsibilities, *Journal of Higher Education, Vol. 56*, pp. 403–418, 1985.

Clark, A.T., The influence of adult developmental processes upon the educational experiences of doctoral students, Doctoral Dissertation, The Humanistic Psychology Institute, p. 196, 1980.

Connell, R.W., How to supervise a Ph.D., *Vestes, Vol. 28*, pp. 38–42, 1985.

Fenton, E., Seminars, Honors Papers, Theses, and Dissertations (Chapter 7), unpublished manuscript on Teaching in Colleges and Universities, Carnegie Mellon University, 1992.

Hart, H. and D.F. Lawler, A Guide to the Preparation of Engineering Theses and Dissertations, unpublished report, Department of Civil Engineering, University of Texas at Austin, October, 1989.

Harte, J., *Consider a Spherical Cow: A Course in Environmental Problem Solving*, Mill Valley, CA: University Science Books, p. 21, 1988.

Hartnett, R.T., Environments for advanced learning, in J. Katz and R.T. Hartnett, editors, *Scholars in the Making*, Cambridge, MA: Ballinger Publishing Co., pp. 49–84, 1976.

Jacks, P., D.E. Chubin, A.L. Porter, and T. Connolly, The ABCs of ABDs: A study of incomplete doctorates, *Improving College and University Teaching, Vol. 31*, pp. 8–15, 1981.

Katz, J., Development of the mind, in J. Katz and R.T. Hartnett, editors, *Scholars in the Making*, Cambridge, MA: Ballinger Publishing Co., pp. 107–126, 1976.

Madsen, D., *Successful Dissertations and Theses*, San Francisco, CA: Jossey-Bass, 1990.

Monaghan, P., Some fields are reassessing the value of the traditional doctoral dissertation, *Chronicle of Higher Education, Vol. 35*, March 29, p. A1, 1989.

Reisman, D., Thoughts on the graduate experience, *Change, Vol. 8*, pp. 11–16, 1976.

Seeman, J., On supervising student research, *American Psychologist, Vol. 28*, pp. 900–906, 1977.

Simon, H.A., *Models of My Life*, New York, NY: Basic Books, p. 84, 1991.

Toombs, W., *Graduate Study as Education*, University Park, PA: Center for the Study of Higher Education, The Pennsylvania State University, February 1974.

Trivett, D.A., The student experience in graduate study, *Graduate Education in the 1970's*, ASHE-ERIC Higher Education Report 7, American Association for Higher Education, Washington, DC, pp. 3–7, 1977.

Ziolkowski, T., The Ph.D. Squid, *The American Scholar, Vol. 59*, pp. 175–195, 1990.

8

GETTING FUNDING FOR RESEARCH PROJECTS

INTRODUCTION

Most beginning faculty members hear a lot about how important it is to bring in research money. For example, department heads (who must balance their budgets) discuss the need for faculty members to support their research program. Faculty colleagues often discuss their proposals—the ones that got funded and the ones that didn't. It is easy to get caught up in this topic and feel that money is the only factor in selecting research topics.

In fact, while funding is clearly important, one should not lose sight of *academic interest* as a key driving force in choosing a topic. After all, one of the joys of being a faculty member is the freedom to work on research that is personally stimulating and rewarding; the previous chapter emphasized this in the context of supervising graduate students. Nevertheless, the previous chapter also admitted that selecting a research topic often involves finding a balance between intellectual interest and practicality in terms of time and money constraints. With these caveats, we now explore the practical matter of how to get funding for your research.

There are literally hundreds of agencies and institutions throughout the U.S. that support research. But there are also thousands of researchers writing proposals, most of whom will be unsuccessful in obtaining funds. The trick to securing research funds is to find a niche—or niches—where you can write excellent proposals for innovative research that will stand up to critical reviews by experts.

113

To many young faculty, the most ominous part of raising funds is competing with established researchers who have years of experience both in writing proposals and in conducting research. This is indeed a challenge. However, many funding agencies have set aside money specifically for recent faculty hires. Furthermore, some agencies have made an effort to bring young researchers into their regular programs. These agencies are aware of the dangers of having a well-entrenched "old boy" network that excludes new arrivals; few researchers are able to produce innovative research ideas year after year. Nevertheless, a new faculty member must make a substantial effort to demonstrate readiness to manage a research project. A well-written proposal indicates this readiness.

The process of obtaining research money through proposal writing is important to you as an individual, to the department, and to the institution—for somewhat different reasons. In terms of individual effort, learning to write proposals can greatly assist your personal development. Identifying areas where research is needed and formulating a research plan require that you develop a broad knowledge base: this means a satisfactory understanding of the way research is conducted as well as in-depth technical knowledge. Personal development also is fostered by interactions with others working in your field; research funding can enable you to attend workshops and conferences where these interactions take place. In some disciplines, particularly science and engineering, preparing proposals is an important part of developing a thriving research program. Money is necessary for the tools of the trade, such as laboratory supplies, equipment, and computer hardware and software. Money is also needed to support the faculty, graduate students, technicians, and other personnel in a research program. Overall, obtaining research funding through proposal writing is an important milestone in a young faculty member's career: success in a highly competitive program is demonstrable evidence of achievement.

For your department, proposal writing is important to secure money for personnel. A primary purpose of research grants and contracts in many departments is to pay for graduate student tuition and stipends. In addition, faculty members are often expected to cover a percentage of their salaries through research funds; these funds are also expected to cover portions of salaries of the departmental staff, such as secretaries. Other personnel hired by the department, such as computer specialists and laboratory technicians, may receive salary support from research funds. Besides salaries, research funding can help the department purchase computers, laboratory apparatus, and other equipment that can be shared among several groups. Furthermore, the department benefits when its faculty members receive public recognition for important research findings, which are usually a direct result of research projects funded through proposals.

For the institution, most grants and contracts contain a provision for overhead, a fixed percentage of the proposal budget that is earmarked for administrative use. Most of the overhead money goes to the central administration. However, a portion is sometimes funneled back to the department or even to the principal investigator to help with expenses not included as line items in the proposal budget. As with the department, the entire institution benefits from research grants when results of a funded project receive positive publicity.

In this chapter, we first explore the types of funding commonly available, including both private and public sources. Then we address the process of identifying topics and potential sponsors. Next we discuss how you might gather detailed information needed as background preparation. Following this, we discuss writing the proposal. Finally, we identify administrative issues that one needs to consider once the proposal is funded and work gets underway.

TYPES OF RESEARCH FUNDING

There are many potential sources for funding research. As a new faculty member, you may be able to obtain seed money or small grants for personal development from your institution. This is usually a good way to start—you may be able to get travel funds to sell your ideas to funding agencies, or money for preliminary laboratory or computer tests to try out ideas. Don't make the mistake of relying on internal funds for more than a start: academic institutions are not funding agencies.

In contrast to funds provided by your college or university, external funding may come from private or public sources. Many private foundations offer support for specific theme areas; for example, conservation-minded foundations may offer funding for environmental research, while industry-supported foundations may provide support to improve industrial competitiveness. Other private money may come directly from a particular industry. This support is often tied to a short-term problem area of interest to the industry, and there are usually specific deliverables. Such funding may be appropriate for faculty if there is a component of basic or applied research that matches academic interests; if not, the work may be better handled by a consulting firm.

Public research support is available at all levels: local, state, and federal. By far, the majority of public research money comes from the federal government, where many agencies support sizeable programs. Table 8-1 summarizes federal support for research and development for fiscal year 1991, taken from a report by the National Science Foundation (1993). Information is provided for basic as well as applied research. In basic research, the objective is to gain an understanding of fundamental phenomena without considering the ways in which this knowledge can be used. In applied research, the objective is to gain knowledge to determine the means by which a specific need can be met. Development refers to the use of the knowledge derived from research to assist with the production of materials, devices, systems, or methods. Funding for basic research

TABLE 8-1

Major Sources of Research and Development Funding
From the Federal government for Fiscal Year 1991
(after NSF Report 93-323)
All values in Millions of Dollars

Agency	Basic Research	Applied Research	Development	Total
Department of Agriculture	558	618	61	1,237
Department of Commerce	34	415	40	490
Department of Defense	994	2,724	28,417	32,135
Department of Education	9	123	39	171
Department of Energy	1,686	1,587	2,709	5,983
Department of Health and Human Services	5,050	3,112	1,593	9,756
Department of Housing and Urban Development	—	9	18	28
Department of the Interior	229	324	39	593
Department of Justice	6	15	28	49
Department of Labor	—	24	20	44
Department of State	5	1	—	6
Department of Transportation	—	115	265	380
Department of Treasury	4	21	7	31
Department of Veterans Affairs	16	178	23	217
Other Agencies				
Agency for International Development	6	352	20	378
Environmental Protection Agency	91	262	79	433
National Aeronautics and Space Administration	1,706	1,666	3,909	7,280
National Science Foundation	1,676	109	—	1,785
Nuclear Regulatory Commission	—	109	—	109
Smithsonian Institute	98	—	—	98
Tennessee Valley Authority	2	17	49	68

by most agencies is somewhat smaller than funding for applied research and development. Total funding for development is dominated by the Department of Defense, which accounts for 84% of the federal money in this category. There are two agencies with high research budgets where basic research funding exceeds funding for applied research and development: the National Institutes of Health (which is within the Department of Health and Human Services) and the National Science Foundation. These agencies, as well as other agencies with significant research budgets, are obviously important to basic research programs at academic institutions.

Research proposals for any of these agencies are solicited through a variety of mechanisms. Some agencies regularly advertise Requests for Proposals (RFPs), often within a particular topic area. Decisions on funding are based on evaluations of reviewers and on the relevance of the proposed work to the topic of the RFP. Submitting a proposal in response to an RFP has the advantage that money is already allocated to a specific program. However, RFPs are widely advertised and there is likely to be stiff competition. If the topic of the RFP is close to your area of expertise, of course, you may be able to compete more effectively. In some cases, a contractor has already been chosen for a project and the agency is required by regulation to advertise; this practice is obviously wasteful and disheartening to those who prepare a proposal only to discover that the RFP is "wired."

In contrast to RFPs, research support is available from some sources through unsolicited proposals. A principal investigator can submit a proposal on any topic within a broad spectrum of interests. The agency will then select experts to review the proposal based on the topic area. Decisions on funding are based on the reviewers' evaluations and the needs of the agency. The primary advantage of unsolicited proposals is that you can choose a research topic relatively unconstrained. On the other hand, you will be competing with other individuals proposing very different projects, many of whom, like you, are experts in their field.

It is apparent that programs involving RFPs and unsolicited proposals are both highly competitive. Some faculty members have found success in negotiating research funding directly from individual program officers at an agency. This requires that you get to know the individual—especially his research interests—and that he gets to know you well enough to have confidence in your ability to do good work. Of course, it is difficult for a newcomer to break into established networks; it may be especially challenging to convince a program officer to fund a new project when his total funding base is not growing. Nevertheless, if you can get to know an appropriate individual and you can make a good impression, this approach sometimes works.

There are two major types of funding awards. *Grants* refer to awards where the terms and conditions are established as blanket policy by the agency: there are no individual negotiations. Grants that are awarded by the National Science Foundation, for example, must comply with the conditions described in their *Grant Policy Manual* (1989). These conditions pertain to many aspects of administration of the project, such as budget restrictions, publication policy, reporting and accounting requirements, and allowable modifications to the project once work is underway. In contrast to grants, *contracts* are awards where the various conditions are negotiable and are generally spelled out in a legal document that is tailored to each specific project. Unlike grants, where the principal investigator and institution must abide by pre-established rules, contracts generally allow more flexibility in negotiating the terms of the award. There is considerable variation in the way both grants and contracts are written; some grants can be rather liberal in the way the rules are specified, while some contracts, once negotiated, may include a long list of rules to be followed.

GROUNDWORK: CHOOSING A RESEARCH TOPIC AND IDENTIFYING POTENTIAL FUNDING SOURCES

There are several tasks to consider when planning research and pursuing funding for it. The first task is to identify a research topic that is familiar to you while at the same time important to a particular discipline. Many new faculty members choose a topic related to their Ph.D. thesis, perhaps an extension of one aspect of the thesis that merits additional work. It is important that the proposed work is not merely a repeat of your thesis—the proposal must plan significant advances. Starting to move away from your thesis research may also be important to avoid direct competition with your Ph.D. advisor. However, tackling a totally unfamiliar area of research is difficult even for experienced faculty members; preparing proposals for a new area should probably wait until you gain experience in raising funds for more familiar topics. If you wish to move into a new area, you may be able to conduct research without funding for a while in order to gain entrance into the field. Or you may be able to get seed money from your school for this purpose. Note that your chances of getting funding are better if you have published a paper on the topic before submitting a proposal. More information about choosing a topic for research is presented in Chapter 7.

A second task is to update your knowledge base in the proposed topic. This applies to concepts as well as tools for conducting the work. Even for a new faculty member who is proposing research as an extension to a recent Ph.D. thesis, there may be new information about the particular topic that should be incorporated into the proposal. Keeping up to date requires scanning recent journals and perhaps making contact with a few well-known individuals in the field. A good place to start might be your Ph.D. advisor. Attending conferences might uncover research not yet published but currently in progress at other institutions that could influence the proposal. However, going to conferences is expensive in terms of time and money; it may be most productive to attend a small specialty conference with many leading researchers in a focused research area rather than a large national meeting. Many departments will provide funding for beginning faculty to attend one or two conferences for this purpose.

A third task is to identify some specific research questions within your chosen topic area. One idea is to determine where there are gaps in understanding that are critical to solving a more general, important problem within the topic you have chosen; think about which of these gaps could be filled by research that you are qualified to conduct. You might also begin to think about how the project would be organized; for example, whether there would be an emphasis on field work, laboratory work, or computer modeling.

A fourth task is to explore organizations that may be interested in funding the work. It is usually helpful to look at the types of projects an agency has supported in the past; you can obtain this information through written material circulated by the agency or by discussions with colleagues. It is also worthwhile to make contact with individuals at these organizations; this is especially important in some unsolicited proposal programs where the personal interests of project officers may influence funding decisions. Colleagues can often provide the names of individuals who may be a starting point for conversation. A literature search can also help identify individuals at funding agencies who may be interested in sponsoring your work. For making contacts at industries, it may be useful to attend meetings of professional organizations (e.g., the Institute of Electrical and Electronics Engineers, American Chemical Society, or dozens of others) where there are opportunities to meet potential sponsors. Note that the purpose of making this initial contact is to determine whether there is an overlap between your interests and those of the sponsor. If there is a poor match of interests, or if there is insufficient funding available, there is no point in trying to convince anyone of the merits of the project.

The ideas presented here should be considered as iterative steps. A literature review may uncover work that makes a planned project obsolete, requiring selection of another topic area. Similarly, discussions with a funding agency may spark new ideas that require you to begin the planning process again. Eventually, a project and one or more potential funding agencies will be identified, and the next phase of preparing to write the proposal begins.

PREPARING TO WRITE THE PROPOSAL

This phase is oriented around two themes: refining your ideas about the proposed project, and obtaining detailed information about the funding agency.

Refining Your Ideas for the Project

In the previous section, we discussed the need to identify key research questions within a topic area that could be developed into a project. Now you need to choose one or more of those questions and use them to write specific objectives. There are important constraints on your choice of objectives: they should be achievable within a limited amount of time and money, yet they must have the potential to provide valuable new information important to the discipline. This often requires a considerable amount of creativity. In many projects, the logistics associated with the tasks of a research project are a limiting factor in how much can be accomplished. Therefore, you may need to get information about the equipment and facilities necessary to conduct the work, including issues such as delivery time, space requirements, and cost. Some options are likely to be too expensive, while others may not be feasible because of limitations in the technology available. The time needed to conduct the work may be too long. All of these problems may require successive refinements of the research objectives to keep the project manageable.

Your research plan may be an individual effort, or it may involve others who have special skills or facilities. Some funding programs specialize in projects that bring together the expertise of several individuals. The concept of a "research team" has been growing in popularity: if properly designed, joint research projects can be far more productive than the sum of individual efforts. Sometimes new faculty members are invited to participate in large field or laboratory projects involving many institutions. These may be good opportunities for exposure to other professionals in the field, individuals who can help you establish a "niche" within the research community.

Even if you are planning the project by yourself, it is sometimes worthwhile to invite an expert in your discipline to participate in the research. For example, you may wish to include a subcontract for an individual with certain analytical skills and laboratory facilities to help with the data acquisition in your project. Or you may benefit by including an expert who can assist with statistical analysis of the data. It may be difficult to arrange more than one or two such collaborations since proposals must be modest in scope and cost.

A final item to consider in planning the proposal is the budget. You will need to gather information from the account administrator in your department on personnel salaries, graduate student tuition and stipend, overhead, and costs required by the department. Line items for travel, equipment, supplies, communications, publications, and other details will generally be of your own choosing. You may already have an idea of what constitutes a reasonable budget through discussions with colleagues and preliminary contacts with funding agencies. If your budget exceeds these expectations, you may need to trim the project.

When you have decided upon the research objectives, the specific experiments to achieve the objectives, the interactions with other personnel, and a budget, you are ready to get the detailed information about the funding agency which you need to write the proposal.

Getting Information about the Funding Agency

A successful proposal requires a clear understanding of the mission of the sponsoring agency as well as the requirements for proposal submission. There are several ways to obtain this information. First, look through written material supplied by the agency. Short pamphlets listing the titles of previously funded projects and stating the goals of the agency are useful in the initial choice of agency as discussed above; at this point, however, you need more detailed written statements, such as proposal submission requirements and possibly annual reports. It is especially important to make sure that you have current written information about preparing the proposal: examples include the requirements for the length and organization of the proposal, details of the budget (including cost-sharing), necessary forms to be completed, timetable for submission, number of copies to submit, and other related information. It is also important to get information on the review process and the criteria for evaluating the proposal; be sure to obtain the written instructions for reviewers. For example, the pamphlet *Grant Proposal Guide* describes in detail the submission requirements for the National Science Foundation (1994). The pamphlet also includes the necessary forms to be submitted with the proposal, evaluation criteria for reviewers, and reporting requirements of the grantee once an award has been made. Similar comprehensive pamphlets are available for most federal agencies; other brochures with descriptions of submittal requirements are generally published by private research foundations.

As a second source of information, you may wish to continue dialogue with personnel from the agency. While the initial contact serves merely to establish common interests, later conversations should be more focused. It is beneficial to discuss details of research objectives, project plan, time schedule, budget, personnel, and overall orientation of the proposal if the project officer is willing. Some agencies have mechanisms for submitting a pre-proposal to provide feedback before you prepare the full-length proposal. Even if there is no formal mechanism for a pre-proposal, many project officers are willing to offer comments on short versions of the research plan; it is generally a good idea to take advantage of this opportunity. Discussing proposal ideas with project officers, particularly if done in person, can also help make a favorable impression that could influence funding decisions. Even though agency research personnel are often swamped with requests such as this, it is worthwhile to make the effort to contact them personally: you are likely to gain valuable information on how to orient your ideas to make them attractive to the agency. Remember that project officers rely upon high quality research results to justify their programs—you may have just the project that appeals to them.

As a third source of information, speak with colleagues who have had experiences in working with the agency you have targeted. Some colleagues may have prepared proposals or received funding from the agency, while others may have reviewed proposals. Look through a successful proposal of a colleague, if possible.

Some new faculty may feel uncomfortable discussing their proposal ideas before a project is funded. Although there are good reasons to be careful, it is generally advantageous to be completely open with project officers in funding agencies. There is no better way to predict reactions to your ideas than to discuss them with individuals who have the interest and resources to sponsor the work. You may also wish to discuss your research ideas with colleagues whom you trust; they can give additional feedback.

> *Exercise: One way to get a few good research ideas is to generate lots of ideas. Successful researchers always have many more ideas for projects than they have time to work on, often because they spend a lot of time thinking about possible projects. List as many ideas in your research field as you can without being concerned about whether they are feasible—try to think of particularly novel or creative projects. Then go through the list and evaluate each one for feasibility. See if you can modify any of the most intriguing ideas to make them feasible and perhaps attractive to funding agencies. This method of separating the creative from evaluative phases of idea generation is an important concept in engineering design, and it works for generating research ideas as well as solving engineering problems.*

WRITING THE PROPOSAL

If you have done a thorough job of preparing for this step, the proposal writing should be relatively straightforward. After all, you have made contact with your potential sponsor, received feedback on some of your ideas, and familiarized yourself with the proposal submission requirements. You also have a detailed outline of the project objectives and work plan, as well as a rough budget. And you know who your collaborators are.

Now you need to pull all of this information together. Think about what the agency is looking for as you start to write. For example, a proposal to a government agency or private foundation that primarily supports long-term basic research should indicate how the work builds on previous research and opens up new frontiers of knowledge. For this type of proposal, it is generally a good idea to begin with a background of the research topic, highlighting critical gaps in knowledge. Then state your objectives briefly and clearly, explaining how achieving the objectives will help to fill these gaps. A project plan describing the methods for achieving the objectives is needed next. Finally, discuss the significance of your expected findings, emphasizing issues that are important to the sponsor. You may also wish to discuss the benefits of your research to the academic community and to the public. Other items which may be necessary for the proposal include a justification of the budget, a statement of the qualifications of personnel involved in the project, and facilities at your institution already available to help you with the research. Statements of how you will disseminate the results and interact with other researchers in the field are also warranted. It is generally a good idea—and often a requirement—to include a short abstract of the proposal.

If your proposal solicits funds from industry, begin by demonstrating a thorough knowledge of the specific problems facing the industry that are relevant to your project. Clearly list the objectives of your work and how achieving them will help to solve these problems. Discussion of specific deliverables with a time schedule is most important. Some of the other sections discussed in the preceding paragraph may also be important in proposals to industry, although you need to determine this on a case-by-case basis.

Independent of where you are submitting the proposal, the preparation of the budget pages may require extra care. You will probably need to work with the account administrator in your department once again to get the exact dollar amounts for each budget item. Be sure to allow enough time to prepare the budget and to obtain all of the necessary signatures from your institution.

If you are planning to work with colleagues or consultants, include letters from them outlining their participation. These letters should go into an appendix, referred to in the main proposal text. Some prior publications or sections of publications relevant to the proposed work can also go into an appendix—provided the funding agency allows this material. You may have written proposals to other agencies for matching funds; clearly identify these arrangements. Be sure to mention whether the success of the project is contingent upon receiving funds from these other sources as well as the primary sponsor. Unless you already have definite funding from other sources, design the project so that it is not entirely dependent upon additional funds.

That's a lot of information to include. Nevertheless, the proposal should be as short and to the point as possible; that requires careful organization and a concise writing style. Many agencies have limits on the length of the proposals, typically 10 to 20 pages, which may include or exclude appendices. Even if there is no page limit, reviewers appreciate short but informative proposals.

Finally, the proposal should be professional in every way. Begin with a well-designed cover page and a table of contents to make a good first impression. Organize the sections in a logical manner, using effective, clear figures to illustrate your points. Be sure to proofread the final product carefully to catch typographical errors and other problems. The type font should be clearly readable, and the output should be on a laser printer, if possible. High quality xeroxes are a must.

Either during the writing process or when the first draft of the proposal is completed, ask a colleague in your department to critique the document. Be sure to allow enough time for the critique and for revisions to the proposal, if necessary.

Because proposal funding is uncertain, you should pursue several research ideas and funding sources. In many cases, a proposal rejected by one agency can be resubmitted to another agency, with modification as appropriate. Be sure you carefully consider comments of reviewers before resubmission. Most agencies provide written feedback on proposals, usually comments written by the reviewers. However, some funding sources do not routinely give feedback in writing; you may be able to get information through discussions with the agency contact person. If your proposal was rejected but the reviews appear to be positive, you may wish to discuss the reasons for decline with the contact person. In most cases, it is not good practice to submit similar proposals to different agencies simultaneously; if such an approach is used, a clear statement to this effect should be included.

For additional help on writing the proposal, a close look at successful proposals by colleagues will illustrate the variety of formats typically used. A recent article by Cohen (1988) outlining the major parts of a proposal may also provide valuable assistance.

Exercise: In the exercise in the previous section, you prepared a list of ideas for research topics. Choose the best ideas from this list and consider two or three possible funding sources with different perspectives. For example, consider a non-mission oriented federal agency such as NSF, a mission oriented agency such as HHS or EPA, and a large industry that supports basic and applied research within its areas of interest. How could your best research ideas, or parts of them, be oriented so as to be attractive to each funding source? Going through this process can help you select appropriate research ideas to sell to funding agencies.

AFTER THE PROPOSAL IS FUNDED

Congratulations! You have just been informed that your proposal will be funded—all that hard work has paid off. How are you to proceed?

To some extent, the next step depends on the type of funding award. If you have received a grant, the conditions of the award are already spelled out in publications of the agency; you need to familiarize yourself with these conditions. Examples include budget constraints, the extent to which the project can be modified, and ultimate disposition of equipment purchased. On the other hand, gaining approval of a contract may require negotiations. Sensitive issues such as confidentiality of results and schedule for payments may need to be negotiated, as well as other administrative matters. Your institution's contract office should be brought into these negotiations. Discussions with colleagues about how they have handled similar issues can help.

For either a grant or a contract, the funding agency may ask you to trim the budget. Many agencies routinely ask their awardees to reduce their costs, in some cases by small amounts but in other cases by substantial percentages. In the former case, the scope of work can usually remain unchanged and the budget categories to trim are relatively inconsequential (e.g., National Science Foundation's mandatory 2% budget cuts in 1990). However, if the budget must be cut deeply, a change in the scope of the project is probably necessary. This will require you to develop a priority scale for individual tasks and to determine which tasks can be reduced. Be sure to submit the revised budget and scope of work promptly. Unfortunately, such belt-tightening is a way of life for most researchers.

Many research sponsors will require you to submit progress reports at intervals throughout the project. In some cases, these need to be substantial documents, while in others a single page summary will suffice. There may also be forms to complete regarding expenditures, publications, and inventions. Some funding agencies allow flexibility in changing the direction of the work as the research progresses, while others are more rigid.

There will almost certainly be a final report to prepare at the end of the project. Again, formats vary greatly. Some agencies require final reports that are tailored to their specifications, and this may include copies of the text as well as data in computer files. Other agencies accept student theses or articles published in books, journals, or conference proceedings. In most cases, published text can be used for at least part of the final report.

Finally, it is worthwhile to think ahead—to the next proposal or beyond. Many faculty members have enjoyed continuous support from a single sponsor for a number of years. You want to make sure that your newly funded project achieves its objectives, and that the results are disseminated through publications and conference proceedings. The best way to secure future funding is to do a good job on your current project.

SUMMARY

In this chapter, we have considered various aspects of writing proposals to obtain funding for research projects. We begin by discussing the types of research funds and mechanisms for soliciting proposals, pointing out differences between private and public sources of funding, and between solicited and unsolicited proposals. Then we address the groundwork needed to begin planning the proposal. This phase includes choosing a research topic, assembling up-to-date information on the topic, identifying specific research questions, and targeting potential funding sources. We then discuss detailed preparation prior to writing, which includes refining ideas for the project and getting specific information on the agency you have targeted for the proposal. Finally, we discuss writing the proposal and attending to administrative matters once the proposal is funded.

There is no question that obtaining research funding is one of the most difficult tasks facing faculty members. However, there are lots of success stories. Carefully choosing a research topic where you have a competitive advantage and writing an excellent proposal can maximize your chances of success. And maintaining excellence from proposal writing to conducting the research all the way through to preparing the final report is the best way to keep research support coming year after year.

In closing, we wish to mention that the concepts presented here must be considered carefully—funding agency expectations vary greatly, and the organization of the proposal should be consistent with these expectations. Every research project is different, and each proposal must be sensibly put together considering the research topic and work plan. Use good judgment as a guide.

REFERENCES

Cohen, J.B., Writing that first proposal, *Graduating Engineer, Vol. 10*, pp. 76–78, 1988.

National Science Foundation, *The NSF Grant Policy Manual,* NSF Report 88-47, Washington, DC, July 1989.

National Science Foundation, *Grant Proposal Guide,* NSF Report 94-2, Washington, DC, January 1994.

National Science Foundation, *Federal Funds for Research and Development: Fiscal Years 1991, 1992, and 1993, Vol. 41,* NSF Report 93-323, Detailed Statistical Tables, Washington, DC, pp.43–45, 1993.

9

WRITING
RESEARCH PAPERS

INTRODUCTION

Developing the ability to write high quality research papers is vitally important to you as a new faculty member. Whether you are composing journal articles, conference papers, research reports, book chapters, or other manuscripts, the quality of your writing is a key factor in gaining acceptance of your ideas. This emphasis on writing is certainly nothing new—we all heard about the importance of written composition beginning in grade school. But effective writing becomes critically important as you strive to communicate path breaking concepts in your field of research to skeptical readers.

The longevity of excellent writing is apparent when one considers the impact of a seminal publication. The Science Citations Index, which provides a listing of written work where technical publications are referenced, shows that some landmark articles have been cited hundreds of times. The message is clear: you can reap the rewards of a good paper for years. This is particularly true if your article appears in a widely circulating publication. The converse is also true; a poor paper may damage your reputation for a long time. And there are lots of poor papers, as evidenced by the fact that some 55% of the articles in top journals worldwide are never cited by anyone. Of course, this figure is related to many factors in addition to the quality of the papers. Differences in the way researchers cite each other's work are reflected in the variability of the percentage of uncited articles by discipline, e.g. 37–41% for chemistry, physics, and biology, 72% for engineering, and 98% for arts and humanities. These figures apply to citations accumulated over a four-year period for articles published during

1984 (results reported by David Pendlebury of the Institute for Scientific Information, cited by Hamilton, 1991). Readers tend to remember the names of authors who have written the worst papers as well as the best papers. Do everything you can to put yourself in the latter category.

In this chapter, we provide a number of suggestions on writing effective papers that present research results. We begin by identifying several categories of research papers you are likely to encounter. We then discuss the collection of background material and the organization of the manuscript. Next we cover many of the details of writing the paper. Finally, we address issues that require attention after the paper is accepted for publication.

TYPES OF RESEARCH PAPERS

Of the many avenues available for publication of research results, the most respected approach is the peer review journal. There are good reasons for this: many journals have circulations in the tens of thousands, providing wide exposure. Furthermore, many journals accept only a fraction of the manuscripts submitted. The decision to publish or decline a paper is based on the quality of the research as well as the quality of the written manuscript, as determined by peers of the author(s). This system is intended to screen substandard research results and poorly written articles so that only the best papers are published. In reality, the reviewers' evaluations themselves have a range of quality. Thus poor papers are sometimes published and good papers are sometimes rejected. Nevertheless, peer review journals generally contain papers of higher quality than most other forms of publication.

A second category is the conference paper. Many conferences on academic topics provide opportunities for participants to submit written manuscripts discussing the research results they present orally. Some conferences require submission of a manuscript as a condition for oral presentation. The manuscripts may be printed in separate folders and sold as reprints, or they may be combined into one or more volumes of published proceedings. For some conferences, the submitted manuscripts are peer reviewed in the same way as journal articles. For others, only the abstracts are reviewed, and decisions on acceptance are based more on the relevance of the subject matter to the conference theme than on the quality of the work.

Research reports such as those submitted to funding agencies make up a third category of research papers. These include progress reports as well as final reports summarizing the results of a funded project. They usually contain far more detail than a journal article or conference paper, with detailed descriptions of experimental procedures, extensive data tables, listings of software code, and similar items. The reports are generally intended only for limited distribution. They may be reviewed and evaluated by agency personnel or external peer reviewers, although this is not always done.

A fourth category of research papers is the book or book chapter. The purpose of manuscripts in this category varies greatly. For example, some books provide a general review of the literature on a particular topic and may be oriented toward lay audiences. Others, for specialists, present focused research results that are more extensive than is possible in a journal article. Some books covering research results are very cohesive, written by a single author with a well-defined scope. Other books are composed of chapters written by different authors on widely varying topics within an overall theme. Some books are peer reviewed, but more often they are not.

There are many other categories of research papers, such as theses, news articles on research, manuals describing computer code, and manuals describing operation of laboratory equipment. Many of the suggestions in this chapter also apply to these other documents.

COLLECTING BACKGROUND MATERIAL AND ORGANIZING THE PAPER

There are several steps involved in planning a research paper. These include collecting material on the publication requirements, assembling the information to be communicated, and finally using this information to outline the paper.

For any type of research paper, you need to gather information on the way the manuscript should be prepared. Journals usually provide a detailed "Instructions to Authors" section, describing formats for typing, style of referencing, length restrictions, review procedures, and other details. If the paper is being prepared for conference proceedings, there are usually similar rules for submitting manuscripts. Preparation of research reports for funding agencies is generally less restrictive, although guidelines are sometimes issued. Finally, book publishers issue guidelines describing their requirements.

Besides instructions for authors, you also want to obtain the guidelines provided to reviewers for their evaluation of your paper. Knowing the criteria by which peers will review your manuscript will help you to prepare the document more effectively. Contact the editor for a copy of these guidelines.

Note that some journals and conference proceedings allow (or require) the submission of camera-ready text. This reduces the time required between manuscript submission and publication, since there is no typesetting necessary. A number of publishers are beginning to allow submission of a computer file for the same purpose. You may need to allow extra time for preparing camera-ready or computer file texts since you will have to consider a number of editorial constraints.

Distinct from acquiring information on the requirements of the paper, you need to choose the concepts that will be the focus of the paper. The amount of detail you can include is a function of the allowable length of the document. You obviously have considerable flexibility in planning a research report that has no page limits. Planning a conference paper that has a limit of four pages, on the other hand, will require you to rank your findings in order of importance and carefully consider the most concise, clear way to discuss them.

After choosing the information to include in the paper, you then need to generate the relevant graphs, figures, tables, and other visuals that will help you write the paper. These visuals should remain in rough form at this point, since you might want to modify them as you write the accompanying text. Note that preparing visuals requires considerable thought, as discussed below.

Finally, you are ready to outline the paper. Include as much detail as you feel comfortable with: some authors use only a few lines of notes describing each major section, while others prefer a highly detailed outline accounting for each substantive comment in the paper. If you have had only limited experience in preparing research papers, the latter approach may provide you with more confidence as you begin writing.

There is wide variation in the way research papers are organized. An example format is shown in Table 9-1. Note that when you develop an outline for the paper, you need to make the entries under each section as specific as possible. Generic outlines lead to generic papers which are of little value in the research literature.

Exercise: Table 9-1 provides one example of the way a research paper might be organized, although other structures are possible. For example, it may be more appropriate in some cases to present the results early in the paper, filling in the details of the experiments later. In other situations, a separate literature review section may not be necessary, but rather previous work can be cited throughout the paper where appropriate. Consider several different ways in which a paper describing your research might be organized. In what types of publications and for what purposes might these other formats be appropriate?

WRITING THE PAPER

By the time you reach this step, you should have a pretty good idea of what the paper is going to look like. But putting those thoughts down in writing can be a difficult task—and more often than not, it involves a lot of revising.

One of the most important concerns of the writer is the intended audience. A journal article should probably be written for individuals familiar with the discipline represented by the journal, but not necessarily for those trained in the specific subject of the paper. A manuscript for the proceedings of a highly focused specialty conference, on the other hand, can be oriented more toward experts in the field. Books are often written to accommodate a variety of backgrounds, both technical and nontechnical.

Style of writing is vitally important. The classic book on the topic is *Elements of Style* by Strunk and White (1979). In the Introduction to the Third Edition,

TABLE 9-1

An Example of the Major Sections of a Paper Reporting Research Results.

1. Abstract or Executive Summary

2. Introduction

   - General Topic Area

   - Specific Problems of Interest, Motivation for the Work

   - Description of Organization of the Paper

3. Literature Review

   - What is Known and What is Unknown: Critical Gaps

   - How Current Research Builds Upon Previous Work

4. Research Objectives

5 Methods of Achieving Objectives

   - Experimental Methods

   - Mathematical Solution Techniques

6. Results

   - Tables

   - Figures

7. Discussion and Interpretation

   - Additional Tables and/or Figures

   - Significance of the Results

8. Future Work

9. Conclusions or Summary

10. Acknowledgments

11. References

12. Appendices

White compares the reader to a person in a swamp, charging the author with the duty to drain the swamp quickly or at least throw him a rope! It is worth reiterating a key paragraph in the book:

> *Vigorous writing is concise. A sentence should contain no unnecessary words, a paragraph no unnecessary sentences, for the same reason that a drawing should have no unnecessary lines and a machine no unnecessary parts. This requires not that the writer make all his sentences short, or that he avoid all detail and treat his subject only in outline, but that every word tell.*

Writing should be definite, bold, and assertive; it should not be hesitating, tame, or noncommittal. Numerous other suggestions for effective writing are included on such topics as using active and passive voices, using proper tenses, and structuring sentences and paragraphs.

Another valuable book covering the mechanics of writing is the University of Chicago's *A Manual of Style* (1982), which lists the rules of punctuation, capitalization, abbreviation, and numerous other details a writer must keep in mind. The book also includes sections on bookmaking and on production and printing. Every faculty member should have copies of *Elements of Style* and *A Manual of Style*.

Assuming the structure of Table 9-1, we will now discuss the paper in some detail, providing ideas on what goes into each section and how the sections can be linked to provide a cohesive paper.

Abstract or Executive Summary

The first section of a research paper, the abstract, is in many ways the most important. In a short essay entitled "A Scrutiny of the Abstract," Landes (1966) points out that many more people will read your abstract than will read the entire paper—by a factor of 10 to 500. With such odds, it pays to give special attention to this part of the paper.

Landes defines the abstract as a concise statement of the essential information in the paper. In lengthy reports, the abstract may be replaced by an executive summary, which represents more completely the content of the full report. Abstracts are typically 50–200 words, while executive summaries may be up to several pages in length.

There are two types of abstracts. The *descriptive abstract* lists the contents of the paper, while the *informative abstract* provides the most important results and their significance. Clearly the latter is preferred. However, often you will need to submit an abstract for a conference presentation far in advance of the conference date itself; you may have to submit a descriptive abstract simply because the substantive results are not yet available. For papers to be published, always use the informative abstract, and write it *after* the rest of the paper is completed. Write in the active voice rather than passive voice whenever possible. Compare the following examples of abstracts; which is more useful to the reader?

> *The importance of high quality writing in research papers is discussed. Various types of research papers are described, and the major steps in organizing and planning a paper are listed. The major sections of a research paper are identified; suggestions on the content of each section are presented. The process of writing the paper is discussed, including details that are particular to the various sections. Finally, steps to be taken after the paper is accepted for publication are identified.*

> *Research papers such as journal articles, book chapters, and manuscripts for conference proceedings require effort in both preparation and writing. The author must be aware of the rules of the publisher and must have available all of the technical information before writing can begin. The content and style of the paper must be appropriate for the intended audience: papers written for lay readers should include more background than those intended for experts in the field. Overall, the quality of writing in research papers is a key factor in gaining acceptance of new ideas.*

The second example, written in the active voice, has more impact, and the information is more immediately usable.

Introduction, Literature Review, and Research Objectives

As indicated in Table 9-1, the introduction to the paper serves several purposes. It describes the general topic area of the paper, lists the specific problems of interest, and presents the motivation for the work. Unless the manuscript is very short, the introduction should also include statements about the organization of the paper: listing the major sections helps the reader understand the flow of ideas that follow.

The writer needs to present a review of the literature as a foundation for the current research. If the primary goal of your paper is to provide a thorough review of a subject, or if your manuscript is somewhat lengthy, a separate literature review section may be warranted. If the main purpose of your paper is to present original research results, however, you may wish to incorporate a brief review into the introduction. This will ensure that the significance of the new information is not eclipsed. Be sure to link any previous work cited to your research; the reader should not have to guess why you included a particular citation. And avoid getting into the habit of citing mainly your own previous work; readers pick up on this form of egotism rather quickly.

The research objectives should follow naturally from earlier statements. If your paper introduces a problem and discusses previously published work that makes progress toward a solution, the objectives of the current work might involve moving closer to that solution. Perhaps the current work fills a critical information gap that will guide the direction of future research. In any case, make sure that the specific objectives of the research and the reasons for choosing them are apparent to the reader. You may want to include lengthy objectives in a separate section, although you can simply list the objectives within the introductory section if they are brief.

Methods of Achieving the Objectives

Having established the goals of the research and their importance, your paper should discuss the techniques that you applied to achieve those goals. For laboratory or field work, the paper might describe the equipment and experimental procedures. For a theoretical study, the paper might discuss the mathematical relations and solution techniques. You can also include brief descriptions of computer software. In a journal article or conference paper, this section should be brief, although a detailed technical report might contain enough information to enable the reader to repeat the work, if desired.

It is customary in this section to cite previous publications that give details of similar experimental procedures or mathematical solution techniques. After all, there is no point in repeating information that is already available in the open literature. Exceptions to this rule include literature reviews where you are summarizing information from a wide variety of sources, technical manuals that summarize state-of-the-art methods, and research reports that are intended to be self-contained.

Results

If the thrust of your paper is quantitative, this section might have only a limited amount of text, with much of the information summarized in tables and figures. Even in this situation, however, there should be enough text to describe the organization and content of the visuals. Note that you should separate data *presentation* and data *interpretation*—either in separate sections or in separate parts of a "Results and Discussion" section.

A common mistake in this part of the paper is attempting to include too much information. Although sometimes there are exceptions, most readers aren't interested in the results of experiments that didn't work—even if you spent more time on them than on the ones that worked well. And most readers aren't interested in raw data; they just want to see the final results, with some explanation of how you got them. Editors are reluctant to accept large tables of data. Try to arrange such data in compact form, perhaps using figures, or simply provide a few examples of the data in short tables. If you choose the latter approach, include results that are truly representative. Overall, be sure to assemble your tables and figures carefully, being honest about including outliers and unexplained values while excluding points known to be invalid. Figures are generally more effective than tables unless the specific values are of interest.

In his books *Visual Display of Quantitative Information* and *Envisioning Information*, Tufte (1983 and 1990) provides a thorough treatment of the design of figures in technical papers. Tufte presents examples of effective graphics and ineffective graphics, and uses them to illustrate several principles of good graphical design. In his own words, graphical displays should:

+ show the data

+ induce the viewer to think about the substance rather than about methodology, graphic design, the technology of graphic production, or something else

+ avoid distorting what the data have to say

+ present many numbers in a small space

+ make large data sets coherent

+ encourage the eye to compare different pieces of data

+ reveal the data at several levels of detail, from a broad overview to a fine structure

+ serve a reasonably clear purpose: description, exploration, tabulation, or decoration

+ be closely integrated with the statistical and verbal descriptions of a data set

These books and others like them (e.g., *The Elements of Graphing Data* by Cleveland, 1989) are valuable tools for faculty; they will help you develop your own graphical displays as well as interpret the graphs of others.

Discussion

This part of the paper should refer back to the results section, highlighting important aspects of the data already presented. You may wish to include additional figures or tables here to illustrate your points. Note that these visuals are not merely presentations of data, but rather the results of interpreting the data in some way—perhaps by applying statistical tests, bringing in the data of others, or combining several of your own datasets. Be sure to relate your interpretations to the research objectives stated earlier.

An inadequate discussion section is one of the most common reasons for the rejection of manuscripts submitted to journals. In some cases, there is a fatal flaw: the research results are simply not significant enough to warrant publication. In other cases, the findings are interesting and worth publishing, but the discussion is inappropriate. For example, the author may be afraid to make a bold statement even when it is supported by the data (perhaps the true significance of the work is not recognized), or conversely the author may make unsubstantiated, sweeping claims when in fact only modest claims are warranted. In either case, discussing a rough draft of the paper with colleagues may head off these problems.

Future Work

It is not always appropriate to include a section on future work, especially when there are length restrictions. When included, however, this section may help the reader further understand the significance and implications of your work. How does your research provide a foundation for additional work? Are the results of your research ready to be applied in some way, or are more research and development needed? Colleagues working in the same discipline may be particularly interested in these issues.

You may have reservations about exposing your ideas for future research in the open literature, since you will want to minimize competition when you submit your next proposal on the topic. However, as a general rule, this section provides only a broad overview of future directions of research rather than details of experimental design that would fit into a proposal. Furthermore, it may be advantageous to have published a statement on ideas for future work; this can help establish your reputation in the field, and it provides a key citation for your next proposal.

Conclusions or Summary

Writers often confuse the difference between the Conclusions and a Summary. According to Webster's Dictionary, conclusions are the *last part of a chain of reasoning; the opinion formed after investigation or thought.* The conclusions are thus an outcome of the work, an extension of the results and discussion. In contrast, a summary is a *brief statement covering the substance or main points* of the entire paper. For a research paper, the summary can include a statement of the problem, the research objectives, the methods used to achieve the objectives, and the results with a brief discussion. Both conclusions and summary might include statements on the significance of the findings and implications for future work. Either a conclusions section or a summary—or both—can be acceptable in a research paper.

It is important to note the distinction between the abstract and the summary. The abstract contains only the essential information in the paper, e.g., the most important results and their significance described in a few sentences. The summary is a more complete retelling of the full paper. The *executive summary* mentioned earlier (see discussion on the abstract) is similar to the summary described here; since the executive summary is positioned at the beginning of the paper rather than at the end, however, it will need to be written assuming no prior knowledge about the paper.

Acknowledgments

Be sure to give credit to individuals and institutions helpful throughout the project and throughout the manuscript preparation. Also indicate the financial sponsors of the work. Usually, the grant and contract numbers are included in this section.

References

Virtually all research papers should include references to previous work upon which the current research is built. Note that each idea or piece of data that is not your own must be referenced, unless the idea is common knowledge not attributable to a single source. (You don't have to reference the original work when you use the Pythagorean Theorem.) To do less is plagiarism.

Of course, there are many instances when you have the option to include a citation that may be marginally relevant. Since too many references can be as annoying as too few, the best guide is to look through other published papers with a similar emphasis. The typical journal article may have as few as 3–4 references or it may have 50 or more, depending on the emphasis of the literature review and the amount of detail in the overall paper.

If you use tables or figures from another publication, whether just a portion or in their entirety, you may need to obtain explicit written permission from both the author and the publisher of the original article. The publisher to whom you are submitting the manuscript can provide the necessary forms.

It is sometimes said that the bane of an editor's existence is the referencing format. More accurately, the true bane is the refusal of many authors to attend to the details of proper referencing. These details include the method of citations within the text as well as the style of the reference list. Some publishers require citations using numbers in parentheses or as superscripts, while others require the authors' names and dates within the text. There are many formats currently in use for the reference list; variations exist in the placement of the authors' first initials, the placement and font of journal volumes, whether the title of an article is included, the placement of the year of publication, punctuation, and other details. We consider attending to such details as part of the overall thoroughness with which one prepares a research paper: when references are sloppy, incomplete, or in improper format, it reflects negatively on the rest of the paper.

Appendices

Appendices should be used for information that would occupy too much space in the main body of the paper or would interrupt the flow of reading the paper, but should be available as reference material. Examples include calculations, lists of data, definitions of terms and symbols, computer programs, or detailed explanations. Appendices are most often used in research reports and books, although they are occasionally used in journal articles. An appendix should include only material that is relevant to the theme of the paper, not for material of marginal interest.

Exercise: In the previous section, we stated that rough forms of the graphs, tables, and other visuals should be generated before writing the paper, since the manuscript must be built around the results of the work. For this reason, it is important to have properly designed visuals, where the key features of the data are easily seen and are represented without distortion. Consider the first graph in Figure 9-1, which has considerable distortion, and the second graph which shows an improvement by Tufte (1983). Now consider published figures you may have seen recently. Can you identify any cases where the data are not presented clearly, or where there is distortion? Can you propose changes in those figures that may help solve the problem?

AFTER THE PAPER IS SUBMITTED: DEALING WITH REJECTION OR WITH ACCEPTANCE

Once the paper is submitted for journal publication, it is out of your control—at least for a while. You need to allow several months for your peers to complete their reviews and for the editor to make a decision.

The decision on your paper will fall into one of three categories: accept, accept subject to revision, or decline. If your paper is declined, read the reviewers' comments carefully. The reasons for the editor's decision are usually quite clear. If you feel that an injustice has been committed, you might wish to contact the editor for further clarification, although don't expect to change anyone's mind. The editor of *Science* magazine, in an essay entitled "The Editor's Quest," describes a set of changes in manuscript review procedures (Koshland, 1985). After presenting the changes, he writes:

> *One rule must accompany these changes—no resubmissions. Each author of a returned manuscript can explain to his or her graduate students that "unfortunately we chose the week in which Darwin, Newton, Priestley, and Keynes submitted their own seminal discoveries." That not only will teach graduate students how statistical fluctuations run the world but will help us give this system a chance to function. A second rule is a must—there will be no lobbying or phoning of review board members to influence their decisions. These individuals were chosen for their Solomonic wisdom, their mercurial response times, and their encyclopedic knowledge, qualities achieved by being extremely busy scientists.*

If your paper is accepted subject to revision, you must submit a revised manuscript as well as an explanation of how you dealt with the reviewers' comments. It is not mandatory to change the manuscript exactly as the reviewers wish, but you must explain your decisions. Be sure to submit your revised paper and explanation promptly. This not only enhances the value of your article as a timely publication, but it also helps the editor minimize the pile of manuscripts

Figure 9-1

The first graph (taken from the *New York Times,* August 9, 1978) exaggerates recent changes in fuel economy standards through use of perspective: the horizontal line segment for 1985 is 7.8 times as long as the horizontal line segment for 1978, despite an actual increase in fuel economy standard by a factor of only 1.53 (27.5/18). The second graph shows a more honest portrayal of the data. For those who argue that the undistorted visual is "too plain," the third graph shows how a figure can be embellished without resorting to distortion. The first graph is reproduced with permission from the *New York Times Company* (Copyright, 1978), while the second and third graphs, taken from Tufte (1983), are reproduced with permission from Graphics Press.

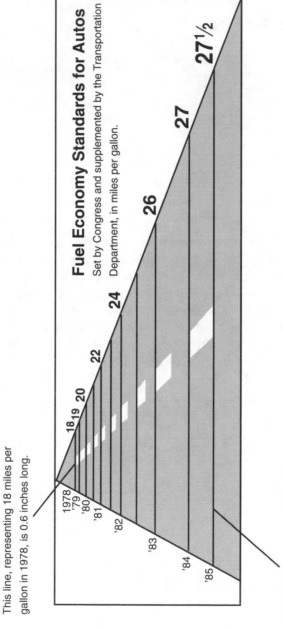

This line, representing 18 miles per gallon in 1978, is 0.6 inches long.

This line, representing 27.5 miles per gallon in 1985, is 5.3 inches long.

Fuel Economy Standards for Autos
Set by Congress and supplemented by the Transportation Department, in miles per gallon.

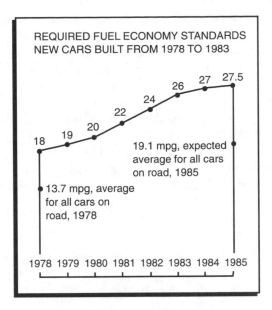

REQUIRED FUEL ECONOMY STANDARDS
NEW CARS BUILT FROM 1978 TO 1983

18 19 20 22 24 26 27 27.5

19.1 mpg, expected
average for all cars
on road, 1985

13.7 mpg, average
for all cars on
road, 1978

1978 1979 1980 1981 1982 1983 1984 1985

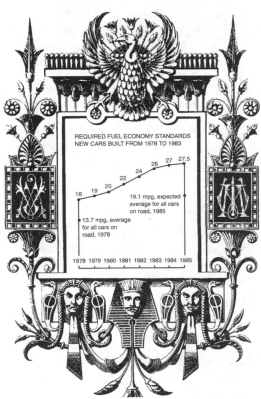

waiting for revision; most editors have a considerable stack of such manuscripts. Obviously, many of these will never be published.

Your revised manuscript may need to be sent back to one or more reviewers, or it may be accepted by the editor without further review. In either case, the manuscript is not officially accepted until you have received a written statement to that effect from the editor. Some authors begin citing their own submitted papers as "in press" before they receive written notification. That can be risky.

When your manuscript is finally accepted for publication, there are a number of issues that merit attention. Unless the submitted manuscript was camera-ready, you will need to check over the typeset galley proofs for typographical errors and other problems. Don't expect the galleys to arrive immediately after the letter of acceptance; a period of several months is typical. This period of time isn't license for a slow turnaround time on your part, however. Publishers generally request return of the corrected galleys within a day or two to avoid the delay of an entire issue of the journal. You may also want to order reprints, using forms provided by the publisher. Furthermore, the publisher will request that you sign a copyright agreement.

Finally, long after you have forgotten about it, the article will appear in print. It is worthwhile to generate a regular mailing list of colleagues to whom you can send reprints—this may enhance your exposure, since many individuals are simply too busy to keep up with the literature. You also need to respond rapidly to requests for reprints of your article as they arrive.

When do you begin to reap the benefits of all this effort? Well, you won't get rich from journal articles or from conference proceedings—in fact, page charges and reprint costs mean a negative cash flow. You may make a little money from books or book chapters. The real reward is when you start seeing your work cited by others—indicating that your efforts are having a positive impact on other research groups and on the discipline.

SUMMARY

This chapter discusses preparation of research papers, including journal articles, conference papers, research reports, and books or book chapters. We begin by listing the background material needed before putting together an outline of the paper. We then discuss the writing of the manuscript, going through each section of the paper. Finally, we discuss procedures to be followed if the paper is accepted for publication or if the paper is declined.

A challenge facing new faculty members is how to deal with the pressure to publish *lots* of papers. An unfortunate product of the "publish or perish" syndrome is that we now have a literature that contains large numbers of mediocre papers, written more to augment promotion packages than to inform an interested readership. Don't fall into this trap; write fewer, better papers. In other words, write for long-term benefits, not for the next promotion hurdle. And be reassured that the trend at most universities is toward evaluation of *quality* rather than mere quantity of research publications.

REFERENCES

Cleveland, W.S., *The Elements of Graphing Data,* Monterey, CA: Wadsworth Advanced Books and Software, 1989.

Hamilton, D.P., Research papers: Who's uncited now?, *Science, Vol. 251,* p. 25, 1991.

Koshland, D.E., An editor's quest (II), *Science, Vol. 227,* p. 249, 1985.

Landes, K.K., A scrutiny of the abstract, *Bulletin of the American Association of Petroleum Geologists, Vol. 50,* p. 1992, 1966.

Strunk, W. and E.B. White, *The Elements of Style,* 3/e, New York, NY: Macmillan Publishing Co., 1979.

Tufte, E.R., *The Visual Display of Quantitative Information,* Cheshire, CT: Graphics Press, 1983.

Tufte, E.R., *Envisioning Information,* Cheshire, CT: Graphics Press, 1990.

University of Chicago, *A Manual of Style,* 13/e, Chicago, IL: The University of Chicago Press, 1982.

10

REVIEWING
RESEARCH PROPOSALS
AND PAPERS

INTRODUCTION

Virtually every research proposal and every research paper you write will be reviewed in some way. Most will be reviewed by your peers, and the process will determine in part whether the agency funds your proposal or the journal publishes your paper. By joining the faculty ranks, you are making a commitment not only to write proposals and papers, but also to participate in the review process.

Peer review activities often become major time commitments. Although financial incentives are offered in some cases, participation is usually expected without remuneration. Nevertheless, the reviews are a vital part of the system that has been developed for conducting research and disseminating the results.

Preparing careful and timely reviews provides a number of benefits to you as a reviewer. Funding agency personnel and editors are likely to remember particularly thorough reviews; such a favorable impression may have an impact when you submit a proposal or paper to the same organization. Furthermore, participating in the review process helps you to identify those criteria that are most important to the organization. Preparing careful critiques also helps you keep abreast of the most current research in the field. Perhaps most importantly, you will have the satisfaction of helping to insure that only the highest quality proposals receive funding and the highest quality papers are published.

In this chapter, we discuss the process of reviewing research proposals and papers using various procedures established by funding agencies and editors. First we discuss a number of issues and questions to keep in mind when reviewing proposals. Then we discuss reviewing research papers for journals, conference proceedings, and books. Finally, we summarize this information and consider implications about the review process for new faculty.

REVIEWING RESEARCH PROPOSALS FOR FUNDING AGENCIES

There are many questions to consider when reviewing a proposal—just as there are many issues to consider when writing one. For example, the criteria for evaluation depend on whether the proposal is for experimental work, theoretical work, computer modeling, or other activity. The criteria also depend on the priorities of the funding agency and even on the priorities of a particular branch of the agency. Therefore, we consider the appropriate questions for a reviewer to ask only at a rather general level. First we discuss proposal reviews conducted by individuals, and then we consider proposal review panels.

Individual Written Reviews

Most funding agencies solicit written reviews through the mail. An agency will probably ask you to review proposals after you have had a proposal of your own funded by them. After all, receiving funding for your proposal is a strong indication that you understand the interests of the organization and know how to design a research project. In some cases, however, organizations will ask you to perform reviews even though you have never received funding from them. As we noted in Chapter 8, most funding agencies have to process a large number of proposals, only a fraction of which will be successful. Considering that each proposal will need anywhere from two to six evaluations (or sometimes even more), it is apparent that the system needs lots of reviewers.

Agencies usually provide written guidelines to assist in your review. Table 10-1 provides a list of topics covered in one form or another in the guidelines from several federal agencies (DOE, EPA, NIH, NSF, and NASA). Note that these guidelines are consistent with earlier discussion on writing proposals: all of the issues mentioned in Table 10-1 have also been discussed in Chapter 8.

The guidelines imply that you need to do more than merely evaluate the research objectives and methods to achieve them. You also must evaluate the research team, the facilities available to support the work, the budget, the proposed time schedule for the project, and the expected significance of the work. Note that you should consider your personal knowledge of the research team members and the facilities when you make your decisions on the merits of the proposed work. Of course, if your acquaintance with any member of the research team prevents you from providing an unbiased review, you may need to disqualify yourself as a reviewer (see Conflict of Interest discussion below).

TABLE 10-1

Typical Guidelines for Reviewing Research Proposals for Federal Agencies

1. Background Information
   - Is the PI aware of previous work related to the proposed project?
   - Has the PI used this existing knowledge base to identify a significant problem in need of research?

2. Research Objectives
   - Will achieving the objectives help to solve the problem identified?
   - Will achieving the objectives be of major benefit? To whom?

3. Methods
   - Can the research objectives be achieved using the proposed methods?
   - Has the PI identified the most appropriate methods for the particular project?

4. Qualifications of the Research Team
   - Do the personnel involved in the project have the necessary education and training to carry out the proposed work?
   - Does the previous research record of the personnel indicate a likelihood of success for the proposed project?

5. Support Facilities
   - Are the available laboratories and equipment adequate for conducting the proposed work?
   - Has the PI justified the need for any new major facilities to be acquired as part of the project?

6. Logistical Concerns
   - Is the budget appropriate for the proposed work?
   - Is the time schedule for each part of the work plan reasonable?

7. General Issues
   - Does the proposal clearly address and justify each of the above topic areas?
   - Is the right amount of detail provided throughout the proposal (just enough to permit evaluation of the project but no more than necessary)?
   - Is the proposal well-organized and well-written? Is it professional, without typographical errors, misspellings, or other problems?
   - Is the project creative and imaginative, employing novel approaches?
   - Has the PI discussed how the research results will be disseminated?

Recall that Table 8-1 listed several federal agencies that support major research efforts. It is useful to consider specific guidelines for reviewers of proposals submitted to these agencies. As an example, we choose the National Science Foundation, which has published information for reviewers (NSF, 1994) and requests comments on the following specific items:

1. *Research performance competence:* Capability of the investigator(s), the technical soundness of the proposed approach, and the adequacy of the institutional resources available. Please include comments on the proposer's recent research performance.

2. *Intrinsic merit of the research:* Likelihood that the research will lead to new discoveries or fundamental advances within its field of science or engineering, or have substantial impact on progress in that field or in other scientific and engineering fields.

3. *Utility or relevance of the research:* Likelihood that the research can contribute to the achievement of a goal that is extrinsic or in addition to that of the research field itself, and thereby serve as the basis for new or improved technology or assist in the solution of societal problems.

4. *Effect of the research on the infrastructure of science and engineering:* Potential of the proposed project research to contribute to better understanding or improvement of the quality, distribution, or effectiveness of the nation's scientific and engineering research, education, and human resources base.

NSF states that Criterion 1 should be applied in a balanced way to all research proposals. Criterion 2 is intended primarily for evaluating proposals that emphasize fundamental research, while Criterion 3 is intended primarily for proposals that deal with applied research. Criterion 4 is included to guide the reviewer in evaluating the overall effect of the research in any categories that are not covered in the first three criteria.

It is significant that NSF requests an evaluation of the effect of the research on the *infrastructure of science and engineering,* addressing the way in which the proposed work can improve the effectiveness of general scientific research and education in the U.S. In contrast, other agencies ask for evaluations of the benefits of the proposed work in specific areas. The areas reflect the missions of these agencies. For example, EPA funds research to safeguard the environment, while NIH funds work to improve public health. DOE sponsors research to improve energy production and utilization. It is important for you as a reviewer to consider how the proposed work contributes to the agency's mission, or in the case of NSF, how the proposed work contributes to basic knowledge.

It is necessary to consider some of the logistical details of the review process. Most agencies request that you complete your reviews within a few weeks, although they often willingly accept reviews that take a bit longer. With the other time pressures of your faculty responsibilities, a review can sometimes sit on your desk for several weeks—be courteous and try to avoid that situation. After all, you will want proposals that you submit to be promptly reviewed.

Most reviews of proposals are one or two pages at most; some may be as short as a paragraph. Although you should avoid unnecessary discussion, remember that the funding agency needs information for their final decision to fund or reject the proposal. You can help the agency by providing specific, detailed comments related to their evaluation criteria. Such detailed comments can also be of help to the principal investigator, at least in cases where the agencies forward reviewers' comments to that individual.

In some cases, you are also asked to provide a grade or numerical score. For example, NSF requests a summary rating in one of the following categories: *excellent, very good, good, fair, or poor*. A rating of *very good* indicates that the proposal ranks in the top one-third of all proposals, with a *good* rating for the middle third and a *fair* rating for the bottom third. Ratings of *excellent* or *poor* are used only in exceptional circumstances.

Many agencies now accept reviews by electronic mail. The agency will provide this information when they send you the proposal for review.

Review Panels

In order to provide a more comprehensive evaluation, many organizations have adopted the review panel approach. The members of the panel are generally chosen by the agency, or perhaps by an individual whom the agency has selected to chair the panel. The members are peer reviewers from academia, government, or private firms who have expertise in the disciplines represented by the proposals. Because of the varied nature of topics addressed in proposals, review panel members are sometimes selected only after the agency has received the proposals. Typical panels have anywhere from a few members to more than thirty.

The major advantage of using a review panel is that a group of individuals has the responsibility of ranking the proposals. This is in contrast to the written review procedure, where often times one individual in the funding agency must rank the proposals based on the written comments received; the comments on a single proposal from different reviewers occasionally disagree, making decisions on how to rank the proposals extremely difficult. A second advantage of the review panel approach is that open discussion in the panel meetings can help to identify important strengths and weaknesses in each proposal. This maximizes chances of a fair review, and can provide better feedback to the principal investigator on ways to strengthen the proposed research.

Despite these advantages, panels are not always used. It is difficult to bring together individuals with busy schedules from across the country—and sometimes from other countries—who must devote a block of time to the panel meetings. It is also expensive for the funding agency to pay for all of the travel costs, and occasionally honoraria, for panel members. These funds might otherwise be used to support additional research projects.

Panels work in a variety of different ways. Some agencies distribute copies of the proposals only after members have arrived at the meeting; the process of reading the proposals, discussing them, and writing the final critiques must be done on-site. In other panels, the members receive copies of the proposals (or perhaps a portion of the proposals) to read ahead of time. Some agencies require reviewers to complete preliminary written evaluations before the meeting or by the time of the meeting. The panel may be asked to write the final critiques at the meeting or within some time interval afterward.

Participation in review panels is especially important for new faculty members. Not only do you have the opportunity to meet influential colleagues in your discipline, you also can witness the proposal evaluation process firsthand. Knowing the issues of importance can help you write your next proposal.

Issues Affecting Individual Written Reviews and Review Panels

The process of peer review requires important distinctions when reviewing proposals of new faculty members versus those of well-established researchers. A newcomer can't possibly have the research record or depth of knowledge of a more senior investigator; although you need to consider the same questions for both, you will have to apply different criteria in the evaluation. For example, a senior researcher who is asking for an extension of current work may submit a very impressive proposal. There is likely to be a wealth of data presented from past projects, with in-depth explanations of the results. A proposal from a recent Ph.D., on the other hand, may be far more speculative. There will almost certainly be less background data and associated interpretation. You will probably want to consider the past record of the senior investigator as a major factor in evaluating his proposal, along with the research objectives and proposed methods. In contrast, you will want to focus more on the objectives and methods in the newcomer's proposal, without an emphasis on past performance. Accounting for this distinction is the only way a newcomer can break into a field. As a new faculty member, you can certainly appreciate the problem.

As you review proposals, it is essential that you respect confidentiality. At many colleges and universities, there are stories of individuals who have had proposals rejected, only to discover that a key innovative idea in their proposal has been copied by someone else. All concepts contained in proposals undergoing review should be treated as confidential. Furthermore, many agencies request that you do not reveal yourself as the reviewer of a particular proposal. Unless the process safeguards the privacy of reviewers, individuals will be reluctant to provide completely honest and candid reviews. Most agencies request that you return the proposal to them or destroy the proposal after completing your review.

You should exclude yourself from reviewing a proposal in the event of a potential conflict of interest. There may be a number of situations that prevent you from giving an unbiased review, e.g., if you have a financial interest in seeing the project funded, or if you have a particularly close relationship with individuals involved in the proposed work. Any financial connection between you and the principal investigator, or between you and the principal investigator's institution, may require you to prepare a separate statement describing the connection so that the funding agency can decide if there is a conflict of interest. The agency will generally provide the rules regarding conflict of interest when you are asked to perform a review.

Finally, when you accept the responsibility to review a proposal, you are obligated to do the best job possible. On one hand, the funding agency is counting on you to be critical to insure the best use of its funds. On the other hand, someone's research program is likely to be affected by your review, with obvious ramifications for that individual's graduate students, research operating expenses, and even promotion and tenure decisions. There is no alternative to an honest and thorough evaluation using your best judgment.

> *Exercise: Difficult issues sometimes arise when reviewing proposals, mostly because there is much at stake in the final decision. Consider how you would write a review for each of the following situations and think about which ones you would be sympathetic toward.*
>
> ✦ *You are reviewing a proposal from a new faculty member that contains some particularly creative research ideas, and you are optimistic that lots of interesting results will come out of the work if the investigator is given a chance. However, some of the administrative aspects of the proposal are lacking in certain respects: issues like descriptions of the facilities and background of the principal investigator are prepared in a cursory manner.*
>
> ✦ *You are reviewing a proposal from a well-known senior scientist with a long history of excellent research and prestigious publications. The proposal has some very good ideas, but it is weak in its description of how the research would be conducted. There are statements to the effect that the "previous record speaks for itself" and the continued high quality research of the past years will be continued, but there is little detail.*
>
> ✦ *You are reviewing a proposal that is excellent in all respects. However, the subject matter does not fit neatly into what is normally considered the domain of the agency to which it was submitted, and in fact does not fit neatly into the domain of other agencies with which you are*

familiar. A corollary to this situation is a proposal that deserves to be funded on its own merit, but does not satisfy some specific (and perhaps narrow) criteria established by the funding source.

✦ *You are reviewing a proposal that is excellent in all respects, except that the goals are overly ambitious given the budget and the time frame allotted. You suspect that the principal investigator cannot complete all of the work proposed, but the project appears to be worthwhile even if only part of the work is completed. A corollary to this situation is a proposal that deserves to be funded on its own merits, where the budget is reasonable given the amount of work proposed, but you know that the agency is set up to fund only much smaller proposals.*

REVIEWING RESEARCH PAPERS

Unlike proposal reviews, which may be conducted by individual efforts or in panels, the review of research papers almost always occurs by individual efforts solicited through the mail. The majority of these reviews are for journal publication. However, many conference proceedings now require peer review, and some technical books or book chapters are also reviewed. We consider each of these categories in this section.

Journal Articles

A visit to any university library illustrates the need for peer review: without it, we would soon be buried in a morass of paper! The number of journals currently published, and the number of manuscripts submitted, demand that every paper be critically reviewed to ensure that only those making significant contributions are published. What constitutes a significant contribution is a matter for each reviewer to decide. Too much leniency promotes a waste of paper and makes it difficult to hunt out truly worthwhile articles. Too much rigidity prevents good research results from being published. It is apparent that faculty careers depend on a peer review system that discourages poor research but allows a certain amount of risk taking and innovation. You should be able to walk this fine line and discriminate between poor papers and good papers after some experience with the peer review system.

In general, journals circulate guidelines for manuscript reviewers similar to those for evaluating proposals. Table 10-2 lists typical topics that may be covered in written guidelines for reviewers of journal articles. Note that these topics are consistent with the parts of a research paper discussed in Chapter 9.

The next-to-last question in Table 10-2 is important: you need to make a recommendation as to whether the paper is acceptable as it stands, acceptable with modifications, or unacceptable. In cases where the paper is of high quality but inappropriate for the particular journal that received it, you may wish to

TABLE 10-2

Examples of Topics Covered in Written Guidelines for Reviewers of Journal Articles

- Is the abstract appropriate, including only the essential information contained in the paper?

- Does the author provide relevant introductory and background material so that the reader gains a perspective on the topic area of the paper? Has an important problem within this topic area been identified for research?

- Do the objectives of the research follow logically from the problem statement?

- Are the research methods to achieve the objectives clearly described?

- Are the data summarized clearly and given with the appropriate level of detail (enough so the reader can follow the interpretation but no more than necessary)? Has the author made effective use of tables and figures that have been designed well for their intended purpose?

- Have the data been interpreted in a reasonable manner using accepted procedures (e.g., standard statistical tests)?

- Does the author draw reasonable inferences or generalizations from the interpretations? Is it clear that the objectives of the research have been achieved?

- Are the most important points of the paper summarized clearly? Does the author reach reasonable conclusions?

- Does the paper contain an adequate number of references? Are the references appropriate and in proper format?

- Overall, is the paper well-organized and well-written? Is it professional, without typographical errors, misspellings, or other problems? Are there any errors in logic, mathematics, or facts?

- Should the paper be accepted for publication?

- If you recommend publication with revisions, do you want to see the revised manuscript before making a final recommendation?

recommend that the author resubmit the manuscript to another journal. Your overall recommendation needs to be supported by answers to the above questions, or to other questions posed in the guidelines. Note that the questions in the table are merely examples—many journals provide lists of questions to be answered, while others send a cover letter simply asking for comments. Some journals ask reviewers to refrain from making a specific recommendation about whether to accept or reject the paper, leaving that decision entirely to the editors. It is clear that each review must be handled on an individual basis.

Conference Proceedings

In general, reviewing manuscripts for conference proceedings is similar to reviewing journal manuscripts—with a few important differences.

Most conference proceedings have strict page limitations. As a result, many of the papers will be constrained by the allowable number of pages: only partial results of a project may be presented. How did the author decide which results to present and which to delete? When and where will the rest of the findings be reported? You generally need to consider these issues when reviewing the paper. Because of length restrictions, some of the sections normally included in full-length journal articles may be greatly reduced or absent altogether. For example, the introductory section may be replaced by a sentence or two citing previous publications. The research methods may not be described in any detail. As a reviewer, you need to ensure that the paper includes adequate references for this missing information, and that there is enough material to support the key findings.

Keep in mind that many conferences are highly specialized. The proceedings for such conferences may be intended more for experts than for novices in the field, and in this case less background and supporting material may be acceptable.

Conference proceedings usually have tight time deadlines for publication. One late manuscript can delay an entire volume, so there is a limit on the revisions an author can make. As a reviewer, you need to take these time limitations into account: a paper that requires extensive revisions may have to be rejected.

Although some conference proceedings publish guidelines for reviewers, many do not. You are usually safe considering the same issues as for journal articles with the added constraints for length and time restrictions. If you are unsure about a particular issue, there is almost always a contact person such as a session chairman or an editor of the proceedings who can assist you.

Books and Book Chapters

Unlike journal articles and conference papers which usually present highly focused research results, books can provide more extensive information such as a broad survey of a topic. As such, books may not be restricted to covering only new, previously unpublished results. The writing style, depth of coverage, and presentation of data may need to be appropriate to a wide audience: readers with a variety of backgrounds may use the book.

The evaluation criteria for books and book chapters are similar to those discussed earlier for journal articles, although there is usually less emphasis on presentation of new and original data. For books presenting a survey of a topic area, the most important considerations are whether the manuscript has attempted to cover a topic area of reasonable scope, whether it adequately covers the topic, and whether it presents a balanced, unbiased treatment. These criteria would also be appropriate for literature review papers occasionally submitted to journals.

Issues Affecting Journal Articles, Conference Proceedings, and Books

Performing a careful review of a manuscript takes time. Fortunately, there are ways to reduce the time commitment and still do an adequate job.

First, you need not—and in fact should not—rewrite portions of a paper. Let the author do that. Your role is simply to point out where problems exist and perhaps to suggest what the author might do to solve the problems. Second, although you want to include enough information to support your final recommendation, you need not include lengthy, detailed discussions. A few sentences may be enough to illustrate a particular problem. Finally, as pointed out by Smith (1990), if you find a fatal and uncorrectable error that invalidates the paper, you are automatically excused from searching for other problems.

You will generally be given two to four weeks to complete the review of a journal article. In cases of short articles intended for rapid publication, or conference papers on a tight publication schedule, the editor may request a quicker response. Sometimes manuscripts submitted to a special issue of a regular journal may require a rapid review. On the other hand, you may be given several weeks or more to review books or lengthy research reports. If you feel you are not qualified to perform a review, be sure to return it to the editor as soon as possible. An editor's nightmare is to wait several weeks for a reviewer who ultimately returns the manuscript without a critique. Be careful not to be too selective; you can probably provide a worthwhile review even if the paper is not in your subdiscipline.

Typically, a manuscript will be sent to two or three reviewers. If these initial statements are in disagreement, an additional reviewer may be sought; an especially short turnaround time may be requested of this last reviewer. In some instances, you may be sent a manuscript that you had previously reviewed and for which you had recommended revisions. If the paper still does not meet your expectations after the author has had a chance to make revisions, it is reasonable to recommend rejection. The final decision on whether to publish the paper is made by the editor(s).

Overall, your report to the editor should be concise, timely, and to the point. Smith (1990) suggests that every review of a research paper should contain the following items:

+ Your recommendation as to the ultimate disposition of the paper

+ A short (1–5 sentence) summary of the main points of the paper

+ An evaluation of the validity and significance of the research goal

+ An evaluation of the overall quality of the work

You should include a list of both necessary changes as well as recommended changes if you feel the paper should be accepted for publication after revision. Be sure your review is polite; insulting and demeaning reviews serve no purpose and may be thrown out by the editor.

Analogous to NSF's guidelines, which state that the best one-third of all proposals be assigned to the *very good* category, Smith recommends the following categories for research papers:

+ Major results; very significant (less than 1% of all papers)

+ Good, solid, interesting work; a definite contribution (less than 10%)

+ Minor, but positive contribution to knowledge (perhaps 10–30%)

+ Elegant and technically correct but useless

+ Neither elegant nor useful, but not actually wrong

+ Wrong and misleading

+ So badly written that technical evaluation is impossible

Papers in the top two categories and some of those in the third category are considered publishable. The percentage of papers accepted for publication can vary greatly from one journal to another, since some journals attract a greater fraction of good papers.

A few final words of caution are in order. Some authors submit papers simultaneously to more than one journal or book publisher. This is permissible only if the author makes it clear that there is a simultaneous submission; it is generally not a good idea to submit papers simultaneously. Related to this problem is the author who attempts to publish material that he has already published elsewhere. If there are substantial extensions of the work contained in the second paper, this may be acceptable, and some journals willingly republish papers. A more serious problem is the author who plagiarizes another author's work without proper citation. Reviewers should be alert to all of these possible problems and should inform the editor if there are ethical questions about the manuscript (Smith, 1990).

Despite the variety of issues you can address as a reviewer, there are some "forbidden topics" for reviewers of research papers (Forscher, 1965). One of these is the goal of the research: the author is free to choose the topic area and specific objectives of the project. It is usually inappropriate for you, as a reviewer, to recommend that the researcher should have pursued a different set of objectives, perhaps of greater interest to you. There is a fine line to tread in this area, however. If the objectives of the research are misguided or irrelevant, then the project results may be worthless and the paper should be rejected. Another forbidden topic for reviewers is the set of research methods. It is generally inappropriate for you to call attention to other methods that would have worked better. As long as the methods employed did achieve the objectives and are clearly described in the paper, that should be satisfactory.

As with proposal reviews, you are expected to respect confidentiality and avoid conflicts of interest when you review manuscripts. The editor will generally ask you to return the manuscript or destroy it after you have completed your review. In rare cases, however, you may want to reveal your identity to the author; this may be desirable if you wish to discuss a particular point with the author, perhaps to call attention to your own work on the topic. Be sure to contact the editor to discuss the situation before making an effort to contact the author. Note that the identity of reviewers may be revealed to authors according to certain editorial policies; for example, Forscher (1965) suggests that reviewers be identified whenever verbatim reviewer comments are forwarded to the author. In practice, however, many editors prefer to keep the identity of reviewers confidential. You will usually be notified of the editorial policy when you receive the manuscript for review.

If this seems like a lot to think about when reviewing a manuscript, remember that good reviewing, just like good writing, takes practice. And because the reviewing and writing processes are related, you will probably find that your own papers improve as you conduct more reviews. The process of peer review is a process of quality control—being a part of the system is an important responsibility of faculty members.

Exercise: In the exercise in the previous section, you were asked to consider how you would write proposal reviews for a few hypothetical situations. Now consider how you would write reviews of manuscripts submitted for publication in the following hypothetical situations.

+ *You are reviewing a paper that summarizes research very similar to your own work. The paper could be substantially improved by incorporating some of your findings, but the author is unaware of your work and has not cited any of your publications.*

+ *You are reviewing a paper that is written by a researcher in another country where the native language is not English. The paper presents excellent results and is likely to have an impact on the field—but the quality of the English in the paper is poor. You start to make comments on how to improve the English but soon realize that this is a bigger job than you bargained for.*

✦ *You are reviewing a paper that is written by a researcher in a developing country. The paper presents interesting results on a research topic you know fairly well. However, the interpretation is not satisfactory because the author did not have access to recent literature on the topic. The library facilities in the country are poor, and it would be extremely difficult for the author to get access to the needed literature.*

SUMMARY

In this chapter, we have discussed procedures for reviewing research proposals and papers. The ultimate goal of these reviews is to help funding agencies decide whether to provide support for a project and to help editors decide whether to publish a manuscript. Proposals can be reviewed either through individual efforts or through panels of reviewers convened by a funding agency. Papers submitted for publication are almost always reviewed as individual efforts. Funding agencies and editors usually provide specific questions for you to address as you review the proposal or manuscript.

Participating in the review process can help you keep up-to-date with developments in your research area and can provide information on how decisions are made that can guide your efforts to obtain funding and publish papers. Conducting reviews can also provide the satisfaction of contributing to the research efforts of many individuals and agencies.

Reviewing proposals and papers is a key part of the current system for conducting and disseminating research results. The peer review process depends on all of our efforts—although imperfect, it is the best system we have to maximize chances that worthy proposals are funded and good papers are published.

REFERENCES

Forscher, B.K., Rules for reviewers, *Science, Vol. 150*, pp. 319–321, 1965.

National Science Foundation, "Proposal Processing and Review," Chapter III in *Grant Proposal Guide*, NSF Report 94-2, Washington, DC, p. 13, January 1994.

Smith, A.J., The task of the referee, *Computer, Vol. 23*, pp. 65–71, 1990.

11

PRESENTING
TALKS ON
RESEARCH RESULTS

INTRODUCTION

You will deliver many talks on your research in a variety of settings through-out your career as a professor. The goals of these presentations might vary widely, e.g., to convey highly focused information to an audience of specialists, or conversely to cover a broad range of issues appropriate for the general public. To cover the spectrum between these two extremes, imagine discussing your research in front of the following audiences: experts in your discipline at a professional conference, students and faculty in your department, a government committee composed of technical and nontechnical people, and a local community volunteer organization. The purpose, amount of detail, and rhetoric of your presentation will vary in these situations. Nevertheless, there are general guidelines that you can use to prepare and deliver effective talks for all of these audiences.

Just as with other skills discussed in previous chapters, you can develop considerable skill in communicating research results; anyone can improve his speaking abilities with appropriate motivation and practice. In this chapter, we discuss a number of ideas to help you become more effective at making presentations on your research findings. We focus on talks at professional conferences because of their importance to new faculty members, although it is clear that many of the items discussed will also apply to other settings. First we describe the research conference environment. Then we discuss how to prepare for a talk of this type. Next, we identify key issues in delivering the presentation. Finally, we summarize ways of evaluating your talk.

In Chapter 4, we discussed preparing lectures for use in the classroom and delivering them effectively. The current chapter expands on some of those concepts but mainly considers new issues involved in presenting research results.

THE RESEARCH CONFERENCE ENVIRONMENT

The most exciting research results are generally published in journals. As discussed in Chapter 9, this is the best way to get wide exposure for your findings. Unfortunately, many journals take a year or longer to publish an article. For this reason, most researchers rely on conferences to disseminate exciting and timely research results prior to journal publication.

It is important to attend conferences in your discipline, both to present your work and to follow the work of others. Furthermore, conferences offer excellent opportunities to interact personally with experts in your field. You may be able to recruit graduate students and postdoctoral researchers through contacts at meetings; these contacts may also lead to cooperative research efforts.

You have a wide variety of conferences to attend—from very large to very small. Although large national or international meetings offer opportunities to meet experts in a number of disciplines, there are some drawbacks. For example, it may actually be more difficult to meet new colleagues at a large conference than at a smaller, focused meeting where everyone shares similar research interests. Furthermore, your talk may be scheduled at the same time as a dozen other talks in simultaneous sessions, and your presentation may draw a disappointingly small audience. Many individuals simply find large meetings impersonal. The process of studying a thick conference program, optimizing the time spent in the most interesting sessions, and attempting to make contact with key individuals may itself be exhausting. Nevertheless, it is sometimes important to attend large as well as small meetings, particularly if there are special sessions in your discipline. Learning how to glean information and make contacts at meetings is a skill worth acquiring.

Unfortunately, there are often high costs associated with attending conferences. In addition to travel expenses, some conferences charge steep registration fees. And as a new faculty member, you are no longer eligible for student registration benefits. Some departments offer limited amounts of funding to beginning faculty to help defray these costs, as discussed in Chapter 8.

Although you may spend several days at a conference, the highlight of the meeting—at least for you—is likely to be those few minutes in which you make your presentation. The rest of this chapter is devoted to that topic.

PREPARING FOR THE PRESENTATION

Chapter 4 summarized four categories of preparation for classroom lectures: determining the objectives of the talk, assessing the audience, organizing the talk, and preparing the visual aids. Some of the issues emphasized in that chapter are also relevant for research presentations, and it may be worthwhile for you to revisit those sections. However, there are a number of important differences. Let us consider each of these four categories in the context of research presentations.

Determine Your Objectives

Your talk may have a variety of purposes. For example, you may wish to make experts at a national meeting aware of some exciting new results of your work that extend the field in some way. Or you might want to pull together the work of several other researchers to draw new conclusions about the state-of-the-art. Alternatively, you may want to question current thinking on a topic by offering a hypothesis that challenges conventional wisdom. If you are invited to give a seminar at another institution, you may wish to emphasize aspects of your work that build upon research underway at that institution to pave the way for possible collaboration. Identifying these kinds of goals for your talk is an important first step.

Assess the Audience

As with lecturing, it is important to assess the audience. But unlike classes, where you can usually get to know quite a bit about the students, you may not know who will be attending your talk. There are ways to get information on your expected audience, however. If you are presenting a talk at a meeting of a national association, speak with individuals who have attended past meetings of that organization. Are they highly focused specialists in your field or are they more likely to come from a spectrum of backgrounds? If you are giving a seminar at another school, you can ask your host about who is likely to attend. Your approach will need to be quite different if there is a large fraction of undergraduates in the audience as opposed to mostly faculty members who are familiar with your discipline.

Organize the Presentation

Organizing your talk requires you to select the central idea of the speech, often called the thesis. This is based on the purpose of the presentation discussed above. As with a class lecture, you need to identify a few main points related to the purpose, and these need to be organized into an introduction, body, and conclusions. You should have an introduction that prepares the audience for the rest of the talk, a body that is cohesive and clearly related to the thesis, and conclusions that tell the audience what you want them to take away from the presentation.

Unlike class lectures where fifty minutes is the norm, you may have to organize your talk to satisfy severe time constraints. Some conferences have such a demand for podium time that there are several simultaneous sessions, and talks are restricted to times as short as ten minutes with an additional five minutes for questions. It doesn't matter whether your results represent the seminal work that will revolutionize the discipline. When your time is up, you must stop talking and let the chairperson take over. Attendees are moving from one session to another according to the published schedule of talks, so it is critical for all of the talks to keep within the time allotted or the entire system breaks down. We heard about a memorable talk at a conference where a miniature traffic light was used to indicate when time was up. As the light changed from green to yellow (the one-minute warning), the speaker was just finishing his introduction. When the light turned red, the chairperson politely asked the speaker to conclude his talk within one minute. The speaker, obviously feeling that his message deserved more time, simply unplugged the light and continued talking! (To deal with problems like this, many conferences hold a special meeting for session chairpersons to discuss how to handle unruly speakers.) If you want the audience to remember your research and not your personality, follow the rules.

Prepare Visual Aids

The final category—preparing visual aids—is an important part of planning a research talk just as it is in planning a class lecture. Many of the rules given in Chapter 4 apply here as well. Most talks at professional meetings use slides or overhead transparencies, although videos, computer demonstrations, and other visuals are also used on occasion.

Preparing visuals for a short conference talk is especially challenging; there is always more information to cover than time to present it, and there is a tendency to make slides or overheads that are crowded. Don't make the common mistake of cramming too much material onto your visuals, no matter how important you feel it is for the audience to see all of the data. Force yourself to choose only the most important material and summarize it clearly. And try to use no more than one slide or overhead for each minute of the presentation, except for photos or very simple slides. Note that most types of visual aids serve best merely as supplements to the oral presentation, not as the primary means of transmitting information (Arthur, 1984).

To cope with the increasing demand for presentation time, many conferences are encouraging the use of posters as an alternative to oral presentations. Although some authors feel that a poster does not have the status of an oral presentation, conference organizers are changing the rules of presentation to make the poster option more attractive to authors. For example, many conferences now have dedicated time slots for poster sessions at times when there are no oral presentations; authors are requested to stand by their posters and explain their work to interested individuals. Furthermore, some conferences offer awards for the best poster presentations. Note that an excellent poster can draw the interest of a large number of people, and does not have the severe time constraints of an oral presentation. The rules for posters vary, but typical space limitations are about 1 m². Because poster presentations are often a combination of text, tables, pictorials, and oral discussion, a variety of considerations apply. These include issues in writing technical papers discussed in Chapter 9, concerns in designing visual aids discussed in Chapter 4, and issues in making oral presentations presented in this chapter. Be sure to use large lettering so that the text can be read by several people at once standing around the poster; this means limiting the amount of information that can be presented. There should also be a reasonable balance between text and other information such as tables, graphs, photographs, and drawings.

Whether you are preparing an oral delivery or a poster, the steps involved in organizing the presentation and designing the visual aids must be done iteratively. As with writing a paper, many research talks are built around the figures and tables. Don't hesitate to revise your outline as you develop your visual aids; many authors rework their presentations several times before they are satisfied.

Finally, you need to allow enough time to rehearse your presentation. This will enable you to get practice in delivering the talk and to get critical comments from others who may help you make improvements. Rehearsals are discussed in the section below on evaluation.

> *Exercise: Recall the sections in Chapter 4 on preparing lectures. What issues are common to both lecturing and giving research talks? In what ways do differences between lectures and research presentations require you to plan differently? Think about how you would plan a poster of one aspect of your current research. In what ways would the organization have to be different from that of a formal oral presentation?*

DELIVERING THE TALK

When the time of your presentation finally arrives, you should feel adequately prepared, but you may still be somewhat apprehensive about the talk. Rest assured that this is normal; confidence comes with experience. Although most of the work is behind you, there are still a number of details to consider about an effective delivery.

As with lecturing, your appearance and speaking style are of highest importance. Chapter 4 emphasized the need to speak loudly and clearly, to avoid nervous mannerisms, to maintain eye contact with the audience, and to provide a feeling of enthusiasm about the subject matter. These issues are just as important in presenting a talk on your research as they are in the classroom. Giving attention to such concerns requires that you know your talk well: being comfortable with the material can help reduce nervousness and allow you to focus on the delivery.

All of us have attended presentations where nervous mannerisms interfered with the delivery of the talk. In one conference talk we attended, the speaker was so nervous that he chose to stand next to the slide projector in the back of the room rather than face the audience. To make matters worse, he had a long pointer intended for use at the screen, but he aimed it in front of the slide projector lens. The audience had to endure a greatly magnified wobbling pointer that filled about a quarter of the screen. (Fortunately, the session chairperson succeeded in bringing him to the front of the room after a minute of this.) Even standing at the screen, laser pointers that are poorly aimed can be a problem; if you see your audience looking around at the ceiling or walls, check where your pointer is aimed. Also remember that laser pointers can magnify the effect of a nervously shaking hand.

Check the room and audio-visual equipment ahead of time. Most conference organizers have session assistants responsible for operating the equipment; you merely need to let the individual know what visuals you plan to use. Some conferences require advance notice for visual aids other than overhead transparencies or slides; there may be a separate fee in this case. If you are giving a seminar at another institution, be sure to discuss your needs for visual aids with your host.

On occasion, you will need to operate audio-visual equipment at a seminar you are giving or at another individual's talk. Be sure you know how to operate the equipment by trying it out ahead of time. And make sure you have a plan in case of a problem: Murphy's Law tells us that when a projector bulb is ready to burn out, it will do so at the most inopportune moment during a talk.

Speaking style is especially important at the beginning and end of the talk. Experienced speakers always begin strongly, with carefully chosen words and phrases that are well-articulated. You need to avoid any impression of boredom even if you have given the same talk seven times before. Visual aids are carefully synchronized with the talk all the way through. Finally, the ending should be especially clear and articulate, giving the audience plenty to think about. An otherwise good speech can leave a poor impression with the audience if the speaker appears to run out of energy. One of the worst ways to end a talk is to say "Well, I guess that's about it." Give the audience the impression that you have enough expertise, enthusiasm, and energy to go on for hours. (But don't.)

In contrast to oral delivery, a poster presentation can be much less formal. A well-timed speech is not necessary, but it is nevertheless a good idea to have a brief overview talk planned, perhaps a few minutes long. This talk will come in handy when an interested individual comes up to your poster and says "Tell me about your research." You must also be prepared to discuss details of your research which are merely highlighted in the poster. The tight time schedule of an oral session will not often permit lots of questions, but there is essentially no limit to the questions in a poster session. Use this to your advantage: be sufficiently knowledgeable and well-prepared to have a good, thorough discussion when the opportunity arises. Of course, there are always chances to discuss your research—whether presented in a formal talk or in a poster—during coffee breaks and other free periods at a conference. For this reason, most well-run conferences have scheduled lots of free time; take advantage of these periods to talk with people.

Given the complex organization of many national meetings, there are always some wrinkles; one of these is the time schedule for the talks. Almost every well-traveled professor has had the honor of being scheduled late in a lengthy meeting. One professor we know was scheduled *dead last* at a major week long conference. As Friday afternoon wore on, the audience grew smaller and smaller. To make matters worse, the session was running late. When it was finally our speaker's turn, the session chairman introduced him to a nearly empty room and then politely excused himself to catch a late afternoon flight. He might as well have said "Oh, and please turn off the lights on your way out."

Scheduling conference presentations is a difficult task. To claim that it is impossible to please everyone is an understatement. Consider the following statement by Baker (1991) published in *EOS,* the Transactions of the American Geophysical Union:

> *During the program planning for my last AGU annual meeting as SPR Magnetospheric section secretary, I realized the need to apologize to those who were scheduled...*

- ✦ on Monday or Friday (I also apologize to those who didn't want anything in the middle of the week)
- ✦ just before lunch or just after lunch
- ✦ just before coffee breaks or just after coffee breaks (I should also apologize to those whose talks were "too early in the morning" or "too late in the afternoon")

> *I certainly express regrets to those who felt their talk was scheduled in a room that was...*

- ✦ too small or too large
- ✦ too dark (sleepy audience) or too light (couldn't see third generation slides)
- ✦ too noisy or too quiet

> *I apologize to those who wanted only oral presentation but ended up giving a poster in Oceanography by putting an "O" in the wrong place on their abstract.*

Finally, I apologize to those scheduled just behind very good speakers (who made you look bad) or just behind very bad speakers (who cleared out the audience).

There was exactly one position at exactly the right time, in exactly the right room, and with exactly the right conditions. Of course, over the two years that I was secretary I assigned my own talk to that one ideal position.

It is apparent that conditions are sometimes far from ideal, ranging from inadequate room space to faulty audio-visual systems to scheduling problems. Successful speech-making requires not only speaking skills but also patience and amenability.

One final point about your talk: be sure to bring a few extra copies of your journal articles or other papers in case there are requests for more information. If your talk is well-received, you may have a number of individuals asking you to mail them additional papers. Similarly, you should feel free to request more information from other speakers whose work interests you.

Exercise: Consider how you would organize a one-hour seminar on your current research for a mixed group of undergraduates, graduate students, and faculty at another institution. Then consider how you would organize a ten-minute talk on the same topic for oral presentation at a conference where the audience is mostly advanced professionals in your discipline. What might be the objectives of each of these talks? How would the visual aids and verbal presentations differ?

EVALUATING YOUR PRESENTATION

Evaluations should be done both before the time of your talk, i.e., during a rehearsal, and also after the formal presentation. Get a colleague to listen to a rehearsal of your talk and offer critical comments. You may also wish to audio-tape or videotape the rehearsal for your own evaluation. Note that you should get critical comments from someone with a background in your field if you are presenting a talk to people in your discipline; comments from a lay person may be more valuable if your presentation is targeted to people not immersed in the field. In either case, you may want your auditor to use a "rehearsal checklist" like the one shown in Table 11-1.

You might consider presenting a seminar within your own department or research group as a rehearsal for a conference talk. This is almost always a good idea, as it allows you to practice your talk in front of a group. It should also be encouraged for graduate students and research staff who are planning conference presentations.

To the extent possible, these rehearsals should make use of the same visual aids you will be using for the presentation. This will help you to determine the

TABLE 11-1

Checklist for Rehearsing a Presentation

(after Mambert, 1968)

Each Question Receives a Rating of Excellent, Good, Fair, or Poor.

Presenter's Attitude
- Is there appropriate enthusiasm and sincerity?
- Does the presenter seem convinced?
- Does the presenter seem "real"?
- Is the presenter nonegocentric?
- Does the presenter suffer from stage fright?

Content
- Is the information valid and accurate?
- Does the presenter display full grasp of the subject?
- Does he appear to have a reserve, to know more than he is telling?

Objective-Thesis
- Is there a clear central idea?
- Is it sufficiently stressed?
- Does it run through the whole presentation?
- Is everything said and done relevant to it?

Structure
- Is there evidence of a single, main structure?
- Is it integrated, unified, and easy to follow?
- Is it sufficiently supported with appropriate detail?
- Is the detail concrete, valid, and specific?

Introduction
- Does it get attention?
- Does it say what the presentation contains?
- Does it relate the presentation to the audience's world?

Conclusion
- Does it tie the presentation together?
- Does it focus attention on the presentation as a unit?
- Does it relate back to the objective-thesis?
- Does it tell the audience what to do next?

Audience Awareness
- Does the presenter understand and empathize with them?
- Does the presenter speak from their point of view?
- Does the presenter use their language?
- Is there audience contact?

Aids
- Are they clear and easy to see and comprehend?
- Does each clearly support or reinforce its related idea?
- Is there a single visual motif-unified and harmonious?
- Is there too much detail?
- Are they "busy"?
- Are they exposed sufficiently for comprehension and retention?

Delivery
- Are language, diction, and pronunciation cultured and appropriate?
- Is the presenter poised and relaxed?
- Is the voice clear, well-modulated, relaxed, and in proper volume?
- Are there irrelevant gestures, actions, mannerisms, etc.?
- Has the presenter a good physical appearance?
- Does the presenter look at the audience—everyone—and maintain contact?
- Is the microphone used properly?

timing and appropriateness of the visuals. Be sure to rehearse your talk with enough lead time to make changes.

Evaluating your talk after the formal presentation can allow you to identify any weaknesses so that corrections can be made for future talks. It can also provide you with the satisfaction of a job well done. Most speakers get feedback on their presentation by talking with members of the audience whom they know well. In some instances, you may be able to arrange to have your speech videotaped. Whatever the evaluation method, be sure to follow up by exploring the strengths and weaknesses in your talk. In this way, you can use your experiences to the maximum extent to develop effective speaking techniques.

Overall, you will find that making effective presentations will be a great asset in developing a thriving research program. And there are few tasks expected of a professor that are more satisfying than giving a talk that commands the respect of a critical audience.

Several books on public speaking are available. The reader may wish to consult Brown and Atkins (1988), Carlile and Daniel (1987), Gilbert (1987), or Kenny (1982) for additional information.

SUMMARY

In this chapter, we have considered issues involved in presenting talks on your research. Preparing for the talk first requires you to define its purpose. You also need to get information about the audience that enables you to be sensitive to their interests and expectations. Next, you must organize the presentation and prepare your visual aids. Finally, you should rehearse the talk, preferably with one or more colleagues, and make improvements.

An effective delivery is necessary to achieve the goals of the presentation. Besides speaking loudly and clearly, you need to maintain eye contact with the audience and show enthusiasm for the material. The visual aids must be clear and synchronized with the talk. Strong beginnings and endings are especially important.

Finally, evaluating your talk after the formal presentation can enable you to make changes for your next talk. Evaluations can sometimes be provided by colleagues in the audience whom you know well.

With some adaptation, many of these suggestions also apply to poster presentations. However, the informality of poster sessions often means more flexibility—and more time during the session to discuss your results with interested colleagues.

With practice, speaking on your research in front of a group can be a rewarding experience: capturing the attention of an audience of experts can be especially gratifying. Most important, becoming an effective speaker is likely to change the way you feel about yourself, thus enhancing your performance as a faculty member in many dimensions.

REFERENCES

Arthur, R.H., *The Engineer's Guide to Better Communication*, Glenview, IL: Scott, Foresman and Company, 1984.

Baker, D.N., An apologia for papers poorly scheduled, *EOS, Transactions of the American Geophysical Union, Vol. 72*, p. 84, 1991.

Brown, G. and M. Atkins, *Effective Teaching in Higher Education*, London: Routledge, 1988.

Carlile, C.S. and A.V. Daniel, *Project Text for Public Speaking*, New York, NY: Harper and Row, 1987.

Gilbert, J., Pronunciation and listening comprehension, in J. Morley, editor, *Current Perspectives on Pronunciation: Practices Anchored in Theory*, Washington, DC: Teachers of English to Speakers of Other Languages, pp. 33–39, 1987.

Kenny, P., *A Handbook of Public Speaking for Scientists and Engineers*, Bristol, England: Adam Hilger Ltd., 1982.

Mambert, W.A., *Presenting Technical Ideas: A Guide to Audience Communication*, New York, NY: John Wiley and Sons, 1968.

12

CONDUCTING GRADUATE SEMINAR PROGRAMS

INTRODUCTION

We have covered quite a bit of material on teaching and research to arrive at this chapter. In a sense, graduate seminars are the endpoint of our education system: a graduate seminar is often the last formal classroom experience of our Ph.D. students. In this chapter, we pull together information from many of the previous chapters to discuss this important educational tool.

A seminar program can be valuable for achieving a variety of goals not possible with a conventional lecture or discussion class format. But what differentiates a seminar from these types of classes? The *American Heritage Dictionary* defines the term as *a small group of advanced students in a college or graduate school engaged in original research under the guidance of a professor who meets regularly with them for reports and discussions.* Although many seminars fit this definition, some seminars are neither small nor advanced; they often cover topics other than research. In fact, a recent survey of several faculty members at Carnegie Mellon University who run seminar programs indicates that no unique definition exists (University Teaching Center, 1988). Rather, there appear to be a number of types of seminars: some have considerable overlap with what is considered a lecture or discussion class, while others are quite distinct.

In this chapter, we describe how seminars can be used to further the educational process and give examples of several types of programs with an emphasis on research seminars. These examples do not represent an exhaustive list; nevertheless, the ideas presented here are intended to provide guidance whether you plan to start a new seminar program or merely provide suggestions for existing programs.

This chapter is divided into two major sections. First, we discuss the objectives of seminar programs, emphasizing the ways in which such programs can help individual participants as well as an entire research group. Then we discuss how you might organize and conduct seminars. Much of the discussion here focuses on programs organized by small research groups, e.g., fewer than a half dozen faculty members with their graduate students and staff, although some of the information also pertains to seminars for entire departments. Similarly, some of the information applies to seminars for purposes other than research, and to undergraduates as well as graduate students. Parts of the chapter are based on work at Carnegie Mellon by Fenton (1992).

OBJECTIVES OF GRADUATE SEMINARS

Most graduate seminar programs oriented toward research are set up to fulfill a number of objectives. Three of the most important include helping graduate students acquire the knowledge and skills to conduct independent research, helping them to develop an appreciation for the diversity of topics within their discipline, and enabling all members of a research group to interact and get to know one another. In this section, we consider each of these objectives. In addition, we present a few examples of seminar programs whose objectives do not involve research.

Acquire the Knowledge and Skills to Conduct Research

In Chapter 7, we discussed five general steps in planning and conducting Ph.D. research. Clearly, a seminar program can go a long way in helping graduate students acquire the knowledge and skills to become independent researchers and complete these steps successfully.

By referring to each of the five steps, we can write examples of research skills to be acquired by graduate students:

+ To identify important research questions and specific hypotheses to be tested

+ To identify the experimental and theoretical research methods used to test the hypotheses

+ To apply the methods and interpret the results

+ To communicate the results orally and in writing

+ To complete the thesis, final examination, and other requirements for the Ph.D.

Many seminar programs focus on a subset of these goals. For example, some departments offer seminar programs devoted entirely to understanding the current literature in order to identify key research questions in a discipline. This can help a beginning student choose a thesis topic. Other programs are oriented solely around research methods. It is clear that all of these skills must be acquired to some extent, either through a seminar program or some other means, if the students are eventually to embark on their own dissertation research.

By focusing on some specific issues, we can see how seminars might provide practical help to students. For example, all graduate students in science and engineering need to be able to think critically about a topic. Although many lecture courses also attempt to promote critical thinking, the format of a seminar is far more conducive to developing and sharpening this skill: the small group size and close interactions in most seminars make it necessary for a student to keep up with the dialogue (Andrews and Dietz, 1982). As another example, a seminar format can be used to help students develop skills in asking good questions. Well-posed questions can serve as a catalyst for promoting active discussion and can draw other members of the audience into the learning process, as discussed in Chapter 3. In addition, seminars can help students to develop higher-level thought processes such as synthesis, analysis, and evaluation (Bloom et al., 1956; see Chapter 1). Finally, many seminars involve presentations by the students, enabling them to gain practice in addressing a group.

This last skill is often viewed as a key focus of student-oriented seminar programs. Despite the importance of oral presentations to their future careers, many graduate students have mixed feelings about getting up in front of a group. On one hand, they would like the opportunity to demonstrate their contributions to the research field; most graduate students work hard on their research, and it is only fair to give them an audience. On the other hand, some of them have never given a professional talk before, and they may be intimidated by the prospect of talking in front of their peers and the faculty. The solution to this problem is to create an appropriate seminar environment: the speaker must feel that the audience is genuinely interested and supportive of her efforts.

Develop an Appreciation for the Diversity of Research Topics within a Discipline

Graduate students embarking on their first research project are often surprised to discover the tortuous path that research may take. Results of preliminary experiments often indicate that the researcher must delve into new topic areas if there is to be hope of making progress; by the time a project is nearing completion, the direction of the work may have changed several times. Coping with this problem requires that graduate students have an appreciation for many topic areas within a discipline besides their own immediate research needs.

Especially important, they must develop a curiosity that provides motivation for learning about new topics as the need arises.

We saw in Chapters 3 and 4 that discussion classes and lectures can provide students with a sampling of topic areas within a discipline. A seminar format enables the students to acquire information at a more advanced level, and to explore particular issues in depth. For example, the instructor of a graduate seminar may frequently change the direction of the discussion in response to questions and comments from the students; the small size of most seminars allows this flexibility. The informality of a seminar also makes it easy to incorporate discussions of recent discoveries into the program. To enable discussions that go into considerable detail, many seminars are based on the assumption that the audience has already achieved a certain level of understanding of the discipline.

Promote Interactions among Members of a Research Group

The final objective of a graduate seminar program is to provide an effective vehicle for bringing together members of a department or research group. This is particularly true of a small research group, where student and faculty presentations can help members of the group to understand many of the current problems of their colleagues. Such presentations can help the entire group be more productive: each student will almost certainly be relying on other individuals during the course of the research. For example, some of the faculty members in the group might be on the student's qualifying exam or thesis defense committees, and other graduate students may provide useful critiques of the data or assistance with operation of equipment. Laboratory technicians or postdoctoral fellows may assist in similar ways. A series of well-presented seminars can therefore lay the groundwork for enabling cooperative work among group members.

Bringing the group together on a regular basis can also help to promote collegiality. In Chapter 7, we stressed the importance of maintaining a graduate school environment which is conducive to productivity. Just as in any organization, individuals need to have colleagues with whom they can interact on a personal as well as professional level. A seminar can help simply by bringing together members of a group or department so they can get to know each other better.

Seminars for Purposes other than Research

Most graduate seminars are oriented toward research, and thus much of the information is usually related to new developments in a topic area. However, some graduate seminars are oriented to communicate well-established concepts rather than knowledge at the cutting edge of a discipline. For example, the discussion may concern a textbook of advanced technical concepts or a critique of a well-known scientific work. The same material might otherwise be used in a lecture course format, but a seminar will permit the participants to probe certain concepts in more detail and with greater flexibility.

As another example, some seminars are set up to assist graduate students with their responsibilities as teaching assistants, discussed in Chapter 6. The goal of these seminars might be acquisition of knowledge and skills on grading papers, tutoring students, and conducting review sessions.

As a third example, some schools have set up seminars to familiarize students with the responsibilities of being a faculty member, covering a wide variety of topics in both teaching and research. Panel discussions involving several faculty members who can provide differing perspectives on these topics is quite appropriate for a seminar program; conveying this information via a single speaker in a lecture format would not be as effective.

It is clear that graduate seminars serve many functions that can benefit the individual members of a research group and also the group as a whole. We now consider possible ways in which faculty can organize and conduct seminars to achieve the goals described above.

> *Exercise: Consider seminar programs on research in which you participated when you were a graduate student. To what extent did these programs attempt to achieve the three objectives discussed above (acquire knowledge and skills, develop appreciation for diversity of research topics, and promote interactions)? Did they attempt to achieve other objectives? Now consider existing research seminar programs at your current institution. In what ways do the goals of the current programs differ from those of your graduate student experience? Are there aspects of your graduate student seminars that could be adopted to improve programs at your current institution? Conducting seminar programs requires iteration and experimentation—making use of past experiences can help.*

ORGANIZING AND CONDUCTING SEMINARS

Seminar programs may be designed in a variety of ways and may use a number of presentation formats, depending on the desired goals. In this section, we first discuss the organization of seminars by considering various categories of speakers who will lead the group. We then discuss organization of seminars by subject matter. Finally, we summarize several possible formats for conducting the individual seminars; we conclude the chapter by discussing how anecdotes and personal experiences can make a seminar relevant and interesting.

Organizing Seminars by Speaker

In general, seminars may be given by faculty and research staff, by students, and by visitors. Each category has particular strengths depending on the ultimate objectives of the program.

Seminars by faculty and research staff are generally intended to convey information to the group about subject areas of common interest or topics of research being pursued within the group. It is apparent that this type of program, when addressing research, can help beginning students choose a research topic and thesis advisor. Such a program can also help experienced members of a group serve as role models for newer members, providing examples of how to conduct research, lead discussions, or make technical presentations. Of course, talks by senior members of a group will not be perfect, but students can learn by negative example as well as positive. Faculty and experienced research staff can also use the seminar to summarize major accomplishments and relate personal experiences, providing the students with a sense of purpose and direction. This issue is discussed later in this chapter.

Seminars by graduate students have some goals in common with those by faculty and staff: both can convey detailed information to the group. However, student-run seminars can provide graduate students with experience in making oral presentations or leading discussions; in many cases, a seminar program is the student's first experience in discussing research results before a group. Experienced members of the group can provide constructive criticism to the student, enabling prompt feedback on the work or the presentation. In fact, a well-run seminar can provide students with a more critical audience than they will encounter at many national meetings. Students who have the benefit of an alert and probing audience in their own department will thus be prepared for presentations elsewhere.

Finally, seminars by visitors can provide opportunities for the group to learn about topics outside of the normal range of expertise of the department. These may include information about new research results, perhaps from other universities, or they may involve discussions of experiences outside academia such as in government or private industry. Such seminars may be especially valuable to students making career decisions, e.g., by acquainting students with potential employers.

Although seminar programs are often designed around one of these three categories, some programs incorporate combinations of speakers. For example, many seminar series include presentations primarily by members of a research group, but often take advantage of opportunities for talks by visitors when they are on campus.

Organizing Seminars by Subject Matter

Graduate seminars can cover a wide range of topics—both in research and in areas of well-established knowledge. Let us consider these two categories as separate entities, focusing on ways to organize seminars for each.

Seminars on current research have become popular primarily because informal discussions provide an excellent format for probing into the details of new knowledge. Pushing forward our understanding of a topic demands creativity and imagination on one hand, but also requires critical thought on the other.

The freeform discussion that occurs during a seminar is useful for both. However, creative discussions and critical discussions should not occur simultaneously since creativity will be stifled in a critical atmosphere.

Seminars covering research should be both backward-looking and forward-looking. Considering the past is important: each member of the audience perceives the material in light of his own background. A well-run seminar will bring out these varied backgrounds during the discussion, letting the group share the collective wealth of experiences. Research seminars should also be forward-looking, probing the impact of the new knowledge. Such seminars involve shared teaching and learning experiences—the instructor is learning along with the students, and the students are teaching along with the instructor at alternate times during the discussion. If the discussion is successful, the overall output of ideas from the group should be much greater than the collection of ideas that would have been generated by individual efforts.

Most graduate seminars on research include students with a wide range of experiences. To allow new students time to get used to the group, many programs begin with seminars by the faculty or experienced students. These programs eventually encourage participation by first-year graduate students, perhaps by making presentations on the research of others, their own preliminary research, or their past experiences (e.g., in the case of students who have worked full-time before entering the graduate program). Of course, not all research seminars need to cover results; good discussions can be conducted simply on hypotheses and ways to test them.

These ideas suggest that research seminars can be organized around current findings within a group, new ideas for research by members of the group, discussions of the research of others, or presentations by visitors. Combinations of these topics are often used for variety.

Seminars on topics other than research, e.g., discussions of advanced textbook concepts or critiques of well-known scientific works, may be organized in a similar way as research seminars, and either faculty members or students may run the discussion. However, there is an important difference between research and non-research seminars: there is usually a greater flow of information from faculty members to students in non-research seminars, since the material is generally well-known by at least one faculty member. This may be true even if the discussion is run by a student.

For example, in one series of seminars at our school, a student was asked to critique Rachel Carson's *Silent Spring* and lead a discussion on the critique. The seminar benefitted from the guidance of faculty members who had read published interpretations of this work. Similarly, discussions of other important scientific works should have input from those who are familiar with them; without such guidance, the participants may not be able to take advantage of the wealth of information already established by others. This suggests the importance of choosing items for discussion where there already exists some expertise. Recall that Chapter 3 emphasized the need to know the subject matter well in order for a discussion to achieve its goals.

Similar statements may be made about seminars on other non-research topics, such as developing the knowledge and skills to be a teaching assistant. Individuals with extensive experience can provide valuable input to the discussion. In this case, senior graduate students who have served as teaching assistants may provide better guidance in seminars than faculty members.

No matter who runs the seminars and what they are about, the format for conducting the seminars must be carefully planned. We now discuss ways of conducting these seminar programs.

Conducting Seminars

Styles within seminars vary considerably. At one extreme, a seminar may be a formal lecture by an individual speaker without much audience interaction. At the other extreme, a seminar may be a freeform discussion without much guidance. Most seminars fall somewhere in between. Often, we call formal lectures "seminars" if they are part of a program that includes less formal interactions, or when the talk is a stand-alone event not connected with a formal program.

The best position along this continuum is determined mainly by the objectives of the seminar. The subject matter, characteristics of the audience, and characteristics of the speaker are also important. For example, a seminar intended primarily to communicate factual information might be conducted as a formal lecture; this is especially true if the speaker is a visitor to the department and does not know the audience, or if the group is large. If the goal is to have a student develop skills at leading a discussion, a less formal approach is desired. Freeform discussions are often most successful in small groups; experience suggests a maximum of perhaps ten persons, although even some large classes have used discussion techniques successfully. Many of the issues in Chapter 3 on leading discussions and in Chapter 11 on delivering presentations are relevant here.

Most seminars are set up to probe some topic in depth. But how can the audience be educated in the details of the topic so that the diversity of their backgrounds can be tapped to the fullest extent in a discussion? One common format is to begin with a presentation followed by a discussion of the topic. In some cases, written material can be distributed to participants in advance, allowing the seminar to be devoted entirely to discussion.

Freeform discussion can be a useful tool to enable the flow of creative or critical ideas. However, guidance from the seminar leader is usually necessary to keep the discussion on track. To facilitate such guidance, many seminars begin by listing several objectives. Participants may then be reminded that all comments should be related in some way to achieving the objectives.

Some experienced faculty members at our institution have developed procedures that greatly help their seminars. For example, in one series of student research presentations, each student in the audience is asked to write a brief critique of the speaker's presentation and discussion. The critiques are then given to the speaker and the faculty advisor, and the speaker must respond to the points raised by discussing them with the advisor. With this format, the audience listens actively to the presentation, and the speaker receives a lot of feedback.

In another program, each beginning student writes a research proposal for distribution in advance, then discusses the proposal at the seminar. The proposal may eventually become the student's thesis topic, although that is not necessarily the objective.

Some guest seminar programs also involve written assignments. In one such program, students must write a critique of each presentation within a few days of the seminar. Published papers related to the seminar topic may also be circulated for comment. The best critiques are circulated in class and discussed the following week. Some brave faculty members even hand out their own research publications for a critique by the students.

It is apparent that a wide range of styles can be used for conducting seminars. Consider your objectives and other factors discussed above and get advice from your colleagues. Also discuss ideas for seminars with the students who will be involved. Whether you are beginning a new seminar program or bringing fresh ideas to an existing program, your input can have a significant positive impact on your research group.

Bringing a Subject to Life:
Use of Anecdotes and Personal Experiences

Sharing relevant personal experiences can help to gain the attention of almost any audience. However, this approach is particularly useful in seminars, where hard-to-grasp concepts on the cutting edge of a discipline may require close attention and careful thought to be understood. The informality of most seminars makes it easy to weave anecdotes into the discussion. Furthermore, many seminars provide a setting where faculty members can discuss their reasons for engaging in a particular research project; enthusiasm about a subject can be contagious. A seminar which does a good job of combining technical detail with interesting personal experiences can make a lasting impact on the audience. Consider the following experience related by a senior faculty member at our institution.

One cold February morning, a barge on the Ohio River was passing under the Interstate 79 bridge near Pittsburgh. The bridge had just been completed five months earlier. The captain of the barge noticed a crack in the bridge, perhaps three inches wide and several feet long. On his return trip underneath the bridge a few hours later, he noticed that the crack had lengthened substantially. Alarmed, he notified PennDOT (the Pennsylvania Department of Transportation). PennDOT sent inspectors to the scene and immediately closed the bridge.

An in-depth study of the problem began. Because the bridge served as a major traffic artery, rapid repair and reopening of the bridge was of highest priority. The same firm that designed the bridge was brought in to analyze the problem, and the results were reported quickly: the crack had occurred in a weld made during the fabrication of the large steel plate flange. The crack, although initially small, progressed until it eventually broke through the entire flange and had progressed through the full web of the bridge. Few people know how close the bridge was to collapse when the crack was discovered.

Fixing the problem was a challenge. A jack was needed to pull the two pieces of the bridge together so that the repair could proceed, but there was no easy way to support the jack. Three ideas were considered. First, a barge could be brought in as a jacking platform; this idea was ruled out because the river had become partially frozen. Second, a new truss could be built and carried across the bridge to serve as a platform. This idea wasn't feasible because the added weight of the truss could have collapsed the bridge. Third, new plates could be added to either side of the crack, and the jack could be installed horizontally between the plates. The third option was adopted.

Although it seemed like a reasonable solution, the repair procedure was untested. A panel of experts, convened to oversee the repair job, therefore recommended that a computer analysis be conducted to evaluate the viability of the repair method. Such computer analyses are difficult to arrange on short notice, however, and PennDOT was pressing to begin the repairs.

Fortunately, a young employee of the Pittsburgh-based firm in charge of the repair work had recently completed his M.S. thesis—on precisely the type of computer analysis that was needed. The computer cards for the analysis program were at his family's home over a hundred miles away in Williamsport, Pennsylvania. This would not normally pose a problem, except that there were problems with the weather: a raging blizzard had begun, keeping planes grounded and closing most of the roads into central Pennsylvania. The repair of the I-79 bridge now depended on getting those computer cards from Williamsport to Pittsburgh.

Enter the Pennsylvania State Police. Working in shifts to avoid exhaustion, state troopers brought the employee from Pittsburgh to Williamsport and back again in their patrol cars, inching over snow-covered roads through the Pennsylvania mountains. With the computer cards safely in Pittsburgh, the program was installed and the analysis was conducted; the results confirmed the soundness of the proposed repair procedure. The method was quickly approved, and repair work began. The bridge was opened for traffic three months later.

Not every graduate can expect that kind of attention to his thesis. Furthermore, not every graduate can expect that his thesis results will be used in a major project for the benefit of thousands of people. Nevertheless, a clear message emerges from the story: a well-planned and thorough research project *can* have a real impact, and this possibility makes it worth the effort.

> *Exercise: Think of a landmark article in your discipline that greatly affected research for a number of years and for which others have published commentary and critiques. How could such an article be used in a seminar discussion to demonstrate certain principles of research? Think about the specific objectives of such a seminar, who would lead the discussion, how the discussion would be structured, and how the success of the seminar could be evaluated. Consider conducting such a discussion with your research group if the opportunity arises.*

SUMMARY

Because of their informality and flexibility, graduate seminars are good forums to present and discuss advanced concepts. For seminar programs on research, several objectives are possible. One key objective is to enable graduate students to develop the knowledge and skills to conduct independent research. Another objective is to provide the students with an appreciation of the diversity of research topic areas within their discipline. Seminars can also provide a vehicle for bringing a research group together so members can get to know one another.

Many research seminar programs are organized around current findings within a group or department. However, a similar format can be used to discuss the previously published research results or ideas for future research projects, or to enable visitors to campus to present their work.

Seminars are also useful for probing advanced concepts in areas other than research. Examples include discussions of technical concepts in a textbook or critiques of well-known scientific works.

A variety of formats exists for seminar programs. They may be highly formal or very informal. They can be led by faculty, research staff, or students. The structure and amount of material presented can vary greatly, depending on the goals of the program.

Overall, graduate seminar programs are important to a research group. They can help members of the group grow in many ways, and they provide a regular forum for getting together—for social as well as technical benefit. It is well worth the effort to organize and continually strive to improve them.

REFERENCES

Andrews, J.D.W., and D.A. Dietz, The self-steering seminar: Improving classroom communication through student participation in videotape feedback, *Journal of Higher Education, Vol. 53,* pp. 552–567, 1982.

Bloom, B.S., J.T. Hastings, and G.F. Madaus, *Taxonomy of Educational Objectives: The Classification of Educational Goals, Handbook 1, Cognitive Domain,* New York, NY: McCay, 1956.

Fenton, E., Seminars, Honors Papers, Theses, and Dissertations (Chapter 7), unpublished manuscript on Teaching in Colleges and Universities, Carnegie Mellon University, 1992.

University Teaching Center, *Conducting Seminars: A Set of Case Studies,* Carnegie Mellon University, 1988.

BIBLIOGRAPHY

Allen, R.R., Encouraging reflection in teaching assistants, in Nyquist, J.D., R.D. Abbott, D.H. Wulff, and J. Sprague, editors, *Preparing the Professoriate of Tomorrow to Teach*, Dubuque, Iowa: Kendall/Hunt Publishing, pp. 313–317, 1991.

American Association of University Professors, *AAUP Policy Documents and Reports*, Washington, D.C., 1977.

Anderson, J.R., Skill acquisition: Compilation of weak-method problem solutions, *Psychological Review, Vol. 92, No. 2*, pp. 192–210, 1987.

Anderson, J.R., *Cognitive Psychology and its Implications*, New York: W.H. Freeman, 1990.

Andrews, J.D.W., and D.A. Dietz, The self-steering seminar: Improving classroom communication through student participation in videotape feedback, *Journal of Higher Education, Vol. 53*, pp. 552–567, 1982.

Arthur, R.H., *The Engineer's Guide to Better Communication*, Glenview, Illinois: Scott Foresman and Company, 1984.

Baker, D.N., An apologia for papers poorly scheduled, *EOS, Transactions of the American Geophysical Union, Vol. 72*, p. 84, 1991.

Balian, E.S., *How to Design, Analyze, and Write Doctoral and Masters Research, 2nd edition*, Lanham, Maryland: University Press of America, 1988.

Bennett, B., B. Joyce, and B. Showers, Synthesis of research on staff development: A future study and a state-of-the-art analysis, *Educational Leadership, Vol. 45*, pp. 77–87, 1987.

Berelson, B. *Graduate Education in the United States.* New York: McGraw-Hill, 1960.

Blanton, J.S., Midwifing the dissertation, *Teaching of Psychology, Vol. 10*, pp. 16–19, 1977.

Bloom, B.S., J.T. Hastings, and G.F. Madaus, *Taxonomy of Educational Objectives: The Classification of Educational Goals, Handbook 1, Cognitive Domain*, New York: McCay, 1956.

Boehrer, J. and M. Chevrier, Professor and teaching assistant: Making the most of a working relationship, in Nyquist, J.D., R.D. Abbott, D.H. Wulff, and J. Sprague, editors, *Preparing the Professoriate of Tomorrow to Teach*, Dubuque, Iowa: Kendall/Hunt Publishing, pp. 326–330, 1991.

Boud, D., J. Dunn, and E. Hegarty-Hazel, *Teaching in Laboratories*, Surrey, England: The Society for Research into Higher Education and NFER-NELSON, The University, Guildford, 1986.

Bransford, J.D., *Human Cognition*, Belmont, California: Wadsworth, 1979.

Braskamp, L.A., Colleague evaluation of instruction, *Faculty Development and Evaluation in Higher Education, Vol. 4*, pp. 1–9, 1978.

Briggs, L.J. and W.W. Wager, *Handbook of Procedures for the Design of Instruction*, Englewood Cliffs, New Jersey: Educational Technology Publications, 1981.

Brown, G. and M. Atkins, *Effective Teaching in Higher Education*, London: Routledge, 1988.

Brown, R.D. and L.A. Krager, Ethical issues in graduate education: Faculty and student responsibilities, *Journal of Higher Education, Vol. 56*, pp. 403–418, 1985.

Canfield, A., *Learning Styles Inventory Manual*, Ann Arbor, Michigan: Humanics Media, 1980.

Carlile, C.S. and A.V. Daniel, *Project Text for Public Speaking*, New York: Harper and Row, 1987.

Chickering, A.W. and Z.F. Gamson, Seven principles for good practice in undergraduate education, *AAHE Bulletin, Vol. 39*, pp. 3–7, 1987.

Civikly, J.M. and D.M. Muchisky, A collaborative approach to ITA training, in Nyquist, J.D., R.D. Abbott, D.H. Wulff, and J. Sprague, editors, *Preparing the Professoriate of Tomorrow to Teach*, Dubuque, Iowa: Kendall/Hunt Publishing, pp. 356–360, 1991.

Clark, A.T., The influence of adult developmental processes upon the educational experiences of doctoral students, Doctoral Dissertation, The Humanistic Psychology Institute, p. 196, 1980.

Claxton, C.S. and P.H. Murrell, *Learning Styles: Implications for Improving Educational Practices*, Washington, D.C.: Association for the Study of Higher Education, 1987.

Clegg, V.L. and W.E. Cashin, *Improving Multiple Choice Tests*, Idea Paper Number 16, Kansas: Center for Faculty Evaluation and Development, Kansas State University, 1986.

Cleveland, W.S., *The Elements of Graphing Data*, Monterey, California: Wadsworth Advanced Books and Software, 1989.

Cohen, J.B., Writing that first proposal, *Graduating Engineer, Vol. 10*, pp. 76–78, 1988.

Cohen, P.A., Student ratings of instruction and student achievement: A meta-analysis of multisection validity studies, *Review of Educational Research, Vol. 51*, pp. 281–309, 1981.

Cohen, P.A. and W.J. McKeachie, The role of colleagues in the evaluation of college teaching, *Improving College and University Teaching, Vol. 28*, pp. 147–154, 1980.

Collett, J., Reaching African-American students in the classroom, in L. Hilsen, editor, *To Improve the Academy, Vol. 9*, Stillwater, Oklahoma: New Forums Press, Inc., pp. 177–188, 1990.

Connell, R.W., How to supervise a Ph.D., *Vestes, Vol. 28*, pp. 38–42, 1985.

Cooper, S. and C. Heenan, *Preparing, Designing, and Leading Workshops: A Humanistic Approach*, New York: Van Nostrand Reinhold Company, pp. 56–103, 1980.

Cortes, C., Chicano culture, experience, and learning: Extracting learning styles from social/cultural diversity. *Studies of Five American minorities*, Southwest Teachers Corps Network, ERIC Document No. ED 158 952.

Cross, K.P. and T.A. Angelo, *Classroom Assessment Techniques: A Handbook for Faculty*, Ann Arbor, Michigan: National Center for Research to Improve Postsecondary Teaching and Learning, The University of Michigan, 1988.

Cusanovich, M. and M. Gilliland, Mentoring: The faculty-graduate student relationship, *Communicator, Vol. 24*, pp. 1–3, 1991.

Davis, B.G., M. Scriven, and S. Thomas, *The Evaluation of Composition Instruction*, Inverness, California: Edgepress, p.7, 1981.

Davis, B.G., *Tools for Teaching*, San Fransisco: Jossey-Bass, p.5, 1993.

Dickinson, L., Credibility, *The Teaching Professor, Vol. 5*, pp. 3–4, 1991.

Eble, K.E., *The Craft of Teaching*, San Francisco: Jossey-Bass, 1976.

Eison, J., Confidence in the classroom: Ten maxims for new teachers, *College Teaching, Vol. 38*, pp. 21–25, 1990.

Erickson, B.L. and D.W. Strommer, *Teaching College Freshmen*, San Francisco: Jossey-Bass, 1991.

Erskine, J.A., M.R. Leenders, and L.A. Mauffette Leenders, *Teaching with Cases*, London, Ontario: School of Business Administration, University of Western Ontario, 1981.

Fenton, E., *In Most Cases It's the Message That Counts, Not the Medium: An Analysis of Research About the Use of Media in Education*, Pittsburgh, Pennsylvania: Carnegie Mellon, The University Teaching Center, 1990.

Fenton, E., Seminars, Honors Papers, Theses, and Dissertations (Chapter 7), unpublished manuscript on Teaching in Colleges and Universities, Carnegie Mellon University, 1992.

Fenton, E., Evaluation: Writing Problem Sets, Quizzes, Examinations, and Paper Assignments (Chapter 8), and Grades and Grading (Chapter 9), unpublished manuscript on Teaching in Colleges and Universities, Carnegie Mellon University, 1992.

Forscher, B.K., Rules for reviewers, *Science, Vol. 150*, pp. 319–321, 1965.

Garner, B., Southeast Asian culture and classroom culture. *College Teaching, Vol. 37*, pp. 127–130, 1989.

Gibbs, G., S. Habeshaw, and T. Habeshaw, *53 Interesting Things To Do In Your Lectures*, Bristol, England: Technical and Educational Services Ltd., 1987.

Gilbert, J., Pronunciation and listening comprehension, in J. Morley, editor, *Current Perspectives on Pronunciation: Practices Anchored in Theory*, Washington, D.C.: Teachers of English to Speakers of Other Languages, pp. 33–39, 1987.

Grasha, A.F., Using traditional versus naturalistic approaches to assessing learning styles in college teaching, *Journal on Excellence in College Teaching, Vol. 1*, pp. 23–28, 1990.

Gronlund, N.E., *Measurement and Evaluation in Teaching, 5th edition*, New York: Macmillan, 1985.

Guerriero, S.J., Multicultural awareness in the classroom, *The Journal of Staff, Program, and Organization Development, Vol. 8*, pp. 167–173, 1990.

Hall, R.M. and B.R. Sandler, The classroom climate: A chilly one for women, *Project on the Status and Education of Women*, Washington, D.C.: Association of American Colleges, 1982.

Hamilton, D.P., Research papers: Who's uncited now?, *Science, Vol. 251*, p. 25, 1991.

Hammons, J.O. and J.R. Barnsley, Everything you need to know about developing a grading plan for your course (well, almost), *Journal on Excellence in College Teaching, Vol. 3*, pp. 51–68, 1992.

Hart, H. and D.F. Lawler, A Guide to the Preparation of Engineering Theses and Dissertations, unpublished report, Department of Civil Engineering, University of Texas at Austin, October 1989.

Harte, J., *Consider a Spherical Cow: A Course in Environmental Problem Solving*, Mill Valley, California: University Science Books, p. 21, 1988.

Hartnett, R.T., Environments for advanced learning, in J. Katz and R.T. Hartnett, editors, *Scholars in the Making*, Cambridge, Massachusetts: Ballinger Publishing Co., pp. 49–84, 1976.

Hatten, J., Why do students fail?, *The Teaching Professor, Vol. 3*, pp. 1–2, 1989.

Hopkins, K.D. and J.C. Stanley, *Educational and Psychological Measurement and Evaluation, 7th edition*, Englewood Cliffs, New Jersey: Prentice-Hall, 1990.

Jacks, P., D.E. Chubin, A.L. Porter, and T. Connolly, The ABCs of ABDs: A study of incomplete doctorates, *Improving College and University Teaching, Vol. 31*, pp. 8–15, 1981.

Johnson, D.W., *Educational Psychology*, Englewood Cliffs, New Jersey: Prentice-Hall, 1979.

Jones, D.J. and B.C. Watson, *"High Risk" Students in Higher Education: Future Trends*, ASHE-ERIC Higher Education Report 3, Washington, D.C.: The George Washington University, 1990.

Katz, J., Development of the mind, in J. Katz and R.T. Hartnett, editors, *Scholars in the Making*, Cambridge, Massachusetts: Ballinger Publishing Co., pp. 107–126, 1976.

Kenny, P., *A Handbook of Public Speaking for Scientists and Engineers*, Bristol, England: Adam Hilger Ltd., 1982.

Kolb, D.A., *Learning Style Inventory*, Boston: McBer and Company, 1976.

Koshland, D.E., An editor's quest (II), *Science, Vol. 227*, p. 249, 1985.

Landes, K.K., A scrutiny of the abstract, *Bulletin of the American Association of Petroleum Geologists, Vol. 50*, p. 1992, 1966.

Levin, T. and R. Long, *Effective Instruction*, Alexandria, Virginia: Association for Supervision and Curriculum Development, 1981.

Levinson-Rose, J.L. and R.J. Menges, Improving college teaching: A critical review of research, *Review of Educational Research, Vol. 51*, pp. 403–434, 1981.

Light, R.J., *The Harvard Assessment Seminars: Explorations with Students and Faculty about Teaching, Learning, and Student Life*, First Report, Cambridge, Massachusetts: Harvard University Graduate School of Education and Kennedy School of Government, 1990.

Lowman, J., *Mastering the Techniques of Teaching*, San Francisco: Jossey-Bass, 1984.

Lowther, M.S., J.S. Clark, and G.G. Martens, *Preparing Course Syllabi for Improved Communication*, Ann Arbor, Michigan: National Center for Research to Improve Postsecondary Teaching and Learning (NCRIPTAL), 1989.

MacGregor, J., Collaborative learning: Shared inquiry as a process of reform, in M.D. Svinicki, editor, *The Changing Face of College Teaching*, Number 42 in the series *New Directions for Teaching and Learning*, San Fransisco: Jossey-Bass, pp. 19–30, 1990.

Madsen, D., *Successful Dissertations and Theses*, San Fransisco: Jossey-Bass, 1990.

Maimon, E.P., Talking to strangers, *College Composition and Communication*, *Vol. 30*, pp. 364–369, 1979.

Mambert, W.A., *Presenting Technical Ideas: A Guide to Audience Communication*, New York: John Wiley and Sons, Inc., 1968.

Maurice, K., Cultural styles of thinking and speaking in the classroom, in P. Byrd, editor, *Teaching Across Cultures in the University ESL Program*, Washington, D.C.: National Association for Foreign Student Affairs, pp. 39–50, 1986.

Mayer, R.E., Instructional variables in text processing, in A. Flammer and W. Kintsch, editors, *Discourse Planning*, Amsterdam: North-Holland, 1982.

McKeachie, W.J., Improving lectures by understanding students' information processing, in W.J. McKeachie, editor, *Learning, Cognition, and College Teaching*, San Francisco: Jossey-Bass, pp. 25–85, 1980.

McKeachie, W.J., P.R. Pintrich, Y. Lin, and D.A.F. Smith, *Teaching and Learning in the College Classroom: A Review of the Research Literature*, Ann Arbor, Michigan: National Center for Research to Improve Postsecondary Teaching and Learning (NCRIPTAL), University of Michigan, 1986.

McKeachie, W.J., *Teaching Tips: Strategies, Research, and Theory for College and University Teachers. 9th ed.*, Lexington, Massachusetts: D.C. Heath, 1994.

Mehrens, W.A. and I.J. Lehman, *Measurement and Evaluation in Education and Psychology, 3rd edition*, New York: Holt, Rinehart, and Winston, 1984.

Milton, O., H.R. Pollio, and J.A. Eison, *Making Sense of College Grades*, San Fransisco: Jossey-Bass, 1986.

Monaghan, P., Some fields are reassessing the value of the traditional doctoral dissertation, *Chronicle of Higher Education, Vol. 35*, March 29, p. A1, 1989.

Myers, I.B. and D.B. Myers, *Gifts Differing*, Palo Alto, California: Consulting Psychologist Press, 1980.

Myers, I.B., *Introduction to Type,* Gainesville, Florida: Center for the Application of Psychological Type, 1976.

National Science Foundation, *The NSF Grant Policy Manual,* NSF Report 88-47, Washington, D.C., July 1989.

National Science Foundation, *Grant Proposal Guide,* NSF Report 94-2, Washington, D.C., January 1994.

National Science Foundation, *Federal Funds for Research and Development: Fiscal Years 1991, 1992, and 1993, Vol. 41,* NSF Report 93-323, Detailed Statistical Tables, Washington, D.C., 1993.

Reichmann, S. and A. Grasha, A rational approach to developing and assessing the construct validity of a student learning style scales instrument, *Journal of Psychology, Vol. 87,* pp. 213–223, 1974.

Reisman, D., Thoughts on the graduate experience, *Change, Vol. 8,* pp. 11–16, 1976.

Sarkisian, E., *Teaching American Students: A Guide for International Faculty and Teaching Fellows,* Cambridge, Massachusetts: Danforth Center for Teaching and Learning, Harvard University, 1990.

Seldin, P., *Successful Faculty Evaluation Programs,* New York: Coventry Press, 1980.

Seeman, J., On supervising student research, *American Psychologist, Vol. 28,* pp. 900–906, 1977.

Simon, H.A., *Models of My Life,* Basic Books, 1991.

Simon, H.A., The information system called "human memory," in M.R. Rosenzweig and E.L. Bennett, editors, *Neural Mechanisms of Learning and Memory,* Cambridge, Massachusetts: MIT Press, 1976.

Simon, H.A., Problem solving and education, in D.T. Tuma and F. Reif, *Problem Solving and Education: Issues in Teaching and Research,* Hillsdale, New Jersey: Lawrence Erlbaum Associates, pp. 81–96, 1980.

Simon, H.A., *The Sciences of the Artificial,* Cambridge, Massachusetts: MIT Press, 1981.

Simon, H.A. and Gilmartin, K.A., A simulation of memory for chess positions, *Cognitive Psychology, Vol. 5,* pp. 29–46, 1973.

Slavin, R.E., Research and cooperative learning: Consensus and controversy, *Educational Leadership, Vol. 47,* pp. 52–54, Dec. 1989/Jan. 1990.

Smith, A.J., The task of the referee, *Computer, Vol. 23,* pp. 65–71, 1990.

Smith, D., *The Challenge of Diversity: Involvement or Alienation in the Academy?* Report No. 5. Washington, D.C.: School of Education and Human Development, The George Washington University, 1989.

Sorcinelli, M.D., Research findings on the seven principles, in A.W. Chickering and Z.F. Gamson, editors, *Applying the Seven Principles for Good Practice in Undergraduate Education*, San Fransisco: Jossey-Bass, pp. 13–25, 1991.

Sprague, J. and J.D. Nyquist, A developmental perspective on the TA role, in Nyquist, J.D., R.D. Abbott, D.H. Wulff, and J. Sprague, editors, *Preparing the Professoriate of Tomorrow to Teach*, Dubuque, Iowa: Kendall/Hunt Publishing, pp. 295–312, 1991.

Strunk, W. and E.B. White, *The Elements of Style*, Third Edition, New York: Macmillan Publishing Co., 1979.

Tannen, D., *You Just Don't Understand: Women in Conversation*, New York: Morrow, 1990.

Tiberius, R.G., *Small Group Teaching: A Trouble Shooting Guide*, Toronto: Ontario Institute for Studies in Education Press, 1990.

Toombs, W., *Graduate Study as Education*, University Park, Pennsylvania: Center for the Study of Higher Education, The Pennsylvania State University, February 1974.

Trivett, D.A., The student experience in graduate study, *Graduate Education in the 1970's*, ASHE-ERIC Higher Education Report 7, American Association for Higher Education, Washington, D.C., pp. 3–7, 1977.

Tufte, E.R., *The Visual Display of Quantitative Information*, Cheshire, Connecticut: Graphics Press, 1983.

Tufte, E.R., *Envisioning Information*, Cheshire, Connecticut: Graphics Press, 1990.

University of Chicago, *A Manual of Style*, Chicago: The University of Chicago Press, 1969.

University Teaching Center, *Conducting Seminars: A Set of Case Studies*, Carnegie Mellon University, 1988.

Weinstein, C.E., D.R. Palmer, and A.C. Shulte, *Learning and Study Strategies Inventory (LASSI)*, Clearwater, Florida: Holt Publishing Co., 1987.

Weinstein, C.E., Assessment and training of student learning strategies, in R.R. Schmeck, editor, *Learning Strategies and Learning Styles*, New York: Plenum Press, pp. 291–316, 1988.

Welty, W.M., Discussion method teaching: A practical guide, in S. Kahn, editor, *To Improve the Academy, Vol. 8*, Stillwater, Oklahoma: New Forums Press, Inc., pp. 197–216, 1989.

Wu, F.W., The trouble with universities' interest in diversity is, they've embraced it as a panacea for racial tension, *Chronicle of Higher Education, Vol. 37*, p. 26, 1991.

Ziolowski, T., The Ph.D. squid, *The American Scholar, Vol. 59*, pp. 175–195, 1990.

INDEX

Abstract of research paper 132, 133
Active learning 20, 21
Active voice, in writing 133
Adaptive production system 13
All But Dissertation (ABD)
    phenomenon 109, 110
Allen, R. R. 90
American Association of University Professors 98
Anderson, J.R. 11, 13
Andrews, J.D.W. and D.A. Dietz 173
Applied research 115–117
Arthur, R.H. 57
Artificial intelligence 12
Assessing audiences
    for course planning 24–26
    for discussion classes 36–38
    for lectures 54–56
    for conference presentations 161
    for research papers 130
Assessment: see Evaluation and also
    Feedback
Assignments 30–32, 65–80
    administering 74–76
    criteria for evaluating 73, 74
    interpreting student performance 76–78
    objectives of assignments 69, 70
    preventing cheating 74–76
    types of assignments 73
Baker, D.N. 165
Balian, E.S. 100
Basic research 115–117
Bennett, B., et al 89
Berelson, B. 100
Blanton, J.S. 102, 104
Bloom's taxonomy 14, 27, 41, 43, 66, 68, 173

Boehrer, J. and M. Chevrier 90
Boud, D. et al. 84
Bransford, J.D. 11
Braskamp, L.A. 48
Briggs, L.J. and W.W. Wager 19
Brown, G. and M. Atkins 62, 168
Brown, R.D. and L.A. Krager 98
Canfield, A. 7, 9
Canfield Learning Style Inventory 9
Carlile, C.S. and A.V. Daniel 56, 57, 168
Case studies 32, 41
Cheating 32, 67, 74, 75, 84, 89
Chickering, A.W. and Z.F. Gamson 20–23
Civikly, J.M. and D. M. Muchisky 90
Clark, A.T. 97
Classroom assessment 30, 48, 62
Classroom environment 39, 40
Claxton, C.S. and P.H. Murrell 7
Clegg, V.L. and W.E. Cashin 71
Cleveland, W.S. 135
Cognition
    expertise 2–4
    learning strategies 8, 9
    long-term memory 11
    organizing and storing knowledge 10–12
    schemas as memory structures 11
    short-term memory 10
    skill acquisition 12–14
Cohen, J.B. 124
Cohen, P.A. 47, 48
Collett, J. 38
Collaboration on assignments 22, 69, 75
Communication skills of students 29
Condition-action pairs 12
Conferences: see Research Conferences

Confidence level of students 6, 23, 38,
   44, 45
Connell, R.W. 96, 102, 105
Contracts, Research 118
Cooper S. and C. Heenan 43–47
Cooperative learning 22, 43, 69, 75
Cortes, C. 38
Coverage in a course 27–28
Course Planning
   assessing student audiences 24–26
   content 27, 28
   evaluating student work and provid-
      ing feedback 21, 29–31
   objectives of a course 6, 26–28,
      30–32
   learning activities and assignments
      28–32, 65–80
   schedule 29, 32
   scope 27, 28
   syllabus 31, 32
   textbooks 28, 29, 54, 69, 87
Cross, K.P and T.A. Angelo 30, 48, 62, 77
Cues for retrieving information 4, 11, 21,
   26
Cultural differences
   see Diversity of students
Cusanovich, M. and M. Gilliland 82
Davis, B.G. 28, 47
Dickinson, L. 60
Discussion classes
   active listening 44
   amount of control needed by discus-
      sion leader 45
   asking good questions 43, 44
   assessing student audiences 36–38
   case study method 41
   difficult student behaviors 45–47
   diversity of students in discussions
      36–39
   evaluating the discussion 47–49
   functions of discussion leader 42–45
   physical environment 39, 40
   preparing for discussion classes
      36–42

   preparing students for discussions
      41, 42
Diversity of students
   cultural and ethnic backgrounds
      37–39, 57–58
   educational backgrounds 36
   gender 37
   international teaching assistants
      90–92
   learning styles and preferences 1,
      5–8, 23
Eble, K.E. 67
Educational Objectives
   of a course 6, 26–28, 30–32, 54, 55,
      69
   of conference presentations 161
   of discussion classes 40, 41
   of exams and assignments 66–70
   of graduate seminars 172–175
   of lectures 54
   taxonomy of educational objectives,
      (Bloom) 14, 27, 41, 43, 66, 68, 173
Eison, J. 62
Erickson, B.L. and D.W. Strommer 70
Erskine, J.A. et al. 41
Ethical behavior of faculty 98
Ethnic backgrounds: see Diversity of
   students
Evaluation
   absolute grading 76
   class curve 76
   of a class by teaching assistants 90
   of class performance using exam
      results 77, 78
   of conference presentations 166–168
   of discussion classes 47–49
   of lectures 54, 62
   of student performance: assigning
      grades 30–32, 66, 67, 76, 77
   of teaching assistants, 89
   of teaching effectiveness using exam
      results 77
Executive summary of a research paper
   132, 133

Exams
  administering 74–76
  criteria for evaluating 73
  designing problems 70–74
  essay questions 72, 73
  final thesis defense 106
  grading 70–72
  interpreting results 76–78
  motivation for learning 66, 67, 76
  multiple choice 71
  objectives of 66–70, 74
  open vs. closed book 70, 75
  proctoring 84
  qualifying exam for Ph.D. 102, 103
  short answer 71
  solution sets 84
  teaching assistant help with 84
  unstructured problems 72
Expertise 2–4
Feedback
  by students and teaching assistants
    on effectiveness of teaching 82
  by teaching assistants on student
    work 81, 84
  on class discussions 47–49
  on conference presentations 168
  on effectiveness of teaching using
    exam results 67, 77
  on lectures 62
  on seminars presented by graduate
    students 179
  on student learning using exam and
    homework results 67, 75, 76
  on student work 21, 29–31
Fenton, E. 59, 70, 77, 100
Fenves, S.J. 107, 108
Feynman, Richard 3
Fisher, Bobby 3
Forscher, B.K. 156, 157
Garner, B. 38
Gender issues in teaching 37
Gibbs, G. et al. 62
Gilbert, J. 168
Grading: see Evaluation

Graduate seminars: see
  Seminars, Graduate
Graduate students (see also Supervising
  graduate research)
  as teaching assistants 81–93
  faculty supervision of graduate
    research 95–112
Grants, Research 117, 118
Grasha, A.F. 6, 9
Grasha-Reichmann Learning Style Scale 9
Gronlund, N.E. 70
Group projects 8, 22, 29, 75
Guidelines by editors and funding agencies
  for reviewing research papers 129,
    152–158
  for reviewing research proposals
    146–148
  for writing research papers 129
  for writing research proposals 121, 122
Hall, R.M. and B.R. Sandler 37
Hamilton, D.P. 128
Hammons, J.O. and J.R. Barnsley 76
Hart, H. and D.F. Lawler 100
Harte, J. 100
Hartnett, R.T. 97
Hatten, J. 67
Hopkins, K.D. and J.C. Stanley 70
Information processing 2–14
International Teaching Assistants 90–92
Jacks, P. et al. 109
Johnson, D.W. 73
Jones, D.J. and B.C. Watson 1990
Journal articles (see also Research papers)
  reviewing 152, 153
  writing 130–138
Katz, J. 98
Kenny, P. 168
Kolb, D.A. 9
Koshland, D.E 138
Laboratory Sessions 83–84
Landes, K.K. 132
Learning
  actively 20
  cooperative learning 22, 43, 69, 75

cues for retrieving information 4, 11,
    21, 26
developing problem-solving skills 4,
    12–14, 27, 28, 30, 35, 72, 85
expertise 2–4
faculty-student contact 22, 29, 35
from exams and assignments 66–70
internalizing information 13, 69
intrinsic rewards 23
learning activities and assignments
    28–32, 65–80
learning preferences 7, 8
learning strategies 8, 9
learning styles 6, 23, 55, 70
learning through writing 41, 42
long-term memory 11
motivation 3, 5, 6, 26, 36, 66, 67, 76
organizing knowledge 10, 11
review sessions for classes 85, 86
schemas as memory structures 11
short-term memory 10
storing knowledge 10, 11
student learning from other students
    22, 43, 69, 75
Learning Styles Inventory (LSI) 9
Lecturing
    assessing the audience 54–56
    delivering the lecture 60, 61
    determining objectives of the lecture
        54
    evaluating the lecture 62
    maintaining student interest 60, 61
    organizing the lecture 56–58
    preparing lecture 53–60
    preparing visual aids 58–60
Levin, T. and R. Lone 26
Levinson-Rose, J.L. and R.J. Menges 89
Light, R.J. 75
Literature review in a research paper 133
Long-term memory 11
Lowman, J. 30, 70
Lowther, M.S. et al. 28
MacGregor, J. 36, 75
Madsen, D. 100

Maimon, E.P. 42
Maintaining information in long-term
    memory 11
Mambert, W.A. 54, 59, 167
Maurice, K. 38, 39
Mayer, R.E. 11
McKeachie, W.J. 1, 8, 9, 11, 48, 53, 56,
    57, 62
Means-ends analysis 12
Mehrens, W.A and I.J. Lehman 73
Memory, short-term and long-term
    10–11
Milton, O. et al. 77
Monaghan, P. 105
Motivation 3, 5, 6, 26, 36, 66, 67, 76
Mozart 3
Myers, I.B. 7, 9
Myers-Briggs Type Indicators (MBTI) 9
National Science Foundation 115, 116,
    118, 121, 148
Novice-expert continuum 3
Presentations on research (see also
    Research conferences and Seminars,
    Graduate)
    assessing the audience 161
    checklist for rehearsing 167
    delivering the talk 163–166
    determining objectives of the talk 161
    evaluating the talk 166, 168
    organizing the talk 161
    poster presentations 162–165
    preparing conference talks 161–166
    preparing visual aids 162
Pre-tests to assess students beginning a
    course 26
Principles of undergraduate education 20
Problem solving 4, 12–14, 27, 28, 30, 35,
    72, 85
    adaptive production system 13
    means-ends analysis 12
    productions as a representation 12, 13
Production systems in artificial intelli-
    gence 12, 13
Qualifying exam for Ph.D. 102, 103

Questioning skills
for a teacher in discussion classes 43, 44
for graduate students in seminars 173
Questionnaires and surveys of students 24, 55, 62, 89
Recitation sessions 83, 87
Reisman, D. 99
Request for proposals (RFP) 117
Research funding
collaborations in research proposals 120
contracts 118
federal agencies supporting research 116
getting information about a funding agency 121, 122
grants 117, 118
organizing and writing proposals 119–124
overhead 114, 115
private sources of funding 115
proposal budgets 120, 123
public sources of funding 115
request for proposals (RFP) 117
unsolicited proposals 117
using proposal reviewers' comments to revise a proposal 124
Research, Graduate
applied research 115–117
basic research 115–117
choosing a topic for a research proposal 118, 119
funding for graduate research through proposals 113–126
reviewing papers 152–158
reviewing proposals 145–152
supervising research 95–112
Research, Undergraduate 96, 103
Research conferences (see also Presentations on research and Seminars, Graduate)
types of conferences 160
using your time at a conference effectively 160, 165
Research papers
abstract 132, 133
acknowledgments 136, 137
appendices 137
books or book chapters 129
collecting background material 129
conclusions 136
conference papers 128
dealing with rejection or acceptance 138, 142
discussion section 135, 136
executive summary 132, 133
future work section 136
instructions to authors 129
introduction 133
guidelines for reviewers 129, 152–158
journal articles 128
literature review 133
organizing the paper 129–131
references 137
reporting research methods 134
reporting research objectives 133, 134
reporting research results 134
reports to funding agencies 128
reviewing research papers 152–158
summary 136
visual displays 130, 135
writing style 130, 131
Research Proposals 113–126 (see Research funding)
Reviewing
books and book chapters 154, 155
conference proceedings 154
confidentiality 150, 157
conflict of interest 151, 157
forbidden topics to address 156, 157
journal articles 152, 153
panels, for research proposals 149, 150
research papers 152–158
research proposals 145–152

Review sessions by teaching assistants 85, 86
Role models 2, 82, 176
Sarkisian, E. 91
Schemas as memory structures 11
Seeman, J. 97
Seldin, P. 48
Seminars, Graduate (see also
    Presentations on research and
    Research conferences)
    objectives of seminars 172–175
    organizing and conducting seminars
    175–181
    presenting seminars 161, 164, 166
    role of seminars in acquiring knowl-
    edge and developing skills 172, 173
    role of seminars in providing breadth
    173, 174
    role of seminars in promoting group
    interactions 174
    seminars for purposes other than
    research 174, 175
    types of seminars 171
    use of anecdotes and personal experi-
    ences 179–181
Short-term memory 10
Simon, H.A. 3, 11, 13, 69, 100, 106
Slavin, R.E. 75
Smith, A.J. 155, 156
Smith, D. 39
Solution sets 84
Sorcinelli, M.D. 20
Sprague, J. and J.D. Nyquist 86
Strunk, W. and E.B. White 132
Students
    attention in lectures 56
    background characteristics 4, 5,
    24–26, 36–38, 55
    collaboration on assignments 22, 69,
    75
    communications skills 29
    confidence level 6, 23, 38, 44, 45
    contact with faculty 22, 29, 35
    difficult behaviors 45–47
    diversity 1, 5–8, 23, 37–39, 57–58

    expectations in a course 6, 23, 26,
    31, 40
    high risk 37, 38
    instructional preferences 8
    international graduate students
    90–92
    learning preferences 7, 8
    learning strategies 8, 9
    learning styles 6, 23, 55, 70
    motivation 3, 5, 6, 26, 36, 66, 67, 76
    personal problems and disabilities
    10, 37
    personality traits 7
    role of personal experiences 41
Student learning from other students 22,
    43, 69, 75
Study strategies 9, 22, 32
Supervising graduate research
    ABD (all but dissertation) phenome-
    non 109, 110
    choosing a research topic 100–102
    collecting and analyzing data
    103–105
    designing the research plan 102, 103
    disseminating findings 105
    expectations of faculty advisors 97, 98
    expectations of graduate students
    96, 97
    facilities for research 101
    faculty advisor role 101–105
    final thesis defense 106
    funding for research 100, 113–126
    interviewing graduate student appli-
    cants 99
    maintaining a healthy environment
    98, 99
    matching graduate students with fac-
    ulty advisors 101
    providing guidance after the Ph.D.
    107
    qualifying exam for Ph.D. 102, 103
    role of creativity 97, 99
    steps in research process 99–107
    thesis proposal 102
    writing the thesis 105, 106

Syllabus 31, 32, 69, 75, 87
  checklist 31, 32
  course schedule 29
  objectives 6, 26, 27
Talks on research results: see
  Presentations on research
Tannen, D. 37
Teacher effectiveness
  conducting discussions 35–51
  cues for retrieving information 4, 11,
  21, 26
  designing learning experiences 21
  evaluating teaching effectiveness
  using exam results 67, 77
  leadership during discussion classes
  42–45
  lecturing 53–64
  providing feedback on student work
  21, 29–31, 67, 75, 76
  receiving feedback from students on
  discussion classes 47–49
  receiving feedback from students on
  lectures 62
  relationships with teaching assistants
  82,83
  roles in graduate research 101–105
  student-faculty contact 22, 29, 35
Teaching Assistants
  attitudes of teachers toward TAs 82
  attitudes of TAs toward their responsibilities 82, 83
  grading papers 84,85
  international TAs 90–92
  laboratory sessions 83
  office hours 85
  proctoring exams 84
  providing feedback on student work
  81, 84
  receiving feedback from students 82
  recitation sessions 83, 87
  relationships with faculty 82, 83
  responsibilities 83–86
  review sessions 85, 86
  solution sets 84
  training teaching assistants 86–90

tutoring 85
  writing exams and homework assign-
  ments 84
Tests: See Exams
Textbooks 28, 29, 54, 69, 87
Thesis
  proposal 102
  writing 105, 106
Tiberius, R.G. 40
Time management 22
Toombs, W. 99
Trivett, D.A. 99
Tufte, E.R. 135, 138
Tutoring
  by faculty 22
  by teaching assistants 85
Visual Aids 39, 58–60, 162, 164
Visual displays of quantitative
  information in research papers 135
Weinstein, C.E. 9, 11
Welty, W.M. 40, 43–45
Writing
  Manuals of Style 132
  importance in the learning process
  41, 42
  research papers 130–138
  research proposals 122–124
  thesis 105, 106
Wu, F.W. 37
Ziolkowski, T. 100